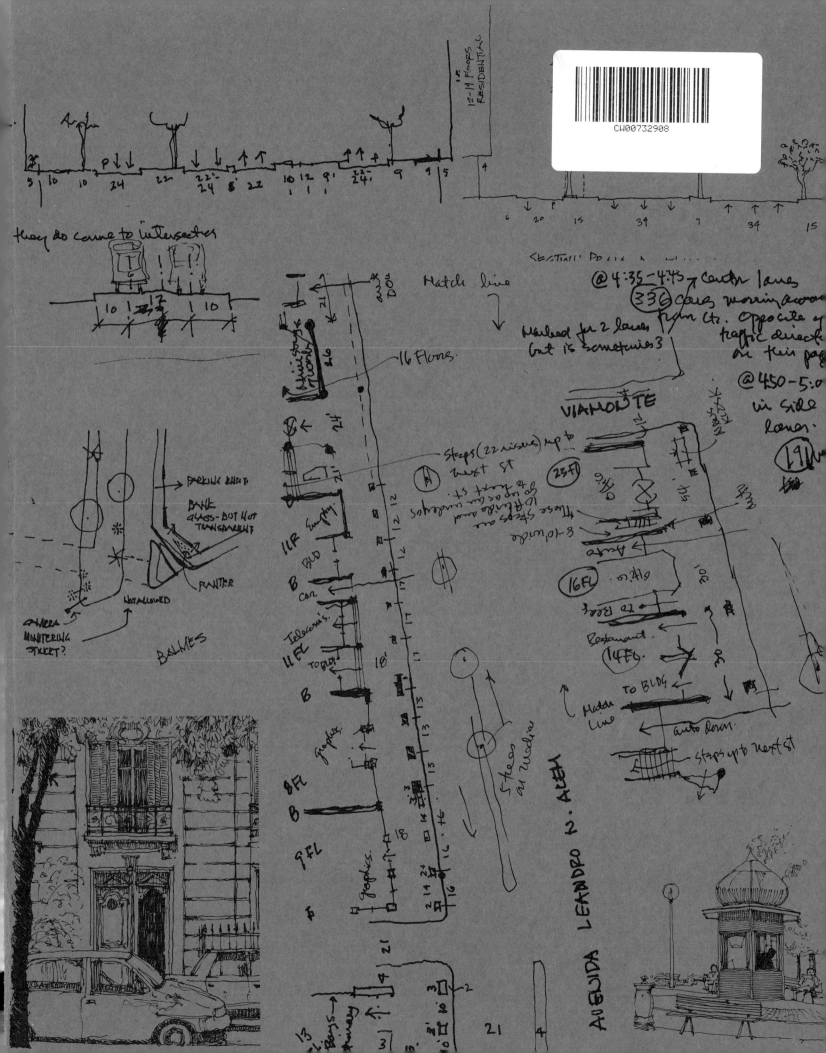

THE
Boulevard Book

The MIT Press

Cambridge, Massachusetts

London, England

The Boulevard Book

HISTORY, EVOLUTION,
DESIGN OF
MULTIWAY BOULEVARDS

ALLAN B. JACOBS, ELIZABETH MACDONALD, AND YODAN ROFÉ

This book was set in Garamond Three by Graphic Composition, Inc.

Printed and bound in the United States of America.

Library of Congress Cataloging-in-Publication Data
Jacobs, Allan B.
     The boulevard book. : history, evolution, design of multiway boulevards / Allan B. Jacobs, Elizabeth Macdonald, and Yodan Rofé.
        p. cm.
Includes bibliographical references and index.
ISBN 0-262-10090-8 (hc. : alk. paper)
  1. Streets—Design and construction. I. Macdonald, Elizabeth, 1959– II. Rofé, Yodan.
III. Title.

TE279.J33 2002
625.7—dc21

To the memory of Jack Kent and Donald Appleyard
and to
Bea and Morris Jacobs
Edy Macdonald and the memory of William C. Macdonald
and
Thom and Maayan Rofé

Contents

ACKNOWLEDGMENTS

Having spent many hours on Avenue Montaigne in Paris and Passeig de Gràcia in Barcelona, measuring their many parts and the buildings on them, counting autos and people, charting their movements, and simply observing these boulevards and people's behavior on them, we were convinced that they were fine streets and wondered why many traffic experts we encountered gave this type of boulevard such a "bad rap." We expressed that concern to Alan Cannel, a colleague in Curitiba, Brazil who specializes in traffic safety, and wondered what it would take to change the apparent bias against them. Among his suggestions—which of course included analysis of accident data—was to make a film that showed how the intersections actually worked, how people and cars actually navigated them. Seeing, he suggested, might lead to believing. That is where the idea for the research that was to be the basis of this book started. Parenthetically, along the way, we completed a twenty-minute video that has been instrumental in getting citizen activists who have seen it interested in multiway boulevards and in making professionals somewhat more open to considering them.

It is astonishing how many people have helped us in our research, particularly professionals from many cities. We have relied on people's willingness to send us information again and again, to gather some of the data, and to help us make sense of it. Specifically, they are: Matthew Thompson from the Engineering Services Department of Chico; Suzanne Rademacher from the Olmsted Conservancy Foundation; Jim Pasakowski and Philip Williams from the Louisville Public Works Department and Jeff Ackerman, also in Louisville; Joe Passaneau, who sent us interesting material on K Street in Washington D.C., as well as Rashid Sleemi, who provided traffic and safety data; Brian Leys and Jae Kang of the New York City Department of Transportation sent us data and drafts of their reports; Jack Knoll from the New York State Department of Transportation sent us accident data; Phil and Ty Ziegler sent us maps of potential streets for study in the Boston area.

In New York, Todd Bressi helped us get oriented, whizzed us around the city on the subway system to see more streets than we thought possible, and actually did some of the fieldwork when we were prevented by bad weather from doing so. Todd was with us again, counting traffic during our second visit to New York.

Obtaining data and information in Europe, where we had language obstacles, was a major worry at the start of the project. The help of Amy Jacobs-Colas and Dominique Colas, and of Jacques Stevenin of the Atelier Parisien d'Urbanisme, was extraordinary in Paris. In Barcelona, doors were opened for us by Jordi Borja i Sebastian, Amador Ferrer i Aixala, Julio Garcia Ramon, and Monica Salada. Hugo Carvalho from Lisbon was kind enough to direct us via Internet communication to streets there and provided some historic information. In Palermo, we were happy to find a fine boulevard and to make new friends. Corrado Marino, Simona Balistieri, and Marina Marino provided us with maps and information, and Marina was with us in Lisbon counting traffic.

In Berkeley, we were fortunate to have the advice of Mel Webber, then director of the University of California Transportation Center; Adib Kanafani, Wolf Homburger, and Robert Cervero, who responded to some of our early notions and whose criticisms and encouragement helped us formulate and improve our work. Wolf was kind enough to read and criticize a complete draft of the manuscript, to its betterment. He even sent us photographs of Melbourne boulevards. Obviously, though, these colleagues are not responsible for what we present.

We undertook a number of case study designs of existing and potential multiway boulevards, in part to see how professionals would respond to them. We thank particularly those who helped us identify the right people to talk to and set up meetings: in particular, City Engineer Dick Asimus of Fremont, Frank Addeo of the office of the Transportation Commissioner, and Gerard Soffian, assistant commissioner for planning in New York City; Michael Kashiwagi, deputy director of public works in Sacramento; Rebecca Kohlstrand in San Francisco; and City Engineer Joseph Loop in West Sacramento. Our thanks go beyond them to the many city staff people who took part in our reviews.

Bimal Patel passed through our office one day, saw some of our boulevard work, and invited us to Ahmedabad, India, where he lives, to design C. G. Road with him as a multiway boulevard. Today, it exists, thanks to Bimal.

Cortus Koehler, from Sacramento State University, opened doors for us in Sacramento and was Jacobs's partner in a study of San Francisco Boulevard in Sacramento. Jose Ureña was our partner in one boulevard study in Madrid and pointed us to another, where he joined us during an afternoon to help measure physical qualities and count traffic.

We could not visit all the cities that have multiway boulevards, much as we might have liked to do so. If we knew colleagues were going to a city that has multiway boulevards, we asked them to help. Clark Wilson was kind enough to research Ho Chi Minh City and the New Delhi boulevards. What a big help! Cheryl Parker visited Buffalo for us, to find out about Olmsted's boulevards. Cheryl also spent time in our cavelike studio in the bowels of Wurster Hall, renewing her graphic skills on street plans and regaining her stippling license. Robert John Adams was kind enough to send us information about the Melbourne streets.

Peter Bosselmann—colleague, teacher, and friend—counseled us from the start. He patiently instructed us in the arts of film and video photography, and in numerous discussions about and reviews of our work he helped us formulate some of the key concepts of the book. His redo of the Appleyard "Livable Streets" study with Macdonald was, we think, a key bit of research. Peter, in so many ways, is the best of friends, and we thank him very much.

Jack Kent died while we were working on this book. He knew about it, and we talked it over with him during lunch from time to time. We know he approved. Richard Bender has always advised us, on matters of substance and publishing. Paolo Ceccarelli brought us to Ferrara, where we found multiway boulevards. Jaime Lerner in Curitiba brought us there to consult on a main road to Paranagua and introduced us to Rio's boulevards.

For a book with multiple authors, it is both informative and useful to know who did what in its research and presentation. It is collaborative in every respect. Jacobs was the focal point and promoter of the original research, which was carried out under his direction and leadership. The evolving research program and conclusions were jointly conceived and evolved from group meetings and discussions. Most of the fieldwork was done together. Early on, each of us was responsible for first drafts of portions of individual working papers and, ultimately, book chapters. The decision to prepare a book based on the early research and its findings was a joint one. Jacobs was responsible for coordinating a first draft of a complete manuscript, and he wrote the initial draft of the Introduction and Conclusion. Macdonald did the writing for the Paris, Barcelona, and Brooklyn boulevards, as well as the history section and all of its research. Rofé was the initial author of the chapters on safety, professional and bureaucratic constraints, and design and policy guidelines. Each of us worked on streets in the Compendium, though Jacobs and Macdonald did the final writing. A penultimate text was collaboratively reviewed and refined by all three of us. Jacobs and Macdonald undertook the final editing. Plans and section drawings are mostly by Jacobs and Macdonald. Most perspectives are by Jacobs and most diagrams are by Macdonald.

This is the fourth of her father's books that Amy Jacobs-Colas has reviewed and helped edit. Kaye Bock, as always, suffered through draft after draft of the manuscript, helping us to get it right.

Two grants from the University of California Transportation Center, with funds provided by the U.S. Department of Transportation and the California State Department of Transportation, enabled us to get started on the research that became the foundation of this book. For sure, there would not have been a book without that assistance. The Institute of Urban and Regional Development at the University of California, Berkeley, helped to oversee those grants and first published our findings. Barbara Hadenfeldt of the Institute helped in the research as well. Small grants from the Committee on Research of the University of California, Berkeley, to hire research assistants, helped to keep us going. A grant from the Graham Foundation funded research in Buenos Aires, Rio de Janeiro, and Lisbon. Some of the Foundation's funds, together with a gracious gift from the Beatrix Farand Fund through the faculty of Berkeley's Department of Landscape Architecture contributed to the quality of the publication. We thank them all.

THE

Boulevard Book

INTRODUCTION

Esplanade, Chico, Cal.

There is a wonderful street in Chico, California, called The Esplanade, reason enough to visit this unassuming northern California city. Leaving downtown Chico by car, you can travel smoothly at 35 or 40 miles an hour on a roadway lined with very large, regularly spaced trees and low plantings. It is like being on a parkway. Driving along, you may notice, beyond the lines of trees, side roads running parallel to the central lanes. You might decide to detour onto one of these one-way access roads for a block or two, just to see what it is like. Life in the one-way side roads is very different than it is in the center: parked cars, sidewalks, and another line of large trees; small apartment houses and single-family residences set back on lawns; a school; some people walking; one block of stores with a restaurant facing the street. Occasional cars move slowly, and every now and then a cyclist pedals by, sometimes moving in the opposite direction to what the law intends. Dappled sun finds its way through the overhead foliage. One can imagine taking a walk here on a summer evening, with or without an ice cream cone. The relaxed, deliberate pace of life along the distinctive edges of The Esplanade and the faster pace of the central movement lanes work together. They are one. The street is a whole.

If you care about streets at all, and most people do—they tend to prefer one street to another, they go out of their way to be on certain streets and to avoid others, they find that travel, shopping, or visiting friends is simply more pleasant on some than on others—you are likely to feel good on The Esplanade. The people of Chico agree: they regularly vote The Esplanade the best street in town.[1]

This book is about streets like The Esplanade, boulevard streets of a particular type; we call them *multiway boulevards*. In many ways, the book is a celebration of these streets, of their grandness and of the many positive roles they have played, and still play, in creating delightful urban environments. But the book is more than a simple voyage of discovery—for who besides the people of Chico knows about The Esplanade?—or a rediscovery of a street type. It is more, too, than a catalogue of such streets and their dimensions. Streets like The Esplanade—or like Eastern Parkway or Ocean Parkway in Brooklyn, the Passeig de Gracia in Barcelona, the Avenue Franklin Roosevelt in Paris, or tiny San Francisco Boulevard in Sacramento—have crucially important, creative roles to play in today's and tomorrow's urban environments. These roles can span a variety of scales, from giving form to an entire metropolitan area and determining the basic physical structure of a city to providing local streets for access to stores, homes, and recreation. This book is about such boulevards, how they came to be and how they work. It is about the reasons that they are currently in disfavor with many professionals responsible for the design of urban streets. Most important, it is about what makes the best of these streets both wonderful and beautiful. In the end, it is about what it takes to design multiway boulevards that can help people live better, more fulfilling, more joyful lives in their communities.

The Esplanade, unlike most other multiway boulevards, is relatively new. It dates from the 1950s. That it exists at all seems a stroke of luck. Perhaps its designers weren't as current as they might have been, not knowing that their peers in the world of traffic engineering generally considered the type of street they were designing to be dangerous and nonfunctional. Or, maybe the opposite was true. Perhaps they were more sophisticated than others of their time.

By the 1950s, multiway boulevards had long been on a downhill slide as an understood and favored street type. They had fallen prey to a narrowly focused way of designing streets, an approach that viewed unencumbered vehicular movement as the overarching concern. Multiway boulevards like Eastern Parkway or Ocean Parkway in Brooklyn were no longer being built; were likely to be reconfigured or otherwise "improved" out of existence; or were simply neglected. To be sure, they continued to exist in Europe, where they were among the most unforgettable of urban places. But not in America!

Boulevards, though rooted in the axial planning of sixteenth-century Italian cities, particularly Rome, follow models refined in Paris during the latter half of the nineteenth century, a part of Louis Napoleon's and Baron Haussmann's modernization and expansion project. In addition to the objectives of beautifying the city and of asserting the public role of city building, they were designed to move people and goods through an essentially medieval city fabric that had become impossibly congested; to improve communications; to add sanitation lines and other infrastructure systems; and to allow police and the militia easy access to crowded neighborhoods where social unrest was fermenting.

Boulevards also provided building sites for new development, accommodating the desires of a growing middle class for new urban residences, cafes, and restaurants. Among their most important functions was that of giving structure and comprehension to the whole city as it grew and diversified under the impetus of industrialization. They were monumental links between important destinations.[2]

Boulevards were imported into the United States as a part of the park movement of the late nineteenth century and were a major part of the formal vocabulary of the city beautiful movement of the early twentieth century. Coinciding with the rapid expansion of cities, they were associated more with new suburban development than with streets cut through old urban quarters. They were often part and parcel of land development promotions. Generally wide and invariably tree-lined, these boulevards were long, quiet, and faced with large homes set apart on deep lawns—quite a different image than the hustle and bustle associated with the European boulevards. Usually built well in advance of the residences that were to line them, they were intended to give a sense of good things to come to the prospective well-to-do homeowner.

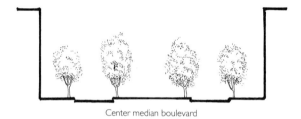

Center median boulevard

Boulevard street

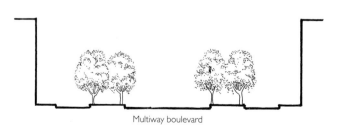

Multiway boulevard

Diagram of 3 types of boulevards

Different kinds of streets with different designs are called *boulevards*. Basically, though, there are three boulevard types. One type has a wide central landscaped median flanked on either side by roadways and sidewalks. The central median may be a pedestrian promenade; or it may simply be planted with grass, trees, and shrubbery. Streetcar lines or horse trails were often located in the central median. Monument Avenue in Richmond, Fairmount Boulevard in Cleveland Heights, and Dolores Street in San Francisco are but three of many examples of this boulevard type.

A second type of boulevard is really nothing more than a street with a wide central roadway and broad, tree-lined sidewalks along each side. It is characterized by gracious tree-plantings, wide walkways, the anticipation of well-designed buildings and, in some cases, a desired high-status address, rather than a distinctive design. Boulevards Saint-Michel or Haussmann in Paris come to mind.

The third type of boulevard, the one we are concerned with here, is distinctly different from the other two. The multiway boulevard is designed to separate through traffic from local traffic and, often, to provide special pedestrian ways on tree-lined malls. Like other streets, it provides access to abutting uses, but often—unlike others—it is also designed for recreation. It is characterized by a central roadway of at least four lanes for generally fast and nonlocal traffic; on either side of this roadway are tree-lined medians that separate it from parallel, one-way side access roads for slow-moving traffic. The medians can be of various widths: some are nothing more than planting strips, while others, in addition to rows of trees, contain walks, benches, transit stops, and even horse trails or bike paths. The sidewalks may or may not have their own lines of trees. The access roads generally allow for one or two lanes of parking and one moving lane.

The multiway boulevard is unique because its parallel roadways serve distinctly different traffic functions. It directly addresses the functional problems posed by the coexistence of through movement and access to abutting land uses on major urban streets. It allows these seemingly contradictory but often complementary forms of movement—both essential to the life of the city—to coexist in the same street space.

However, increasingly in the twentieth century, boulevards of this type have been maligned. They are held by important professionals to create complicated, difficult, and often dangerous intersections.

As much as any reason, it was a new way of thinking and of classifying streets that resulted in the decline of boulevards in the United States.

Beginning in the 1930s and intensifying after World War II, the emerging field of traffic engineering, in order to resolve the conflict between fast movement and access to abutting properties on streets, embraced the notion of "the *functional classification* of streets." In essence, this approach to transportation planning concentrated on auto traffic and strove to achieve a specialization of urban streets according to the movement functions they were primarily intended to serve. It paid much less attention to other appropriate uses of streets.[3]

In the context of functional classification, multiway boulevards present a problem because they do not fit into any of its categories. They usually serve arterial street functions in terms of vehicular movement, but they also allow continuous access to abutting properties. Analogous to mixed land uses—another victim of city planning and development preferences since World War II—the boulevard is a mixed-use public way that is by its very nature complex.

Multiway boulevards have also fallen prey to changing standards of road building. Over the years, there has been a tendency to widen lane widths, for example, from eight or nine feet to twelve or thirteen feet. Acceptable distances between parallel roadways have also increased, left and right turning lanes have become standard, and turning radii at intersections have grown. Parking lanes have become wider, and acceptable tree-spacing standards and norms have become greater, especially the required distances from intersections. In combination, the impact of such guidelines has meant that the essential form of the multiway boulevard has been eroded, particularly the local, protected character of the side lanes.

The reasoning for these changing standards always includes a major safety component. But safety considerations are often based on geometric and physical assumptions and applied logic and not necessarily on observation of the actual behavior of drivers and pedestrians. For multiway boulevards, these considerations are especially focused on intersections. The sheer number of possible conflicting movements—weaves from side access roads to the central lanes or from the central lanes to the access roads, possible right turns from central lanes across straight-moving traffic on the access roads, to name only a few of many examples—suggests logically that boulevards must not be as safe as other streets. Our research shows otherwise.

Indeed, this book stems from what are largely safety and function concerns thought to be associated with multiway boulevards. It is also born of our experience. During the 1980s in Los Angeles, while participating in the design of a major new development through which a high-volume arterial road passed, we proposed building one-way access streets to serve the adjoining commercial and residential properties that were to be developed on each side of the artery. That seemed like a simple and straightforward way of dealing with both the fast through traffic and the more deliberate circulation and access needs of the envisioned development. But we learned very quickly that lane-width standards for the access streets were so great that the local character we desired would be lost. More important, we were advised, intersections along such streets would be exceedingly dangerous. Satisfying the engineers' requirements would have taken so much space under operative standards and norms that the idea died. Years later, proposals to modify an existing arterial street in San Francisco into a multiway boulevard met with similar objections.

In contrast, while doing research for an earlier book, we had occasion to spend considerable time on a variety of boulevards, mostly in Paris and Barcelona.[4] Recalling our unfortunate experiences in Los Angeles and San Francisco, we decided to take a closer look at the European examples. Spending hours observing intersections and the behaviors of motorists and pedestrians, we did not get the impression that they were particularly dangerous. Rather, the overwhelming characteristic of the traffic at the intersections was adaptation. People simply adapted to what was there, and they did so safely. Most important, these streets were delightful places to be as a pedestrian. They were, and are, peopled, full of activity and life. Pedestrians, local motorists, and those passing through seem to get along well together.

Looking at them, observing them over extended periods, it was hard to believe that these multiway boulevards were more dangerous than other major traffic carriers. That became a major question: in reality, are these boulevards unduly dangerous? At the same time, another question emerged: even if it turned out that these boulevards were not particularly dangerous, could one be built today, especially in the United States? Would today's standards and guidelines permit them? The Los Angeles and San Francisco experiences suggested not. It would be depressing to learn that we could not emulate something of value, something desirable, something perceived to be pleasurable and useful for the community. Of course, this would not be the first time that an eminently livable environment could not be reproduced, at times for good reasons. The low wood-frame structures of many a downtown in the United States were at a human scale, easy to build, and they helped provide pleasant places to live and do business. But they were often prone to fires, and concerns for safety have made them impossible, and maybe inappropriate, today. But what if those buildings weren't unsafe? More to our point here, what if existing multiway boulevards proved safe, or at least not less safe than other major urban roadways? Shouldn't we be able to build them?

These questions of safety and reproducibility were the initial concerns that invited an exploration of multiway boulevards. During the research, however, we became aware of the role of the functional classification of streets as a major obstacle to the creation of new boulevards and the improvement of old ones. We became aware that the boulevard epitomizes a completely different paradigm for urban street design—one that embraces complexity and coexistence of movement over simplicity and separation, and one that insists that access to abutting uses is as central to the functionality of city streets as swift through movement. Pedestrian movement, too, is as important to the life of the city as vehicular movement, and as such should have space devoted to it and protected for it on all city streets.

There was a period after World War II when a strong case for single-purpose roadways could be made—though probably never as forcefully and comprehensively as was visited upon U.S. cities. At the time, the country was behind in road building; the number of automobiles and trucks had vastly increased. Vehicular travel needs between distant locations required legitimate routes that could be traversed speedily; some existing roadways were simply too narrow to accommodate both slow and rapidly moving traffic. At the turn of the twenty-first century, there exist occasional justifications for limited-access roadways or other streets serving single or limited functions. The arguments for these roads are generally more convincing in nonurban environments than in complex urban settings: the long-distance freeway in large single-use areas, industrial enclaves, large and low-density single-family housing areas.

It is clear in hindsight that the freeway, expressway, and arterial improvements of the 1950s, 1960s, and 1970s were not always changes for the better. One need only look at the countless urban environments through which widened, limited-purpose arterials configured for fast traffic were pushed, or visit the areas through which the new expressways or freeways were built to wonder seriously if there were not better solutions.[5] There are good reasons why the people of San Francisco had a freeway revolt in 1966 and why some freeways in that city and in Boston have been removed. City people at the turn of the century are less likely to stand by and permit significant changes to streets that pass through their neighborhoods than they were earlier, particularly if the purpose is only to speed auto traffic. People understand that single-purpose roads attract traffic and that width tends to induce speed. The lower-income areas through which arterials were pushed, with attendant dislocation of neighborhoods and loss of property, may still have the same people in them; but they are more sophisticated now, more politically capable of defending their turf. Moreover, there are no longer funds available to clear long swaths of right-of-way for new or widened roadways in urban areas.

As we come to understand and appreciate that complexity is a positive and necessary attribute of urban areas, it will become more natural to use creatively the resources that we have, adapting and changing physical environments, including streets, to accommodate many uses and varieties of activities. Multiway boulevards can accommodate both slow and rapid traffic and can solve the problems occasioned by the conflict between movement and local access.

Before considering the major issues of safety and reproducibility, however, it is important to get a more intimate picture of the kinds of boulevards that are our concern. Like streets of other types, all multiway boulevards are not alike. Their dimensions, the uses along them, the amounts and speed of vehicular traffic they carry, the pedestrians that use them, their settings, and a host of design details differ from one boulevard to another. To give a feeling for their variety, purposes, original and current contexts, and how they have been treated over time, we start in Part One by visiting multiway boulevards in Paris, Barcelona, and across the United States. To permit comparisons among boulevards, the various graphics are drawn to the same scale.

Once we know some boulevards more intimately, we look back at their history—from their beginning as tree-lined avenues atop late-Renaissance fortifications, to their nineteenth-century use as major urban form-givers, and to their decline in the twentieth century. This history is the subject of Part Two.

Part Three describes the results of empirical research showing multiway boulevards to be as safe as comparable major urban streets. The empirical results are explained theoretically by the concept of "the pedestrian realm." This zone lies between the buildings facing the street and the center roadway and includes sidewalks, access streets, and tree-lined medians; it mediates between fast vehicular movement and slow pedestrian movement.

The research also found a conspicuous lack of empirical data to back up professional assumptions that boulevards are unsafe. Part Three concludes with a discussion of the present-day bureaucratic constraints on building boulevards.

Part Four is a celebration of multiway boulevards. They exist all over the world—grand ones, modest ones, even tiny ones (a seeming contradiction in terms). Although they have certain common features, there is great variety as well, and they all have something to teach us. Even so, our compendium of plans, sections, details, and contexts is not all-embracing; we could not include all important boulevards. But within the limitations of time and money a representative variety is presented, including an old and very narrow one in Ferrara and an incredibly complex, chaotic intersection of two multiway boulevards in Rome. There are examples of boulevards that work poorly, but more of those that work well. Included as

well is a new boulevard in Ahmedabad, India, whose design is derived in large measure from
the research carried out in preparing this book. Finally, there are two design case studies,
one a possible reconfiguration of a presently unsafe boulevard and the other of a possible conversion of an arterial street so that it can incorporate light rail mass transit within a multiway boulevard arrangement.

At this point in the investigation and narrative a new promise emerges about boulevards
and their prospects. If, indeed, they are not inherently unsafe, and if they are or can be what
they were always intended to be—eminently livable, enjoyable, multipurpose urban
streets—then those that remain can and should have a future. Even more challenging and
exciting are the prospects for creating new and extended boulevards in the making of urban
environments. Where and how might we build them? Part Five, Building Boulevards, includes, in Chapter 1, design and policy guidelines for creating such new multiway boulevards. The guidelines are aimed at helping people identify potentials for them in their own
communities and providing solutions for the recurrent problems that arise in designing
them.

Multiway boulevards have had a bad press and have long needed a new look. They remain a workable street form that can resolve many of the problems related to movement and
access in urban areas, especially the need for balance between the needs of the city as a whole
and those of local people. Moreover, the concept of the pedestrian realm applies to more than
multiway boulevards. For a city to regain its urbanity and civic life the pedestrian realm has
to be introduced and protected on all its streets. Boulevards are but one, unique example of
how to integrate this principle into the design of city streets.

Cities are wonderful inventions of diversity—people, things, activities, ideas, and ide-
ologies. Multiway boulevards are an urban form that responds to many issues that are central to urban life: livability, mobility, safety, interest, economic opportunity, ecology, mass
transit, and the need for open space. Multiway boulevards can help to achieve the best that
urban life has to offer. Let us see how.

Σm

Chapter One

PARIS BOULEVARDS, A GRAND VARIETY

Think about Paris and sooner, rather than later, the word *boulevard* will come to mind. Boulevards—the word itself, perhaps as much as their physical reality—define this city. The word conjures up images of broad tree-lined sidewalks, elegant buildings, attractive stores, corner cafes, crowds of people, and the warm light of street lamps.

Paris has many boulevards, and they have great variety. All are wide compared to other streets in the city and have regularly spaced trees and buildings that generally complement each other in height, materials, and architectural details and that define their edges. Elegant and beckoning as most of them are, however, not all are multiway boulevards—our concern here.

Although some Paris boulevards date from the seventeenth century, most were built in the mid-nineteenth century under the direction of Baron Georges Eugène Haussmann, Napoleon III's prefect of the Seine. Many of the latter, including some of the most impressive ones, were multiway boulevards. These streets established the basic form of the multiway boulevard used worldwide. In Paris, many retain their original form, and all are in

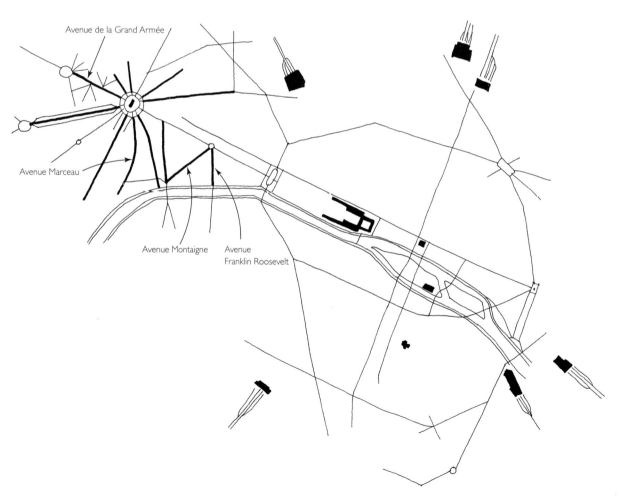

Avenue de la Grand Armée

Avenue Marceau

Avenue Montaigne   Avenue Franklin Roosevelt

The Etoile Boulevards

normal use as part of the street system. Most are valued and well cared for. What better place to study such streets?

The biggest single concentration of multiway boulevards, twelve in total, is in the western part of the city near the Place de l'Etoile and the Avenue des Champs Elysées—itself a multiway boulevard until recent renovations. From the wide Avenue de la Grand Armée to the relatively narrow Avenue Montaigne, the multiway boulevards of the Etoile area differ markedly from each other in width, length, uses of the land along them, amounts of traffic carried, and traffic arrangements. While most are very similar in basic form and in the way they function, differences in their spatial qualities and use, and in design details, lend them distinctly individual characters. As a group they illustrate the adaptability of the multiway boulevard form. In this chapter we concentrate on four of these streets: Avenue de la Grand Armée, Avenue Montaigne, Avenue Franklin Roosevelt, and Avenue Marceau. Two additional Paris boulevards located in other parts of the city are described in Part Four, A Compendium of Boulevards.

Avenue de la Grand Armée

The Avenue de la Grand Armée extends the line of the Champs Elysées west of the Place de l'Etoile. The layout of the street is very similar to that of the Avenue des Champs Elysées before that more celebrated street was reconfigured in the early 1990s to widen the sidewalks and eliminate its side access roads.[1] Like the Avenue des Champs Elysées, the Avenue de la Grand Armée is wide—approximately 230 feet.[2] At slightly over a half mile from the Etoile to Porte Maillot, it is three-quarters as long as the famous commercial section of the Avenue des Champs Elysées that runs from the Etoile to Rond Point.

For a passerby the strongest impression of the Grand Armée might well be one of traffic. Ten lanes operate in the 89-foot central roadway, pumping some 92,000 vehicles per day in two directions.[3] Yet there is more to the street than just this traffic realm. The central traffic lanes are bordered on each side by 8.5-foot-wide medians lined with trees planted 33 feet apart. Next come the side access lanes, which are 25-feet wide and marked for one traffic lane and two parking lanes. The sidewalks are quite wide—37 feet—and have curbside trees that mirror those in the medians. The center, then, with all that traffic, takes up slightly less than 40 percent of the total right-of-way, leaving about 60 percent for uses of a much more relaxed character.

Besides the traffic, the passerby might be impressed by the street's elegant structures, residences of well-to-do people and businesses and commercial ground floors dominated by automobile showrooms and computer and electronics outlets. A yet-closer scrutiny of a single block would reveal bakeries, cafes, a delicatessen, a florist shop, and a clothing store—more locally oriented uses than one would expect to find on a street carrying so much traffic.

There are always vehicles on the access lanes of the Avenue de la Grand Armée. Generally it is not easy to find a parking space, but there is always hope. People enter an access road, assess the situation, and, if all spaces are taken, may wait for one to open up. Delivery

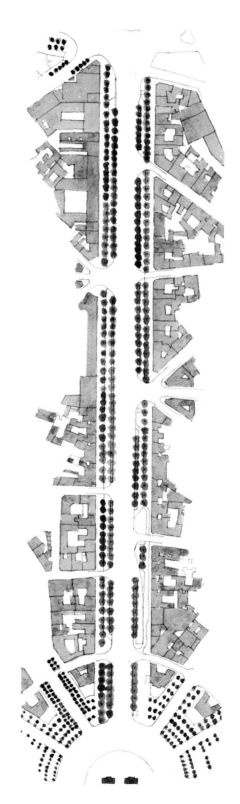

Avenue de la Grand Armée:

street and building context

Approximate scale: 1″ = 400′ or 1:4,800

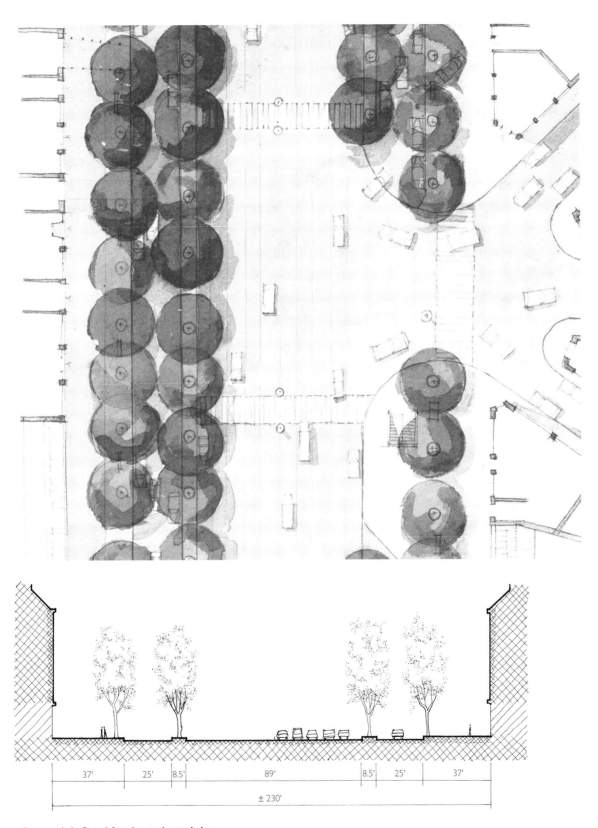

Avenue de la Grand Armée: section and plan

Approximate scale: 1″ = 50′ or 1:600

trucks also commonly double park, making passage difficult or impossible. Traffic moves very slowly on these lanes.

There are only a few intersections, but they are generally complex, with movement permitted in all directions. Each one has a traffic light; when it is green for the central roadway, traffic moves along it as fast as possible, except for vehicles turning into the side access lanes or intersecting streets. All other traffic simply moves when permitted to, carefully.

The wide sidewalks along the street provide room for many things: stairs to the Metro below, large news kiosks, Paris's famous circular information kiosks, benches, and pay phones. While the pedestrian volume is not heavy, there is usually a steady flow of people, and the telephone booths always seem to be occupied, especially when you want to use one. There is more than enough room on the sidewalks for all the uses and for everyone who wants to be there—which perhaps is why they are also used, in places, for parking motor-cycles and, sometimes, cars.

The Avenue de la Grand Armée has both some of the grandness of the Avenue des Champs Elysées and some of the problems the latter had before it was reconfigured. Its width, together with its large trees and its focus on the Arc de Triomphe at the Etoile, to

which the street rises, gives it great presence and formality. The buildings that line it, all of a similar height and regularity, reflect conscious design. At the same time, the width of the central roadway makes it difficult to cross on foot. As a consequence, the two sides seem divorced from each other. Furthermore, pedestrian areas along the street have the sense of being whittled down and look somewhat neglected. The Avenue de la Grand Armée displays the same deterioration as the earlier Avenue des Champs Elysées, where severe parking problems along the access roads led to a breakdown of rules and norms as parked cars and trucks spilled onto the walks and medians.

In fact, the present configuration of the Avenue de la Grand Armée is the result of an erosion of its pedestrian areas. In its original nineteenth-century form, the street had 50-foot-wide medians planted with double rows of trees and a center roadway only 60 feet wide.[4] Over the course of many years the street has become more and more oriented toward traffic needs—vehicles passing through and parking—and this trend seems to be continuing. Nonetheless, it is not a fast-traffic wasteland but still has grandness and elegance. The boulevard form truly helps.

AVENUE MONTAIGNE

Avenue Montaigne has come a long way since its days as a country path in the sixteenth century.[5] Its tree-lined form, too, predates that of most boulevards near the Etoile; as early as the 1770s it served as the location of *bals,* evening entertainments, and dancing.[6] By the late 1800s it had become, as it remains, among the most fashionable of Paris streets.

The Avenue Montaigne runs for only five uneven blocks—or about two thousand feet—from the Rond Point on the Champs Elysées southwest to the Seine. There, it offers a grand view of the Eiffel Tower. Block length varies considerably, and there is only one through cross street; the others are T-intersections. The street is lined with chestnut trees and elegant six- or seven-story buildings, many with designer salons, cafés, and banks on the ground floor. There is also a major hotel and an embassy. Except for those in the hotel, upper floors are a mixture of residential and office uses.

Avenue Montaigne is narrow for a multiway boulevard and has an unusual traffic arrangement. It is approximately 126-feet wide from building to building. At 42 feet, its center roadway is less than half the width of that of the Avenue de la Grand Armée. It carries four lanes of traffic. The side medians are approximately seven feet wide and contain

Central Roadway on Avenue Montaigne

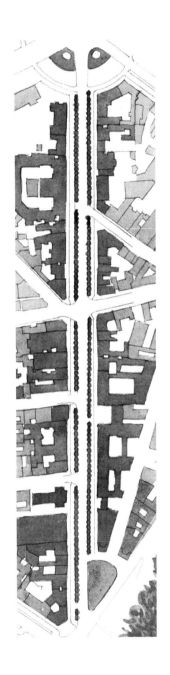

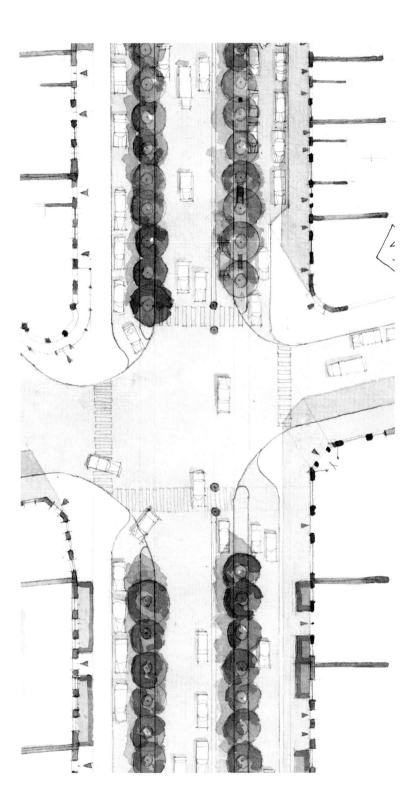

Avenue Montaigne: street and building context

Approximate scale: 1″ = 400′ or 1:4,800

Avenue Montaigne: plan

Approximate scale: 1″ = 50′ or 1:600

Avenue Montaigne, Paris

chestnut trees closely spaced at 15 to 18 feet apart and forming a dense screen of trunks and foliage. The width of access roadways and sidewalks varies. At some places the access road is 21-feet wide, with two parking lanes and one through lane and 14-foot-wide sidewalks. Elsewhere the dimensions are reversed: a 14-foot-wide access lane with only one parking lane and a 21-foot-wide sidewalk. Sometimes, this sidewalk space narrows to 10 feet to allow for a landscaped area in front of the buildings. The planting beds are surrounded by elegant ironwork rails and are well tended.

Traffic movement is arranged so that all lanes, central roadway and side access roads alike, move in one direction, toward the Seine, except for a central lane reserved for buses and taxis, which move in the opposite direction, toward Rond Point. Within this arrangement, movement between the access roads, center lanes, and intersecting streets is unrestricted. The access lanes curve toward the central roadway at intersections (and the sidewalk becomes wider), which means that traffic enters or exits them just after or before the intersections.

Avenue Montaigne carries a good deal of traffic, overwhelmingly in the center roadway. An hourly volume of approximately 850 vehicles was counted in the center, about 115 of them in the contra-flow bus/taxi lane; only 42 vehicles were moving in the access lanes during the same period. Traffic moves considerably more slowly in the access roads than in the center.[7] Vehicles slow down upon entering the access roads because of an elevation change—a small curb of about one and a half inches—a detail common to many Paris boulevards. Once in the access lane, drivers slow to look for parking places and often must wait behind other vehicles stopped for unloading or other reasons. Drivers also slow for pedestrians, who regularly walk along or cross the access road. Illegal vehicle movements can be observed with regularity: drivers backing the wrong way into or out of an access road, parking at the end of medians, and double parking. While there may not be a great deal of

Access Lane on Avenue Montaigne

this activity, there is enough to give a sense of confusion to a casual, unfamiliar observer. But the street works. When traffic along the access lane does flow, speeds of only thirty-two kilometers per hour (nineteen miles per hour) were observed, compared to the observed speeds of forty-eight kilometers per hour (twenty-nine miles per hour) in the center roadway.

Pedestrian volumes are high. At one intersection, approximately 1,330 people were counted along the sidewalks in one hour, and almost 1,200 people crossed Avenue Montaigne.[8] People often walk for some distance on the access roads and gather there carrying on conversations. Mothers push baby carriages down the access roads. A few pedestrians walk along the medians—which contain bus and taxi stops and two or three benches per block—but in general the medians are not used as walkways. Tree wells that take up the full width of the medians make continuous walking difficult. The benches are used mostly by people waiting for buses.

Pedestrians wishing to cross the street can do so with ease. They move to the medians from the sidewalks regardless of the traffic signals. From there, the relatively narrow center is easy to cross. For those who don't make it, a pair of bollards separating directional lanes serves as a pedestrian haven—a simple well-designed detail common to most Paris boulevards.

Avenue Montaigne contains many physical elements within a relatively narrow cross-section—fast moving lanes, slow moving lanes, sidewalks, planting strips, and trees—and it all works. Drivers can move in the center roadway with some dispatch, but the pace in the side zones is slower and more relaxed. Avenue Montaigne is an elegant, extremely pleasant, and intensely urban place to be.

Contemplating the varying access road and sidewalk layouts of Avenue Montaigne suggests that an even narrower boulevard could function quite well —one with, say, a right-of-way of 112 feet—and still provide for substantial through-going traffic and high pedestrian use.

AVENUE FRANKLIN ROOSEVELT

Avenue Franklin Roosevelt is similar to Avenue Montaigne, except that it is one-sided: there is one side access lane rather than two. On its western side, the street is lined with buildings similar to those on Avenue Montaigne. The eastern side is bounded by the park surrounding the Grand Palais museum. There, a wide sidewalk with two rows of trees occupies the space where the access road would typically be. This arrangement makes sense, as there are no buildings requiring access. It also has the happy effect of visually extending the park into the street.

Like Avenue Montaigne, Avenue Franklin Roosevelt starts at Rond Point; it runs some 1,400 feet to the Seine, where it meets the Pont des Invalides. The median and the access lane on the western side of the street are similar in dimension and layout to those along the Avenue Montaigne: a 7-foot-wide median planted with chestnut trees at 15-foot intervals and a 21-foot-wide access lane with one through lane and two parking lanes. The sidewalk is 13 feet wide and has no trees.

Here, too, the access road functions as a shared vehicle and pedestrian realm. There are a number of restaurants in the first block down from Rond Point, as well as quite a few shops. This makes for a goodly number of pedestrians on the street, especially at the lunch hour. When the sidewalk becomes overfull—or, as was observed on one occasion, when the sidewalk is disrupted because of maintenance work—people walk in the access lane, seemingly (but not actually) oblivious to vehicles. Drivers move slowly among them, rarely tapping a horn. They seem to understand that this is a shared domain. Pedestrians walking or standing in conversation move briefly aside when they become aware of a vehicle. They seem comfortable in the street—it is their realm.

Drivers along the access lanes are not so docile about getting into and out of parking spaces. Parking spots are difficult to find, and a driver who spots one may do bizarre things, like driving over a median, despite the high curbs, maneuvering between two trees, or reversing to capture a space that has just opened up. A stationary delivery truck up ahead can occasion the same behavior. To an outsider accustomed to clear rules and prohibitions—all abundantly displayed on signs spaced every four or five car lengths and regularly enforced—the surprising aspect of this behavior is its apparent normalcy.

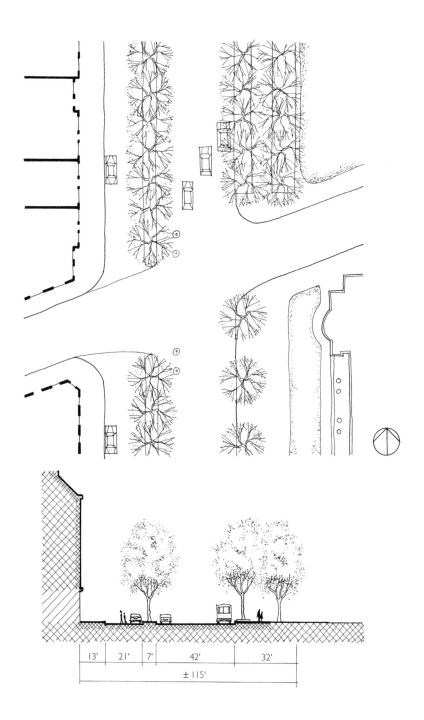

Avenue Franklin Roosevelt: plan and section

Approximate scale: 1″ = 50′ or 1:600

AVENUE MARCEAU

If there is such a thing as an "everyday boulevard," then Avenue Marceau might well be it. It is one of twelve streets that radiate from the Etoile, seven of which are multiway boulevards. With a right-of-way of approximately 134 feet, it is neither very wide nor very narrow. It is difficult to say that, by itself, it is very memorable; other nearby streets, like the Avenue de la Grand Armée and the Avenue Montaigne, are much grander or more elegant. Still, it is a presence and contributes to the entire boulevard ensemble that makes this part of the city so memorable.

Avenue Marceau runs some three thousand feet from the Etoile to Avenue President Wilson and a bridge that crosses the Seine from the Place de l'Alma. While the buildings lining the street are not all that different in height, size, and general appearance from those on the Grand Armée, they have considerably less commercial presence at ground level. For the most part, the residential and office uses of the upper floors continue to the ground floors, although there are occasional small concentrations of shops. Thus there are few entrances into buildings and relatively little street-level activity.

There is also a slight harshness to the street that is created by too much parking: six lanes at most locations, two on each of the access roadways, and two along the median curbs of

Along Avenue Marceau

the central roadway. As parking is at a premium in this part of Paris, all lanes are usually full. Walking along Avenue Marceau can therefore feel a bit like being in a linear parking lot. Perhaps this, along with the abutting land uses, explains why there are few pedestrian strollers there compared to some of the nearby boulevards.

So, while it may not be a particularly memorable or outstandingly beautiful example of a boulevard, Avenue Marceau has an ordinary day-to-day character that is in itself important when considering the many possibilities of the street type.

Its basic physical arrangement is not all that different from the parking-oriented sections of Avenue Montaigne. At 46 feet, its center roadway is 4 feet wider; the medians, at 9 feet, are 2 feet wider; the 23-foot access roadway is 2 feet wider; and the 12-foot-wide sidewalks are 2 feet narrower. Individually these are small differences, but combined with traffic arrangements and design details they add up to a very different street.

The center roadway accommodates two moving lanes in each direction as well as the two parking lanes—two more lanes in total than on Avenue Montaigne. How can there be so many lanes in 46 feet? If the lanes were actually marked, there would probably not be that many of them. As there are no markings, what happens is that when necessary—such as when there is a rush of traffic or when one or more vehicles are turning at intersections—two very wide moving lanes become four narrow moving lanes.

Like those on Avenue Montaigne, the medians on Avenue Marceau have lines of trees and contain bus shelters, benches, and parking-chit machines. However, here too, small differences become significant. First, the median trees are spaced about twice as far apart—at 33-foot intervals, like those on the Avenue de la Grand Armée—which means that the tree trunks create a less dense line separating the center from the side. Second, there are wide breaks in the medians, at least one per block, to permit vehicles to exit from and enter the central lanes. These breaks substantially erode the pedestrian character of the medians; fewer people venture along them than they do on Avenue Montaigne.

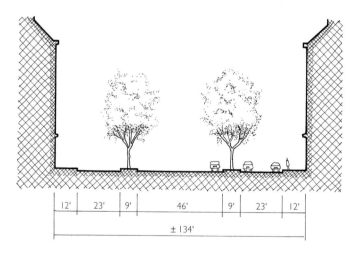

Avenue Marceau: section

Avenue Marceau carries only moderate traffic volumes. As on the other Paris boulevards, that traffic is concentrated in the central lanes: of a total of approximately 1,000 vehicles counted in one hour, some 88 percent were in the center, while only 120 vehicles used the two side access roadways.[9] Traffic in the center doesn't flow as smoothly midblock as it does on Avenue Montaigne or on the Avenue de la Grand Armée. From time to time it is disrupted by drivers slowing to look for parking spaces along the median curb, or pulling out of parking spaces, or entering or exiting the roadway via the midblock median breaks. On the access roads, drivers generally move slowly because they are usually looking for a parking space. Pedestrians rarely walk along the access road other than to cross to or from a parked car or bus stop.

A particularly interesting feature of Avenue Marceau is its complex intersections, which make turning possibilities even more complicated than on most multiway boulevards—and yet the street still works. Of the seven intersections along the street, only one has crossing streets that meet the center roadway at anything close to a right angle. Thus, turning angles to and from the boulevard are both obtuse and acute, and often several angled side streets come into the same intersection from one side. In spite of all this complexity, there are no restrictions on movements among side lanes, center lanes, and cross streets. For example, the intersection of Avenue Marceau with Rue Newton, Rue Galilée, and Rue Euler—one intersection away from the Etoile—offers some forty-two separate permitted movements, not counting U-turns from the center lanes, which are also legal. There is no traffic light, just a subtly raised circle near the center of the intersection that most drivers use as an informal traffic circle. Yet the accident rates at this intersection, and all along Avenue Marceau, are not dissimilar to those on other major streets in Paris. Drivers seem to recognize that there are many possibilities, that there is a risk, and, therefore, that it is prudent to be careful. Avenue Marceau makes it apparent that the boulevard form, already complex, can absorb additional complexity and still function well.

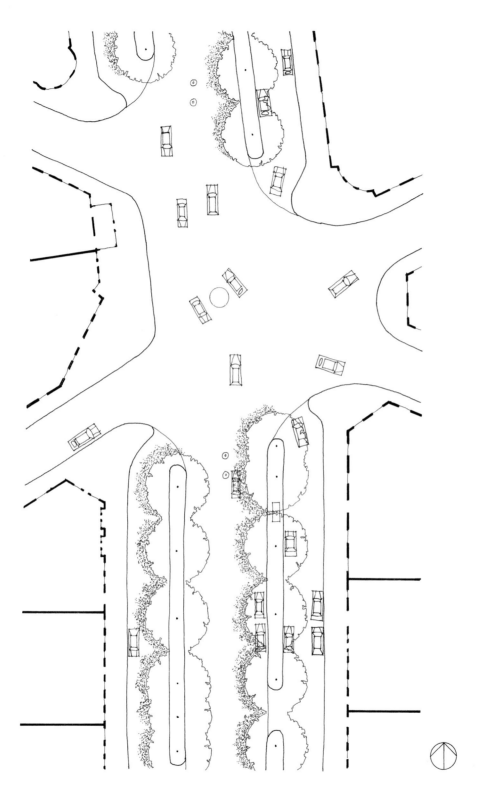

Avenue Marceau: plan

Approximate scale: 1″ = 50′ or 1:600

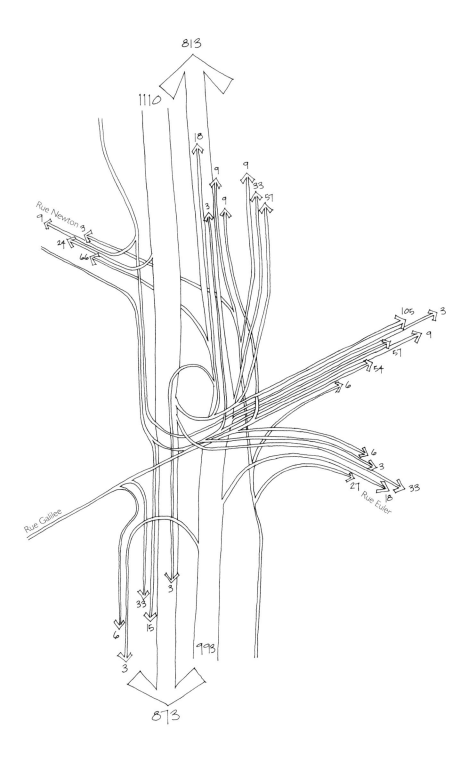

Traffic movements on Avenue Marceau at Rue Galilee

The Etoile Boulevards in context

We have visited four of the many boulevards concentrated in one notable area of Paris. Each has a distinctive character determined, in large part, by its particular physical qualities. It is remarkable that there are so many others close by, that each one has its own distinctive character, and that most are memorable in very positive ways. Avenue Georges V may, like Avenue Marceau, have too much parking, but it is alive with people attracted to the mostly upscale shops, restaurants, and hotels. Here it is the uses of the buildings along the street that are most distinctive. Avenue d'Iena, one boulevard over from Avenue Marceau, is more modest and locally scaled than Avenue Georges V. Avenue Foch, at 400 feet, is the widest of the Paris boulevards. Its breadth, especially its 100-foot-wide medians that seem to separate the center and side roadways into separate streets, may tempt us to see it as something other than a multiway boulevard, though in basic form it is the same as its more modest relatives.

So, the Paris multiway boulevards are all similar and yet different. They all still seem to work well today, even though they were designed for a period well before the proliferation of motor vehicles. They are all wonderful places to experience.

Avenue George V

Chapter Two

BARCELONA'S ELEGANT BUT THREATENED BOULEVARDS

If one were intent on studying the best streets in the world but could visit only one city, that city might well be Barcelona. So many of its streets are tree-lined and elegant, with particularly generous areas for pedestrians to gather and stroll. Within the area of the city known as L'Eixample—the famous mid–nineteenth-century city expansion grid designed by Ildefons Cerdá that has memorable beveled corners at intersections—are several major multiway boulevards: the Passeig de Gràcia, the Avinguda Diagonal, and the Gran Via de les Corts Catalans. These boulevards give structure to the grid, connecting L'Eixample with the old city in very visible and appropriate ways, at the same time creating strong lineal pathways within the newer area.

Like other streets in the city, the boulevards are elegant. And yet, because they are the widest streets in the city, they also serve as major traffic thoroughfares—a function that some of Barcelona's other great streets, such as the Ramblas, do not have to shoulder. In recent times, their traffic-movement functions have perhaps received more attention than their more pedestrian-oriented uses—and this is unfortunate.

Passeig de Gràcia

The Passeig de Gràcia starts at the Plaça de Catalunya, a major public square that connects it to the old Gothic Quarter and the Ramblas and runs north for about a mile. However, it is more than its geographic position and width—some 200 feet—that give this boulevard its strong presence: it is the most elegant shopping street in the city, intricately complex in its design details and always lively with activity. Along both sides of the street are stores, offices, hotels, theaters, restaurants, and residential quarters in an unending procession. Wide sidewalks are for strolling or for sitting under a line of closely planted plane trees.

There are side access lanes for slow-moving traffic, parking, and access to an underground carpark. There is another row of trees on each median, as well as bus shelters, places to walk, benches (near the intersections), and entrances to the parking garage and subway. In the sub-

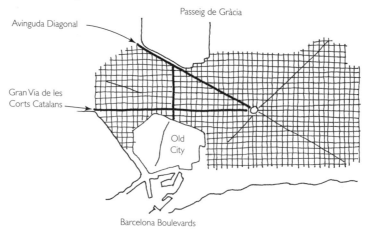

Barcelona Boulevards

Barcelona boulevards

Passeig de Gràcia

way, there is even a regional and national train station where one can board trains to major European destinations. Fast traffic occupies a center roadway some 60 feet wide. While traffic arrangements here have changed from one decade to the next, there are always, it seems, buses running in both directions. The last time we looked, there were four lanes in one direction and two in the other.

Block lengths along the Passeig de Gràcia are relatively short, so there are plenty of intersections, mostly with one-way streets, but also with the two-way Avinguda Diagonal and Gran Via de les Corts Catalans. The system of alternating one-way streets is pervasive throughout the city, an attempt to facilitate traffic flow.

The 70 feet on each side of the central roadway is where the intricacy and richness lie. The sidewalks are wide, about 36 feet, and they are comfortable to walk on under the trees. Indeed, they are wide enough to hold generous café seating and still have space for such regularly scheduled events as book fairs. Sidewalks are edged in many places by planting beds that hold well-tended shrubs and flowering plants. Benches placed under the trees at regular intervals face toward the sidewalk activity. There are numerous kiosks selling newspapers, magazines, lottery tickets, and various things to eat. At the corners there are wonderful round tiled benches with planters in the middle—designed by Antonio Gaudí—and sidewalks are paved with his magnificent hexagonal tiles. The medians have a different version of Gaudí's tiled bench, with a lacelike iron streetlight growing out of it—one of at least four different streetlight designs that embellish the street.

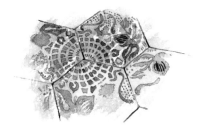

The access lanes vary in width to accommodate different parking arrangements: one lane of parallel parking in some places, one each of parallel parking and diagonal parking in others. And yet, it is always possible to walk along the medians under the trees. Though not

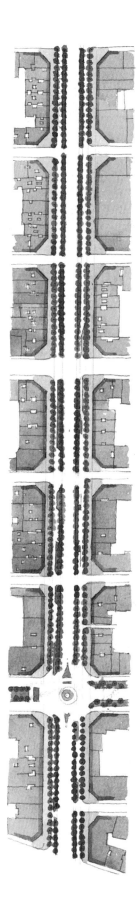

Passeig de Gràcia: street and building context

Approximate scale: 1″ = 400′ or 1:4,800

all the buildings along the street are richly detailed, many of them are; some feature elaborate bay windows that overhang the sidewalk. Then there are the fanciful and colorful buildings by Gaudí and Josep Puigi Cadafalch—including the well-known Casa Milà and Casa Batlló.

As good as this boulevard is, it could be better. There is often a steady flow of traffic along the access roads, and it moves a bit too fast, averaging almost 32 kilometers per hour.[1] It seems that the asymmetric arrangement of traffic lanes in the center and the fact that left turns cannot be made from the center forces traffic onto the side roads. Drivers desiring to make a left-hand turn move first into the access lane and then, at the intersection, turn left across the whole center roadway.

In general, cars on the cross streets seem to make more turns into the access roads than into the center. At one block, 108 vehicles per hour were counted turning left into the southbound access road, while only 24 made a left turn into the southbound center.[2] Many of these vehicles are taxis cruising for fares and cars headed for the entrances to the underground garage.

Traffic on the one-way cross streets is often heavier than it is on the Passeig de Gràcia, especially on a particularly wide one called Aragó. Here, an hourly count of 3,564 vehicles per hour were observed, versus 1,956 on the boulevard.[3] The one-way configuration of the cross streets makes for an interesting traffic flow out of the access roads at intersections. In order

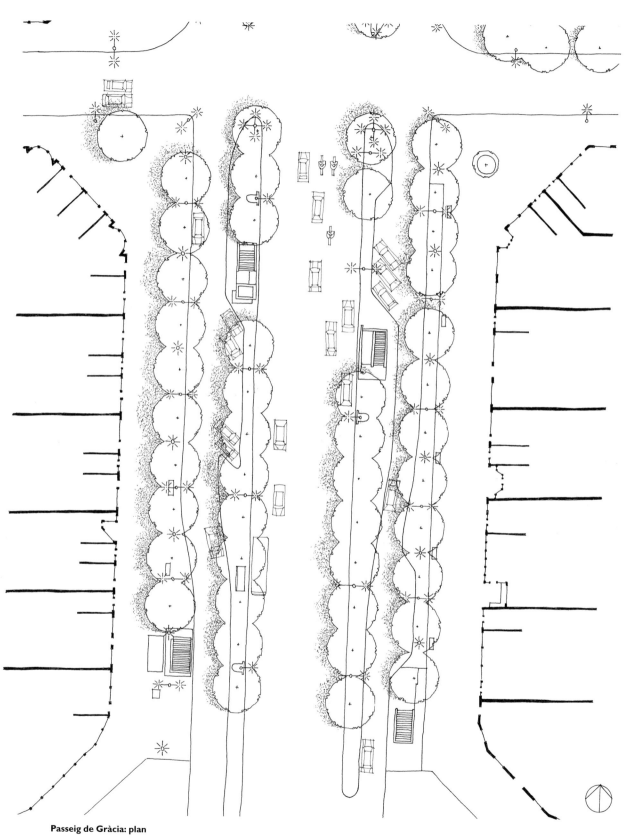

Passeig de Gràcia: plan

Approximate scale: 1″ = 50′ or 1:600

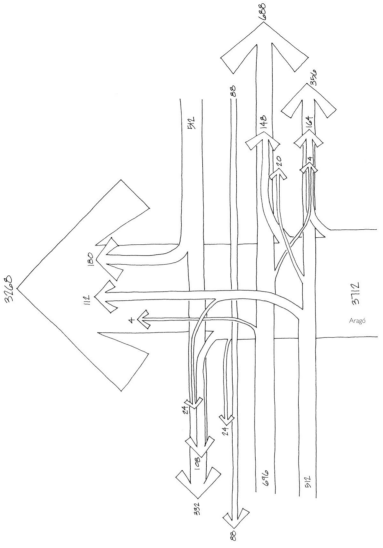

Traffic Movements on Passeig de Gràcia at Aragó

to make left turns out of the access roads, vehicles pull into the space defined by the median, where they wait for the cross traffic light. Often six or seven cars stack up there during a signal phase.

In spite of the traffic on the access roads, pedestrians often mingle with the vehicles, cutting through to parked cars or to the bus stops and benches on the median. They also make use of the wide and boldly zebra-striped crosswalks provided at intersections. There are always many pedestrians on the Passeig de Gràcia; at times their numbers exceed the number of vehicles. In one location, a total of 3,304 pedestrians per hour was counted along the sidewalks, while during the same period only 1,808 vehicles were moving along the center and side roadways.[4]

Along the Median on Passeig de Gràcia

The current cross-sectional configuration of the street, though not new, is not original. The side roadways apparently were narrower and the medians wider, and each held two rows of trees. That sounds better. In 1994, the trees were pruned in what seems a brutal way. So change has occurred on the Passeig de Gràcia, and it could be made better—perhaps by restoring it to the way it was. In the meantime, it remains a wonderful street.

THE AVINGUDA DIAGONAL

The Avinguda Diagonal is also no small presence in Barcelona: it extends some five miles from the northwest corner of the city at the Jardins de Cervantes to the Placa de les Glories Catalans, where it intersects with the Gran Via de les Corts Catalans. Aside from its length, its diagonal orientation to the grid laid out by Cerdá—hence its straightforward name— renders it special, easy to recognize and recall. Along this boulevard, particularly near its intersection with the Passeig de Gràcia, office and commercial uses predominate in buildings of generally seven stories, with some taller.

Many triangular open spaces are created by the angular intersections, and there are three traffic circles where other major streets meet Avinguda Diagonal. The wide, irregular intersections, combined with its multiway boulevard form and generous tree plantings— memorable in their own right—tell us immediately that the Diagonal is a special passageway in the urban landscape. Its width, almost 165 feet from building to building, is significantly less than that of the Passeig de Gràcia. But it feels wider because of the size and openness of the intersections.

More than the Passeig de Gràcia, Avinguda Diagonal is geared to moving traffic, though its cross-section design might not at first suggest as much. The central roadway, though only 50 feet wide, is striped for six moving lanes, the outer ones reserved for buses and taxis. The side access lanes, while narrow at 17 feet, do not permit parking but carry two lanes of traffic. Vehicles move fast, almost as fast as they do in the center roadway. More total traffic travels in the center than on the access roads, but the numbers per lane are similar.[5]

There is no auto parking whatsoever along the Diagonal. Sometimes people wanting to dash into a building will tempt fate by pulling halfway onto the sidewalk, but recently a line of round granite bollards at the curb line were installed to discourage such behavior.

Bollards.

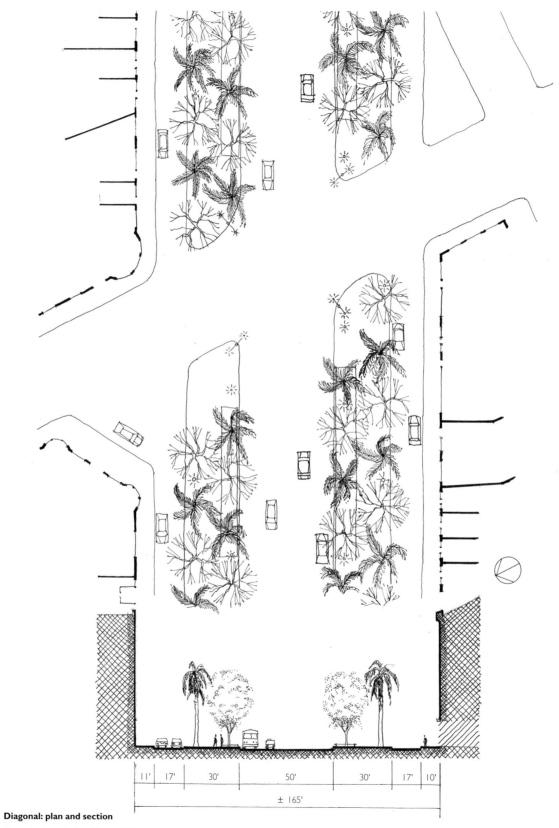

Diagonal: plan and section

Approximate scale: 1″ = 50′ or 1:600

11'   17'   30'   50'   30'   17'   10'

± 165'

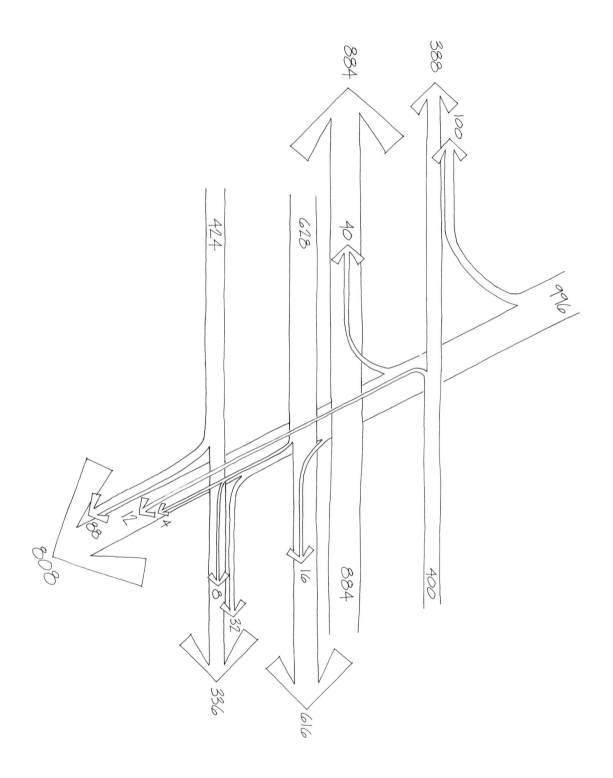

Traffic movement on Diagonal at Balmes

Clearly this is a traffic street. Given its length and the connections it makes between distant parts of the city, this is understandable. Yet the emphasis on traffic movement is somewhat at odds with the 30-foot-wide tree-lined medians that appear designed for strolling and sitting at leisure. In fact, while there is far less pedestrian activity on the Avinguda Diagonal than on the Passeig de Gracia, there are still many walkers—though their activity often seems more purposeful than leisurely. Most pedestrians use the medians rather than the narrow 10.5-foot-wide sidewalks. Many walk for some length, crossing from median to median at intersections. Bicycle lanes have recently been installed on the medians, so pedestrians must share the space. In addition, large numbers of motorcycles are often parked adjacent to the walking path, and this activity is seemingly without consequence.

Nonetheless, the medians are handsomely detailed and include a planting arrangement not observed elsewhere. One doesn't normally associate palm trees (*Phoenix canariensis* type) with plane trees, but here they are planted together in a staggered pattern. Planters set back about a foot from the curb on the central side of the medians are 11 feet wide and planted with grass and shrubbery; they are approximately 10 inches high and form a double high curb along the center roadway. This design detail may be intended to discourage pedestrians from midblock jaywalking across the center roadway. There are also attractive pedestrian-scaled lampposts on the medians and benches between the trees that face toward the center.

Time spent on the Avinguda Diagonal is less enjoyable than on the Passeig de Gràcia. Though its wide medians suggest leisure, the boulevard is programmed and regulated for moving great volumes of traffic at great speed, and that leaves it not as pleasant a street as it might be.

Along a median on Diagonal

Barcelona's other centrally located multiway boulevard, the Gran Via de les Corts Catalans, is similar in its cross-sectional configuration and traffic flow. Its main difference from the Avinguda Diagonal is that it is aligned with the overall grid pattern rather than crossing it diagonally; its intersections therefore are not as wide. Its medians are planted solely with plane trees. Like the Avinguda Diagonal, it functions more as a traffic-moving street than as a strolling street.

Barcelona's boulevards are elegantly designed and detailed streets, and the Passeig de Gràcia is very much a lively multipurpose street that serves equally well local users and through traffic, pedestrians and drivers. But the other boulevards seem to be devoted more and more to a single purpose, and even the Passeig de Gràcia is a less-inviting street than it once was. We fear for these boulevards.

Chapter Three   BROOKLYN'S CLASSIC SUBURBAN BOULEVARDS:
EASTERN PARKWAY AND OCEAN PARKWAY

For most people the thought of New York City readily brings to mind images of broad avenues and endless numbered streets—not boulevards, let alone multiway boulevards. Parkways may come to mind, particularly if one knows of New York's twentieth-century history and can recall or has read about Robert Moses. Moses attached the name "parkway" to many of the limited-access highways he pushed through the crowded boroughs of New York in the 1930s, 1940s, and 1950s, displacing countless people and destroying many neighborhoods in the process.[1] But parkways have an earlier, positive, even bucolic, history in New York. Moses borrowed the term from Frederick Law Olmsted and Calvert Vaux, who used it to describe the suburban boulevards they designed and built in a number of American cities in the 1870s and 1880s. They began in Brooklyn.

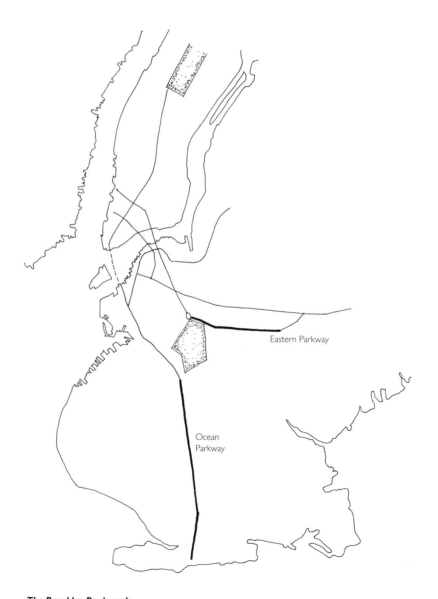

The Brooklyn Boulevards
Approximate scale: 1:100,000

Brooklyn has two Olmsted and Vaux multiway boulevards. Eastern Parkway is two-and-a-half-miles long and runs east from the Grand Army Plaza, at the main northeast entrance to Prospect Park, to Brownsville, which marked the city limits when the parkway was built. Ocean Parkway is five-and-a-half-miles long, beginning at the southwest corner of the park and running to Coney Island. Both streets were laid out through open countryside and built in less than five years—which seems, at the start of the twenty-first century, a very short time. Their physical form remains much as originally designed and built, although how they are used has evolved along with transportation technology and social norms.

The parkways are as wide as the grand boulevards of Paris and Barcelona: a distance of 270 feet separates buildings across the street. The parkways themselves are 210 feet wide and have 30-foot front yard setbacks. The center roadway of Eastern Parkway is 65 feet wide, while Ocean Parkway's is 5 feet wider. Modest 25-foot-wide access roads line the sides of both streets. Between the center and the side roadways are generous 30- or 35-foot wide pedestrian medians locally referred to as "malls."

What is most impressive about the parkways are the six rows of mature, closely spaced trees that continue the whole length of the streets with barely a break at intersections. On both parkways, one row of trees lines each sidewalk edge, and two rows line each of the malls; they are planted 25 to 30 feet apart. On Ocean Parkway they are a dense, low-canopied mix of maple, oak, and sycamore. On Eastern Parkway they are stately London plane trees.

The medians of the two streets are configured slightly differently. On Ocean Parkway, the inner edge of each median features an almost unbroken line of wood-slat benches, each 20 feet long and facing toward the center. A wide cement walkway runs down the middle of the median. On the west median, the walkway is divided down the middle by a low rail that designates half of it as a bicycle path. On Eastern Parkway, the medians have newer, more widely spaced benches set under the trees along both sides, wide flagstone walks, and closely spaced ornamental, antique-style lampposts. Many of the trees are newly planted. Recent improvements are the result of Eastern Parkway's designation as a historical land-mark. The medians there also carry several entrances to the subway (built in the 1910s), which runs under the western part of the parkway.

Both of these streets are truly wonderful, human, community places. Forget, at least for a moment, the volume of traffic, which is sizable, and look at the people. People *use* the park-ways. On Ocean Parkway families stroll, women in groups push baby carriages, old men and women sit on the benches watching street life. People jog singly and in pairs, and bicyclists ride at a leisurely pace along the western mall. At the northern end of the street, groups of older men gather daily to play cards at fixed tables set near the benches. Many of them pass long hours this way. On Eastern Parkway, people sit on the benches, alone or in groups; and throughout the day there is a constant flow of pedestrians along the malls moving to and from the subway entrances. On warm days, people congregate on the malls, on the side-walks, and in front yards. Strangers are usually greeted with a nod.

Ocean Parkway passes through a series of generally well-kept neighborhoods. Some are moderate-income neighborhoods and others are more well-to-do. Numerous Italian and Jewish families live in these neighborhoods, which carry names like Bensonhurst and Mid-

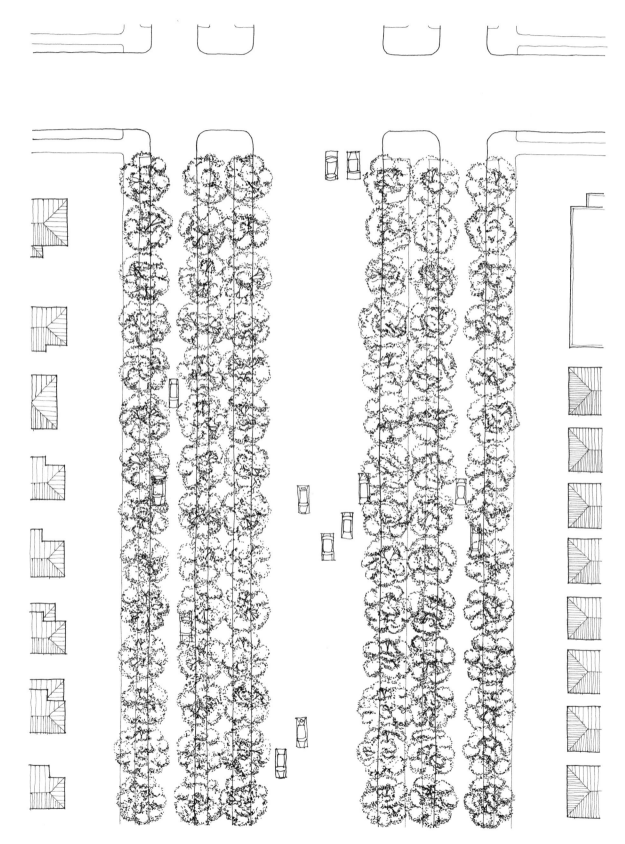

Ocean Parkway: plan

Approximate scale: 1″ = 50′ or 1:600

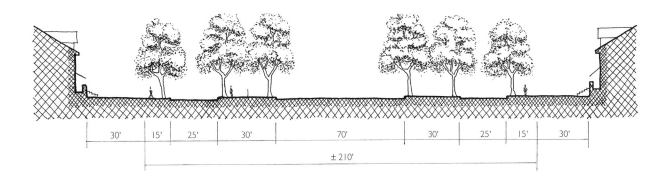

| 30' | 15' | 25' | 30' | 70' | 30' | 25' | 15' | 30' |

± 210'

Ocean Parkway: section

Approximate scale: 1″ = 50′ or 1:600

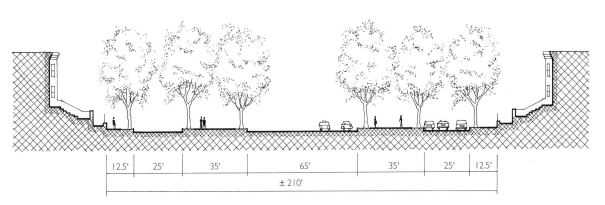

| 12.5' | 25' | 35' | 65' | 35' | 25' | 12.5' |

± 210'

Eastern Parkway: section

wood. Many of them have lived on the parkway or in the nearby neighborhoods for a long time.[2]

Ocean Parkway today still has much of the suburban character that Olmsted and Vaux envisioned for the Brooklyn boulevards. A stretch of tall apartment buildings at the park end of the street quickly gives way to neat two-story duplexes and, farther south, large single-family homes. Nearing Coney Island, after the boulevard passes under the Beltway, the apartment buildings begin again, taller and more closely spaced and oriented toward ocean views. Along the length of Ocean Parkway there are a number of Jewish community centers and religious schools. Several are large and recently built. Other than these institutions and a handful of nursing homes, there are only residences on the parkway. The apartment buildings at either end of the street are relative newcomers, dating from the dislocation and redevelopment associated with Moses's freeway building. In the 1950s, the Prospect Expressway built in central Brooklyn was designed to feed traffic directly onto the northern end of Ocean Parkway. The perimeter Shore Expressway (Beltway) was built slightly later, girdling Brooklyn and substantially cutting off the city from its waterfront.

Eastern Parkway has a very different feel and look than Ocean Parkway. It is more densely built, lined for the most part with tightly packed brownstone rowhouses three and four stories tall, most of which have stately stairs leading to second-floor entrances. Some of the rowhouses have been converted into offices, but most are divided into three or four residential flats. There are some large apartment buildings, mostly congregated near the park, and, at several major street intersections, a few small stores and medical offices. There is also a large Jewish community center and several churches. The Prospect Park end of Eastern Parkway is home to two important cultural institutions, the Brooklyn Museum and the main branch of the Brooklyn Public Library. Everywhere the prescribed 30-foot setback remains intact. Many of the people who live on Eastern Parkway have lived in the neighbor-

Subway Entrance on Eastern Parkway Median

Ocean Parkway, Brooklyn '94.   A.B.J.

The Sidewalk on Ocean Parkway

Ocean Parkway Median

hood for a long time. In some brownstones, extended families live in flats on different floors of the same house, and many young married couples live down the block from the house where they grew up.[3]

The people who live along Eastern Parkway are different from those who live on Ocean Parkway. Eastern Parkway runs through Crown Heights, which since the 1960s has been home to a vibrant and thriving West Indian community. Surrounding residential streets look like those in any other well-kept neighborhood, but an ethnic flavor pervades the colorful commercial cross streets, where one can buy West Indian newspapers and broiled goat. On warm spring and summer days, entrepreneurs sell syrupy shaved-ice drinks from pushcarts set up along the parkway malls.

Today, both parkways function as major arterial streets within Brooklyn and carry a lot of fast-moving through traffic. Between 60,000 and 75,000 vehicles travel on the center lanes of each parkway every day, but the streets handle these volumes gracefully.[4] In spite of the constant blur and noise of fast traffic, there is a noticeably lazy feel to the parkways. Even the rush of southbound traffic hurtling onto Ocean Parkway from the gaping underground mouth of the Prospect Expressway is absorbed into a more gentle ambiance within one or two blocks. On both streets, the tree-lined malls and side roads are slow-moving realms. People stroll or linger on the malls and often walk down the middle of the access roads. Drivers on the access roads proceed slowly, hemmed in by the parked cars on both sides and forced to stop at every intersection by stop signs. Often, cars creep along behind pedestrians who are undeterred by their presence. Delivery vehicles and double-parked cars often block passage. Not many drivers drive along the access roads for more than a block or two.

Along Eastern Parkway Brooklyn.   6/99

At a few places along both streets, parking restrictions on one side of the access road are slowly changing the pedestrian character of the side roads. On Ocean Parkway, in an area of single-family houses, the restrictions are intended to deter nonresident parking. On Eastern Parkway the restrictions apply only during the day to reserve space for transit-police vehicles. In these areas, drivers on the access road often move faster than in other areas because the roadway is more open. There the pedestrian realm is not so friendly.

Traffic in the center roadway of both parkways is controlled by traffic lights. On Ocean Parkway there are three through lanes in each direction, with left-turn lanes added at some intersections. Eastern Parkway has three lanes running east and two in the other direction, plus center turn lanes. On both streets all movements are allowed at the intersections. Drivers in the center can go straight, turn into a cross street, or slip into the access road on either side. Drivers on the access roads can go straight, make a right turn onto the cross street, or turn out into the center. Cross-street traffic can turn into the side or into the center. When stopped by a signal, cross traffic stops at limit lines painted at the sidewalk edges. Drivers who want to make a right-hand turn are then free to pull out into the space protected by the medians and wait for an opening in the traffic. Linear travel by pedestrians and bicyclists along the medians is given de facto priority; most continue across the intersection from median to median in what have become informal crosswalks.

The pervasive atmosphere of both Eastern Parkway and Ocean Parkway is that of a lineal neighborhood meeting place. Their wide public spaces provide settings for the public life of the community. On Sundays, large congregations of people converge on the several churches on Eastern Parkway. As services let out, friends greet each other and socialize,

Eastern Parkway Median

drifting onto the access roads and the malls. Small children in their Sunday best cling to parents' hands. Older children skirmish or lounge in groups. There is a general air of festivity that dissipates only slowly as drivers cruising the side lanes pick up family members and groups of pedestrians drift away down the parkway malls.

On Saturdays, Orthodox Jews of different sects observe the Sabbath by walking along the parkways to their synagogues and yeshivas. Sometimes, groups of celebrants surrounding a rabbi make a slow progress up Ocean Parkway, stopping every hundred feet or so, raising the Torah in the air and chanting.

On Labor Day people in the millions take over Eastern Parkway. Revelers come from all over New York City and more distant places to watch the colorful West Indian Carnival parade. The food is spectacular. People who live on the parkway speak enthusiastically of the parade and say it is an important reason for living on the street. The tall rowhouses offer great views, and family and friends come for the party.

Other annual rituals that occur along the parkways are the long-distance bicycle races and runners' marathons that yearly use the streets as part of their route. Runners or bicyclists take over the tree-lined malls in a long, spread-out line while cross traffic is held at bay by police, who follow the participants along the course. The parkways also host everyday bicycle trips and weekend outings. They are a part of the Brooklyn/Queens Greenway, a forty-mile bicycle and pedestrian path system that runs from Coney Island to Long Island Sound.

In 1969 Donald Appleyard, Mark Lintell, and Sue Gerson completed a well-known study in San Francisco; *Livable Streets* measured residents' responses to high-volume through traffic streets.[5] Those who lived on high-volume streets complained vehemently about the traffic's effect on their quality of life. The Brooklyn boulevards, as well as The Esplanade in Chico, California, are high-volume residential streets. Yet according to a 1997 replication of the Appleyard study, the boulevard configuration—with its access lanes separated from

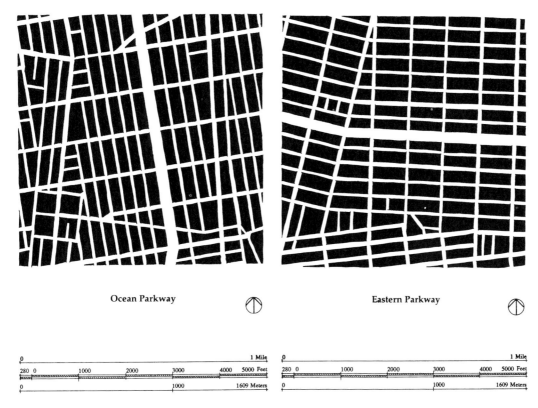

Ocean Parkway

Eastern Parkway

Ocean Parkway, square mile map

Eastern Parkway, square mile map

the center by tree-planted medians—successfully mitigates the impact of heavy traffic.[6] Residents rated all three of these boulevards as more livable than neighboring, conventionally designed streets with medium traffic volumes.

Ocean Parkway and Eastern Parkway are remarkable streets. They are remarkable because they have retained their complex form in spite of the fact that for years they have been major carriers of traffic and are classified as arterial streets by city traffic engineers. Yet in spite of the heavy traffic, they are highly valued streets on which to live and spend time. Their community value is further attested to by successful local resistance to federally generated reconstruction and repaving proposals for Ocean Parkway in the 1960s—changes that would have widened lane widths in the central roadway and decreased the widths of the medians. Moreover, designation of these boulevards as historic landmarks, which protects their basic designs, would not have happened without community support. These are not bucolic, meandering parkways; nor are they settings for displaying the homes and gardens of the wealthy. They are working multiway boulevards that carry a lot of vehicular traffic at the same time as they provide gracious focuses for local life, including everyday recreation and neighborhood meetings. They both shape their local communities and give structure to a large part of Brooklyn. They are boulevards for everyone.

Chapter Four   THE GRAND CONCOURSE:
A BOULEVARD IN NEED OF HELP

A sadness accompanies the Grand Concourse in New York City's Bronx. It comes from knowing how it once was as compared to how it is now. It is a sadness not without hope, of knowing that this boulevard could be much better than it is. Ironically, the street is now what it
was originally envisioned to be in the late 1890s: a speedway concourse, though one with a
far different character than the pleasure drive connecting Manhattan with the northern Bronx
parks intended by its engineer designer.[1] Speed then was different than speed now.

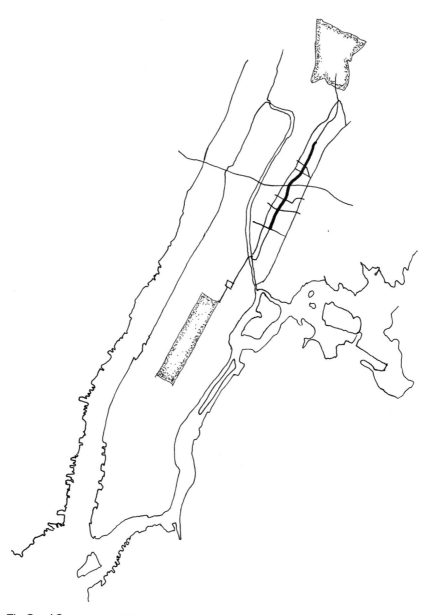

The Grand Concourse: context
Approximate scale: 1:100,000

The Grand Concourse is a major north-south throughway of the Bronx, and it has a multiway boulevard configuration for most of its four-and-a-half-mile length. It runs along a natural ridge that bisects the Bronx. If Manhattan continued north along the line set by Central Park, Fifth Avenue, and Park Avenue, the Grand Concourse would be the extension of that spine. That was its designer's intent. By its location and size, it gives structure to the Bronx. The ridgeline location was chosen because it allowed cross streets to be tunneled beneath it without disrupting through traffic.

The basic character of the street is determined by the stretch between 161st Street and the Bronx County courthouse in the south and Fordham Road in the north. The street is lined with five- and six-story apartment buildings with a few ground-floor shops—usually at corners. Local shopping areas, for the most part, run perpendicular to the Grand Concourse on the cross streets that burrow through the ridge. The few commercial concentrations are mostly near stops for the major subway line that runs beneath the street. The Bronx Museum is located near the southern end of the street; and Joyce Kilmer Park, which is directly in front of the Bronx County courthouse, has long been a place to walk, sit, meet friends, and talk while the kids run around and do what kids do. Fordham University and the Bronx Zoo are not far from the Fordham Road intersection, but the once-busy commercial hub where the two streets cross has a moribund quality to it.

Socioeconomically, the area is stable. Long a middle-class, predominantly Jewish area, much of the street and most of the surrounding neighborhoods are now occupied by lower-income African and Hispanic Americans. Toward Joyce Kilmer Park, though people's eth-

Along Grand Concourse

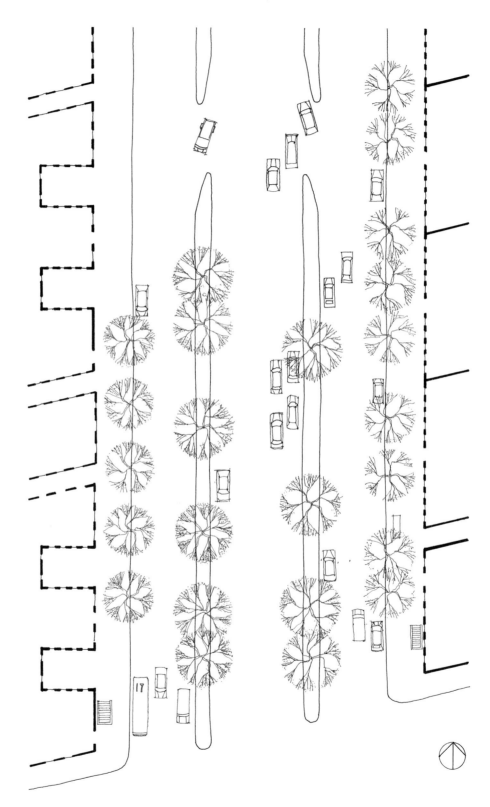

Grand Concourse: plan

Approximate scale: 1″ = 50′ or 1:600

A "sleeve" from the central roadway to the
access roadway on the Grand Concourse

nicity has changed, their carriage, manners, and dress seem similar to or the equivalent of those of the early 1950s—but that may be a superficial observation.

The changed physical qualities of the Grand Concourse—the lack of maintenance, the absence of recent public and private investment, and the changed nature of vehicular behavior along it are what generate the sadness.

This was once a relatively gracious street. The people who lived there were by no means wealthy, but the address was a good one. The six-story buildings were in fine condition. There were no graffiti. If it was not a strolling street in the sense of the Passeig de Gràcia in Barcelona or Ocean Parkway in Brooklyn, it was nonetheless a walking street. To walk from 165th Street to Fordham Road—a distance of almost three miles—to attend the Loews Paradise Theater or to shop at Bloomingdale's—might not have been a daily habit, but it was certainly not an extraordinary event. Trees lined the medians, good-sized if not large London planes. As long as one stayed to one side of the street, traffic was not a problem, because traffic on the access lanes moved slowly.

But whereas crossing the side access lanes used to be easy, now one had better be careful. The cars really zip along, and gypsy cabs, always on the prowl, speed up or make stops at any angle. The central, fast-moving lanes, always a reason for pedestrian caution, are all the more so now. Many of the trees along the medians are missing, giving a moth-eaten appearance to what once were continuous lines—the moths have won.

Maintenance is an issue perhaps best illustrated by the Andrew Freeman Home near 164th Street. A retirement home for the elderly until the 1950s, it is set well back from the street between a low wall and a transparent cast-iron fence; the once-immaculate building

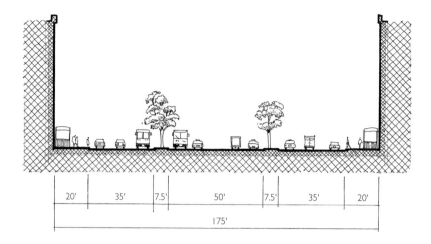

Grand Concourse: existing section
Approximate scale: 1″ = 50′ or 1:600

and grounds are now shabby. Everything seems in need of repair.

Why did things change? We are not sure but suspect that many factors, all acting to-gether, made the difference. By the mid-1950s and early 1960s, traffic movement—speed, high volumes—was a high priority, and those in charge were not overly concerned with, or may not have recognized, the slower-paced life that took place along the street. One need only recall the construction of the Cross-Bronx Expressway in the 1950s and the chunks of neighborhoods that it decimated to understand the prevailing official attitudes of the times. Not too many people cared about local streets then. The ensuing migrations and disinvest-ments of the South Bronx in the 1960s had to have spillover impacts along the Concourse. The city's finances were stretched, and spending on maintenance was not at an all-time high. Streets can deteriorate slowly, just as they often improve slowly. One day someone looks anew, or there comes a community awareness that the street has changed and it is not as good as it once was—seriously not as good.

Currently the Grand Concourse is a fast-moving traffic street. A good many pedestrians use it, but the overall impression is that people are incidental to the primary objective of moving vehicles. If this was once a multipurpose roadway—for fast traffic, slow traffic, people, local public transit buses, strolling, even sitting—it is no longer. There is a missed opportunity here, an opportunity for the Concourse to be a focus for the community. And that is unfortunate.

The Grand Concourse is 175 feet wide, 25 feet narrower than the Passeig de Gràcia in Barcelona, though it seems as wide. There are many fewer physical things to catch the eyes and to keep them occupied. Buildings generally abut the property line. The central road-way, which is 50 feet wide, has two through lanes in each direction and a left-turn lane at intersections. Medians, paved, are narrow, at 7.5 feet, and are planted, seemingly at random, with an assortment of large and small trees. Much of the median paving is broken up by large grates covering the air vents for the subway below. There are also "sleeves" cut into

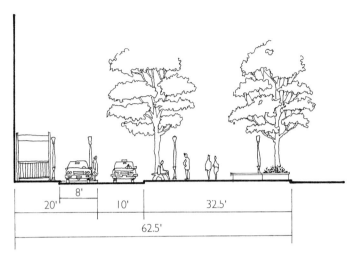

**A possible reconfiguration to create an extended pedestrian realm
on the Grand Concourse**

some of the medians to permit vehicles to make the transition between the center roadway
and side access lanes. It is not surprising that, with so many interruptions and no positive
reasons to be there, few pedestrians walk along the medians. People do, however, use them
at intersections as safe havens in the long crossing of the whole street.

The 35-foot-wide access roads allow for two lanes of through traffic and one parking lane.
Their 11.5-foot moving lanes are wider than the center lanes. No wonder traffic speeds
along them! Buses also use the access lanes. (Strange that Americans almost always relegate
public transit to a secondary position rather than giving it the dominant location in the center.) The 20-foot sidewalks are planted randomly with an assortment of trees. Stair access to
the subway occurs at the sidewalk.

Block lengths along the Grand Concourse vary considerably, and most minor intersecting streets do not cross it. Rather, they stop at the side access lanes, barred from the central
lanes by the medians. Major cross streets have through lanes that pass under the Grand Concourse, as well as side lanes that come up to the Concourse, forming the intersections. This
arrangement permits, even encourages, speed in the central lanes and does nothing to slow
traffic along the access lanes.

Movement at intersections is restricted. Traffic may not merge from the center lanes into
the access roads, or vice versa. Neither right turns from the center nor left turns from the access roads are permitted; these transitional movements are presumably accommodated by
the midblock sleeves in the medians. At most intersections, the center, the access roads, and
the cross streets are all controlled by signal lights.

The Grand Concourse has a reputation as one of the most dangerous streets in New York
for pedestrians—the other being Queens Boulevard, which has a similar physical configuration. It doesn't take long to understand why. There is almost as much traffic using the access roads as the center roadway. An average northbound volume of over 850 cars per hour

was counted in the center, and almost 800 in the access road.[2] The ratio of traffic in the central lanes to that in the access lanes is a far cry from that of Brooklyn's Eastern Parkway or Ocean Parkway. This is a much-used street: over one day in 1992, almost 58,000 vehicles used the Grand Concourse.[3]

But the problem is not only the number of cars using the access lanes, it is their speed. On a snowy winter morning, we rode for about twenty blocks in a taxi on one of the access roads, traveling at least as fast as vehicles in the center lanes. These side lanes are wide—wider than in the center. Why go slow? Generally, movement restrictions at intersections are respected by motorists, but if a rule is broken, it is a reasonable bet that a gypsy cab driver will be the wrongdoer. They are big users of the access roads.

Given the density of population along the Grand Concourse and nearby, it is not surprising that pedestrian activity is high.[4] There is considerable midblock jaywalking, which might be expected, considering the long distances between intersections with the central lanes. Youngsters especially tend to jaywalk. Essentially, people jaywalk whenever they think it is safe to do so, across the access lanes with their fast traffic and across the central lanes with theirs. But people don't walk along the narrow medians. We have seen that the medians flanking Avenue Montaigne in Paris are even narrower, at seven feet, but they have benches, bus stops, kiosks, and plentiful trees. People use those medians. But pedestrians on the Grand Concourse do not treat the access lanes any differently than they do the center roadway. Both are fast-moving realms clearly meant for cars.

There is hope for the Grand Concourse. During the spring of 1995 a group of professionals and citizens were meeting regularly to address the problems of the street. Money seemed shy, but a start was being made. What is hopeful, too, is that it is easy to see not only ways to fix the street and solve its problems—making it as good as it was—but also ways to make it better than it ever was. The state of the Grand Concourse today is, in large measure, a consequence of applying overwhelmingly a single point of view, that of moving vehicles swiftly, without giving much, if any, consideration to other values and needs. It is indisputable that the Grand Concourse moves vehicles. But it does so at a cost of accidents and with disregard for the people living along it. Why is it that roads such as these are regularly found in areas where people have lower-than-average incomes and where minorities of color live? Need that be so?

Obvious possibilities for improvement shout out to an observer walking along the Grand Concourse today. Given the unseemly width of the access roads and the likely need for parking in the area, simply permitting parking along both sides of the access roads, thereby reducing the moving lanes to one instead of two, would force the fast-moving traffic to the center lanes, would slow traffic on the side roads, and would calm and humanize the street, if only a little. The capital cost—for new signs showing the regulations—would be minimal. It is the kind of improvement that could be achieved in less than a month and would have a great impact on the livability of this part of the Bronx.

But why stop at a minimal intervention? This is New York, and this is the Bronx. Why not make the Grand Concourse grand? It has the potential to be a fine boulevard, primarily because of the active and diverse street life along it and its width. First-rate alternative designs almost cry out for recognition. It is not too early in our exploration of boulevards to consider one of them.

The Grand Concourse would be a much safer street, and a more pleasant one, if it were reconfigured with narrow access roads and wider medians. Making these changes might well stimulate neighborhood revitalization. Further, since the densely built residential neighborhoods surrounding the Grand Concourse offer little in the way of public or private open space, there is an opportunity to think of the street as a linear park and an expanded public realm.

The central roadway for fast traffic can remain as it is now, but the medians can become much wider, 33 feet, and the access roads and sidewalks narrower. The medians can become pedestrian promenades with paving, light fixtures, benches, and planters. Two rows of closely spaced trees could line the edges of the promenades. To discourage midblock jaywalking, the center edge of the medians could be lined with either a raised planter with high shrubs or a continuous bench. The access lanes need be no wider than 10 feet, with continuous parking on one side cut into the existing sidewalk, which would also be reduced to an adequate 10 feet wide. If additional parking is needed, perhaps near commercial corners, some diagonally angled spaces could be located on the medians, between the trees. The level of these diagonal spaces would be raised slightly above the roadways so that median edges would remain distinct. The pedestrian realm thus created would account for 73 percent of the total right-of-way, as compared to its current 23 percent.

Hope for the Grand Concourse lies in the reality that nothing, thus far, has been done to it that cannot be undone. People concerned with its future could do worse than to simply look at the models of the best existing boulevards and adapt one of them; Eastern Parkway and Ocean Parkway in Brooklyn are close at hand. Then, the Grand Concourse can be redesigned into a truly fine street.

"Jaywalking" on the Grand Concourse

Chapter Five

THE ESPLANADE: A RELATIVE NEWCOMER

The Esplanade in Chico, California, is a relatively new multiway boulevard and it is un-expected, but it plays second fiddle to none of the others.

The Esplanade comes out of (or into) an attractive, small-scaled downtown, moves north-west past the remarkable Bidwell Park, which defines the older town center, then through an early city extension to Lindo Channel at West 11th Avenue. After that it ceases to func-tion as a boulevard.[1] The Esplanade is a multiway boulevard for about fifteen blocks, just shy of one and one-quarter miles. A major north–south traffic street, it serves the city as a whole as well as the local residential uses along its path. It runs parallel to Mangrove Street, an important commercial carrier about half a mile to the east, and to Route 99, the freeway that bypasses the city on its way north.

One would not expect to find a multiway boulevard in a small, agriculturally-based com-munity in the northern Central Valley of California about 75 miles north of Sacramento. Boulevards of this type are so often associated with formal structure and strong, centrally directed design—qualities not usually characteristic of agricultural communities. Often, too, boulevards start out as such; they are designed and built that way from the outset. Not so The Esplanade. It began as a private road on Rancho Chico, the 25,000-acre Bidwell fam-ily estate, and was first used principally by farm wagons. But by as early as 1898 it had been planted with four rows of trees and become a public roadway for buggies, wagons, bicycles, and pedestrians. By 1905 there were streetcars on The Esplanade, part of what was to be a remarkably comprehensive public transit system in a small city, one that permitted travel as far south as San Francisco. Rail service along The Esplanade was also used during the es-tate's annual nut harvest. Shortly after World War II the streetcars were removed, and in the 1950s the street was reconfigured as a multiple-roadway boulevard. Its central roadway was

The Esplanade: context
Approximate scale: 1:100,000

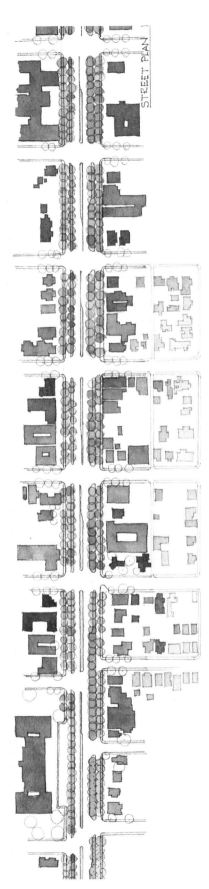

STREET PLAN

The Esplanade: street and building context

Approximate scale: 1" = 400' or 1:4,800

Along the access roadway on The Esplanade

widened and traffic signals were installed in the 1960s. Yet it remains a classic boulevard and a beloved street.[2] Moreover, it is an example that runs counter to the trend of removing such roadways in the late–twentieth century. It is all the more important because it is such a delightful street to walk or drive along.

Quiet graciousness characterizes The Esplanade. From the moment you're on it, you know you are in a special, a different place. *In* is perhaps an appropriate word here, better than *on,* or *along,* because of the strong "placeness" of this street. It matters little whether you come to it from the faster-moving and less-structured northern section, from the tight, pleasantly urban downtown near Bidwell Park and its historic mansion, or from one of the fifteen or so side streets that cross it—gracious as these are in their own right. To be sure, The Esplanade seems wider than other streets in Chico, much wider than any of those that cross it or run immediately parallel to it, and as such it gives pause and focus. It provides structure. But wideness doesn't necessarily mean graciousness or quietness. Often the opposite is true. It is, we think, the trees, the set-back houses and other buildings on well-kept lawns, the short blocks with frequent views up tree-lined streets of modest houses, and the simultaneous separateness of the two side access streets and their oneness with the whole. And it is the quality of the light, summer or winter, playing through the leaves and branches that gives both a spaciousness to the whole and an intimacy to the parts.

Four, and sometimes five, rows of trees, mostly London planes and mostly large, line The Esplanade. Overhead, their branches join and, during hot sunny summer days in Chico it is dark and cool on the tree-lined access roads. Branches and leaves permit bright splotches of sun and shadow and light to constantly move and intermingle. The shrubs along the median strips, along with the trees, partially hide the fast-moving cars in the central lanes. Vehicles move slowly along the side access lanes, through the dark-light of shade and sun. There is a stop sign at every intersection, so you could not drive fast for very long even if you wished to. You're not likely to be on one of these lanes unless you have a destination on the block. In the winter it is cooler, sometimes cold, and the sun, unhindered by leaves, is welcome. Then the pattern is a tracery of shadows from branches and limbs, while tree trunks and shrubs still separate the central traffic from the access lanes.

The Esplanade is the kind of street that you might expect to be lined with large, old houses well set back on manicured lawns. Indeed, that may be your first impression, before you look more closely. The buildings generally *are* set well back from the street, perhaps 20 to 30 feet. But except for a few larger residences at the southern end and along the east side, the single-family homes are not large; most are bungalows of one to three floors. They don't give a sense of great wealth, now or in the past. Their maintenance is adequate, but not outstanding. The houses do not appear much different from those on the surrounding streets. The exceptions are several newer, two- and three-story apartment buildings. These, too, are set back from the street, though not as far back as the older houses. They appear to be the residences of middle- and lower-middle-income people.

There are some institutions along the street—among them a school that takes up most of a block and the historic Bidwell mansion, now a tourist destination. There are also some doctors' offices in new and converted buildings, a bed and breakfast inn at the southern end, and other miscellaneous newer residences.

There are two commercial areas, one at the northern entry to the street and a second about midway along it. The second has a more urban character: buildings there are closer to the street and have display windows but no visible off-street parking. They look like buildings that might once have housed a local grocery store, a pharmacy, or a creamery. Now they are occupied by an inexpensive restaurant and an electrical appliance store.

Cars in the center lanes move along at a reasonable pace, without speeding. Traffic lights every second block are timed to permit continuous flow at 28 miles per hour. As some people drive a bit faster—about 31 miles per hour—the lights stop some of them.[3] The relatively slow pace provides the opportunity, whether driving or stopped, to take in the surroundings: the double rows of trees on either side of the enclosed side access roads, the houses beyond, and the trees planted along the center divider that separates the directional traffic lanes of the central roadway.

Coming from the striplike suburbanized northern streets or the urban downtown to the south, the sheer physical differences in size, plantings, and layout of The Esplanade call attention to its distinctive character. Leaving The Esplanade, one is aware of passing into an-

Houses along The Esplanade

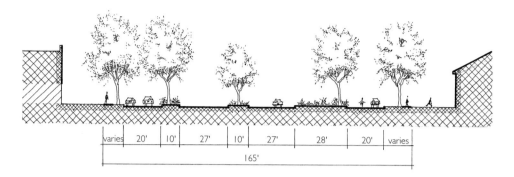

| varies | 20' | 10' | 27' | 10' | 27' | 28' | 20' | varies |

165'

The Esplanade: section

Approximate scale: 1″ = 50′ or 1:600

other environment, moving north with some regret, or moving south with anticipation as the road curves through and over Bidwell Park into downtown.

The Esplanade may be no less noisy than other major streets, but it seems quieter. Perhaps it is the strong division of the central lanes from the side access lanes, or perhaps the overall width of the right-of-way, the set-back buildings, or the three distinct but joined sections of the whole street. Maybe it is all those qualities together. To further understand the street, we need to look more closely at its physical attributes.

The Esplanade's right-of-way is 165 feet wide, which places it near the center of the multiway boulevards we studied. The 64-foot center thoroughfare has two wide lanes in each direction, with left-turn lanes cut into the 10-foot-wide center median at every second intersection. The center median is sparsely planted with sizable trees.

The two medians separating the access roads from the center roadway have different widths: the one on the west side is 10 feet wide, while the eastern median—where the railroad track was formerly located—is approximately 28 feet wide. The eastern median accommodates right-turn lanes. The mature London planes and sycamores planted along the medians' access-road curbs are between 30 and 35 feet apart. There appears to be no rule regarding spacing of trees near intersections. The ground surfaces of the side medians are as notable for their reddish-brown packed soil as for their plantings. The exceptions are the informally arranged shrubs along the tree line, particularly on the wide eastern median. They provide a visual barrier to the central traffic lanes and discourage jaywalkers.

The side access roads, typically 20 feet wide, provide one lane of parallel parking and one moving lane. At commercial areas the access lane may widen to 28 feet to provide for diagonal parking.

Typically, though not consistently, 10-foot-wide planting strips separate the sidewalk from the access road. Sometimes the planting strip is 4-feet wide, and sometimes there is none at all. Trees are planted along the walks on the right or left side, but most often on the street side. They tend to be less regularly spaced than the trees in the medians, but they are close enough to the latter to allow the branches to meet overhead.

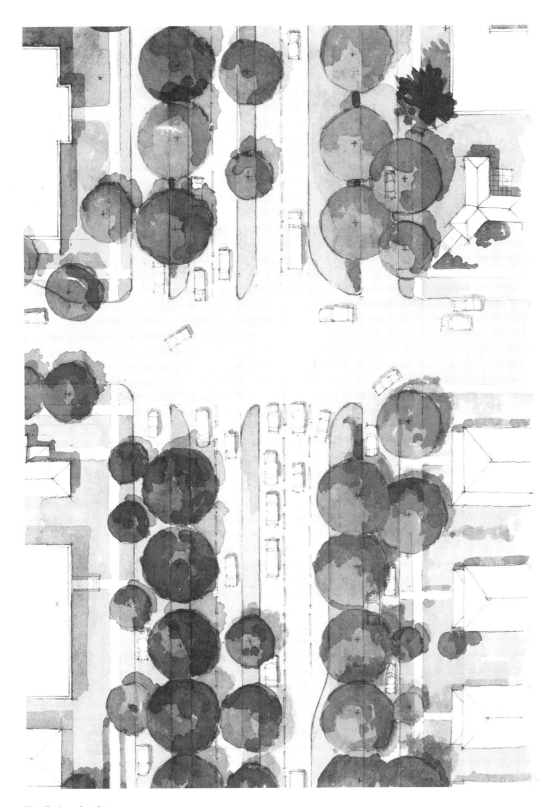

The Esplanade: plan

Approximate scale: 1″ = 50′ or 1:600

68 EXPERIENCING BOULEVARDS

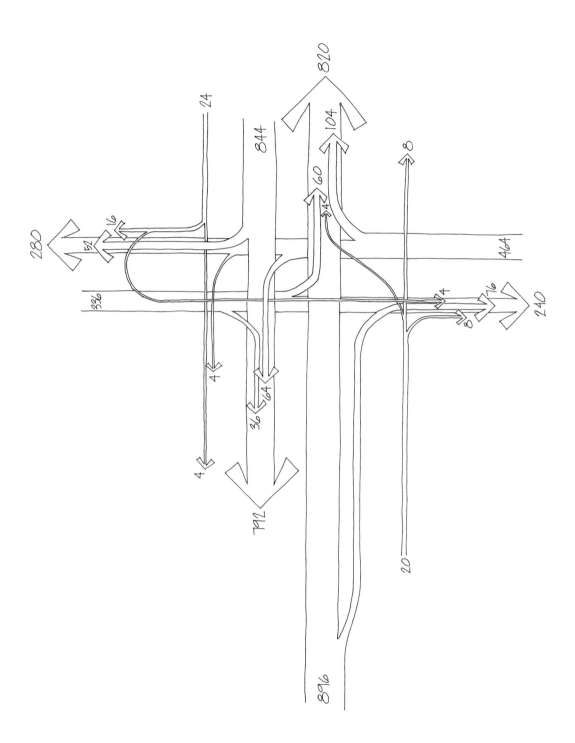

Traffic movement on the Esplanade at First Avenue

Local bus lines run on the side access roads as well as in the central lanes, but the stops are on the access roads. There are no designated bicycle lanes.

Traffic movement possibilities on The Esplanade are nothing short of amazing and fly in the face of traffic-engineering standards and norms. Most notable is the lack of restrictions in movement between the center and the access roads at intersections. The center and the cross-streets are controlled by signal lights at every second intersection. At these intersections, left turns are not allowed from the center. But there are no traffic lights at the alternate intersections, where left turns *are* allowed. Access lanes are controlled separately, with a stop sign at every intersection. Cross traffic waits at the median edge. A clear hierarchy is established: traffic in the center lanes always has preference, except where there are stoplights. Second priority is given to the cross streets, where vehicles proceed past the access road traffic, without having to stop, to the edge of the center lanes, where there is either a stop sign or a traffic light. Drivers on the access roads are last in the pecking order; they have to stop at every corner. Pedestrians, as usual, have the right-of-way at crossings, except where a traffic light controls movement.

Drivers use The Esplanade the way they were meant to: almost all traffic travels in the center lanes.[4] Very few vehicles travel along the access roads for more than a block. Why would they, as they are compelled to stop at every corner, about every 400 feet? As would be expected, traffic travels much more slowly on the access roads than in the center: 21 miles per hour compared to 31 miles per hour. There is far less distance for building up speed.

Theoretically, this arrangement permits some forty-two points of conflict at a typical intersection, where one vehicle can cross the path of another; but people recognize this potential and act with caution. The main conflict is between drivers on the center roadway making a right-hand turn and those on the access road going straight ahead (which is rare) or making their own right or left turns from their stop sign. In general, observation shows that central roadway drivers make the right turn more cautiously when there is a car on the access road or approaching the intersection. They look to see what the driver in the access lane is planning to do, slow down, and wait. Access-lane drivers, too, are very cautious about entering an intersection, looking in more directions than are required at a normal intersection. It is necessary to look back over the left shoulder to see if there is traffic approaching in the center roadway, especially if the light is green, and also to be sure no turns are in process or likely. This is an unusual direction in which to look, but drivers learn fast in such situations, especially after encountering a car unexpectedly crossing in front of them when they failed to check.

Cars on cross streets pull up to the center roadway to wait for a green light or an opening in traffic that will permit them to pass.[5] When cross traffic is heavy and more than two or three cars have to wait, drivers find themselves sitting in the intersection as the access lanes become blocked. When that happens, drivers on the access road intending to proceed straight may turn right instead. More often, drivers of waiting cars notice the situation and back up or pull forward to allow the car on the access road to maneuver through. When only one or two cars in the cross-streets are stopped and blocking traffic, access-road drivers wishing to go straight simply maneuver around them. Buses frequently do the same thing.

Chico, Calif. Esplanade

People obey the rules on The Esplanade. Illegal moves by autos are few and far between. Cyclists also use the access lanes and, more often than not, they move in any direction, regardless of the one-way nature of the street. But there are few moving cars, and no one seems to mind, and the cyclists can proceed swiftly and with a certain sense of freedom. For pedestrians, however, there is a sense of being in a no-man's land when crossing a cross street. There are no crosswalk markings, so a specific pedestrian zone is not established. One feels vulnerable to traffic moving from many directions. It is a small problem that could be easily solved.

If one were convinced that all those possible turning and weaving movements and potential conflicts on The Esplanade make for a dangerous street, then one would expect Mangrove Street, which runs five blocks east and parallel to it and carries about the same amount of daily traffic, to be relatively safer.[6] Within its 65- to 67-foot-wide roadway Mangrove Street carries two lanes of traffic in each direction, plus a left-turn lane; thus it has close to the same number of fast lanes as The Esplanade. But the number of intersecting streets on Mangrove Street is about half the number as on The Esplanade and, more important, the number of potential conflict points has been effectively reduced to zero. Its intersections have traffic controls that give each major movement, especially left turns, its own green cycle. Each movement has a place and time, largely separate from others, to minimize potential conflicts. Moreover, the uses along Mangrove Street are significantly different than those along The Esplanade; this is a commercial strip. Nonetheless, given all the potential conflicts—at least according to prevailing traffic-management wisdom—there should be more accidents on the boulevard than on Mangrove Street. But there are not. The accident rates of the two streets are virtually identical: 0.19 accidents (per average daily traffic count divided by 1,000) on The Esplanade, compared to 0.18 on Mangrove Street.[7]

It is hard to know with certainty why the accident rates on these two streets are so similar. Close observation over extended periods at different times of the year offers some explanations. All of those complex traffic lights on Mangrove Street may give a false sense of security ("Everything is taken care of, I don't have to worry.") that decreases drivers' awareness and preparedness. Also, the lights and longer blocks may encourage speed. If I know that I'm going to have to wait through three traffic-light intervals before my turn comes again, I might just try to get through the intersection on the caution light now, while there is a chance. And that might prove to be a mistake. Then, too, uses along Mangrove Street give vehicles access directly onto and off the street, creating zones where through traffic and local traffic must mix. Not so on The Esplanade, where local traffic (though light) and through traffic are kept apart. The very complexity of the intersections on The Esplanade suggests caution and the importance of paying attention to one's surroundings.

The Esplanade could be a better street—what street couldn't? Gestures to the needs of pedestrians at crossings would help. The commercial area at the northern end of The Esplanade could use some tightening up—perhaps by eliminating some of the parking spaces abutting the street. And one might wish that the storeowners near the midpoint of the street could somehow find space for an ice cream shop. The only thing missing from The Esplanade is people walking along on a summer's evening, with ice cream cones.

On the Esplanade.

Part Two INVENTION, EVOLUTION, AND DEMISE: A HISTORY

Ocean Parkway, Brooklyn, in 1890
Drawn from a photograph, New York City Parks Photo Archive

There is a larger story about boulevards than their current conditions and the ways they are used. It is the story of how they came to be in the first place and why they were designed and laid out as they were.

THE FIRST BOULEVARDS

Most people associate boulevards with the mid–nineteenth-century reconstruction of Paris undertaken by Napoleon III and his prefect, Baron Georges Haussmann. At that time many straight and wide tree-lined streets called *boulevards* were cut through the medieval fabric of the old city and extended outward into new areas of urban expansion. But boulevards were not new to Paris, nor to other European cities at the time. Haussmann's boulevards were a formalized and modernized reinterpretation of an earlier, popular urban street form.

Today the word *boulevard* has lost much of its original meaning; developers use it loosely to describe streets of all kinds in an attempt to convey an aura of specialness. Originally, however, a boulevard was a *very* special type of street in a particular location.

The French word *boulevard* (related to the English *bulwark*) has a medieval origin and originally referred to the raised, strengthened part of a fortified town wall. In the sixteenth century, the walls of European cities were elaborate systems of defense comprised of inner and outer earthworks, masonry walls, moats, and towers. The *ramparts,* the wide and elevated inner earthworks, were staging areas for heavy weapons. After defensive town walls became obsolete in the seventeenth century, the tree-lined walkways built on these ramparts came to be called boulevards. As early as the late-sixteenth and early-seventeenth century, still-functioning ramparts in some cities had been planted with trees and were used for limited public recreation; Lucca, Ferrara, Antwerp, Amsterdam, and Strasbourg all had such areas. The first transformation of city ramparts into a significant public way, however, occurred in 1670 when Louis XIV abandoned the walls of Paris and ordered them turned into public pleasure promenades.[1]

The *promenade* was a public ritual that developed as European urban culture grew to embrace a new concept of society and associated ideas about leisure. During the Middle Ages, most cities had few public spaces that could function as settings for public social rituals. As polite society developed in newly prosperous cities in the sixteenth and seventeenth centuries, rituals of public display became increasingly important ways to define who belonged to society—and who didn't—and to provide a milieu for social interaction. Promenades were built as places where the nobility and the new bourgeosie could display their status and interact with others of their class.

The first such promenades, built in the late sixteenth century, were tree-lined paths in enclosed private gardens. These *allées* were often the main structural component of a formal garden. By the early-seventeenth century allées were being built beyond garden walls to visually extend the garden allées into the surrounding countryside. The most notable of these allées, which became the Avenue des Champs Elysées, lengthened the central allée of the royal Tuileries gardens for a mile and a quarter. Around the same time, members of the royalty and the nobility began building within their estates broad tree-lined paths called

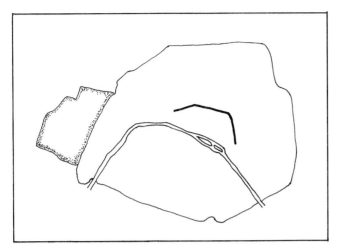

The Grands Boulevards

cours to serve for carriage promenades. The most important, the Cours de la Reine, was built in 1622 for Marie de Medici, second wife of Henri IV, on the western edge of the Tuileries gardens, adjacent to the River Seine. Around 1660 a cours was built in the Bois de Vincennes, a royal hunting ground outside the eastern edge of the city walls.[2]

The transformation of Paris's ramparts into public promenades took many years and was accomplished in sections. The masonry walls around the northern part of Paris were taken down, surrounding moats were filled in, and the remaining raised ramparts were planted with multiple rows of trees. Between 1670 and 1705 promenades varying in length from 660 feet to over 2,000 feet were developed on eleven separate rampart segments. They varied in width, because of the uneven breadth of the old ramparts, but most were between 100 and 125 feet wide—much wider than the average Paris street at that time (24 feet). Each promenade segment was planted with two, four, or in some places five rows of trees that defined a wide center way and narrower, protected sidepaths known as *contre allées.*

The promenades—first called *cours,* and then *remparts*—finally came to be known as *boulevards,* in reference to a particularly large bastion called the Grand Boulevard that stood on the ramparts north of the Porte St. Antoine.[3] Over time the boulevards were connected, eventually forming a three-and-a-half-mile-long semi-circular elevated promenade around the northern edge of the city. Each original promenade segment bore its own name, which they carry to this day: Boulevard Beaumarchais, Boulevard des Filles du Calvaire, Boulevard du Temple, Boulevard St. Martin, Boulevard St. Denis, Boulevard de la Bonne Nouvelle, Boulevard Poissonniere, Boulevard Montmartre, Boulevard des Italiens, Boulevard des Capucines, and Boulevard de la Madeleine. Collectively, they became known as the *grands boulevards.*

Because the rampart boulevards were elevated and only accessible at a few street crossings marking locations of the old city gates, they were not initially integrated into the general street system of Paris. Their social uses evolved over time and may have varied from segment to segment. At first, because of their isolated position at the city's edge, they were apparently little used; but by the 1750s, when the city had expanded into the surrounding areas, they had become fashionable gathering places.

The uses of the boulevards were restricted from the start. Early on only pedestrians and pleasure vehicles were allowed; carts and commercial vehicles were prohibited.[4] Later, though all kinds of traffic were permitted, their uses remained regulated. The police ordinances of 1763 and 1766, for example, stipulate that the contre allées of the promenade known as the Filles du Calvaire were reserved for pedestrians, while the center roadway was for horses. Horses had to be driven *au pas* (at a walking pace) in the center and kept at least six feet from the trees to protect them from damage. Carriages were not allowed to park in the center; if they wished to stop they had to pull over to the edge and could not block pedestrian access. Pushcarts of any type were forbidden on the center way. On some rampart segments pedestrians apparently used the whole promenade, at least some of the time. A 1760 engraving shows elegantly dressed people strolling in both the center and the side allées and being served food and drink at tables set under the trees.[5]

As the city grew around the boulevards, cafes, restaurants, and theaters were built along their edges, contributing to the pleasure milieu. Later, fashionable residential neighborhoods grew up around the western boulevards, and monuments—such as the triumphal arches commemorating war victories built at Porte St. Denis and Porte St. Martin—marked boulevard access points.

In spite of their initial purpose as pleasure promenades and their isolation from the city's street system, the rampart boulevards provided a direct route around the northern part of the city, and early on they assumed a traffic-movement function. In the early nineteenth-century, when the grands boulevards were lowered and they were integrated into the general street system, their use increased dramatically.[6] Today the grands boulevards remain a major tree-lined traffic route through the northern parts of the city. Most of them as currently configured do not have side access roads but rather wide, tree-lined sidewalks; the exception is the Boulevard Beaumarchais (see Part Four), whose access roads are of a recent vintage.

The Paris rampart boulevards established the form and purpose of the seventeenth-century boulevard street type. Boulevards became known as wide, tree-lined streets with separate spaces for pedestrians, riders, and vehicles of different types. They were principally associated with pleasure, but also with through-traffic movement. During the eighteenth century, such boulevards were built on the abandoned ramparts of many European cities.

NINETEENTH-CENTURY BOULEVARD SYSTEMS

The mid- to late-nineteenth century witnessed a second major period of boulevard building. It began with Haussmann's reconstruction of Paris in the 1850s and continued in major cities in Europe and the United States into the early 1900s, and in Asia, India, and Central and South America into the 1940s.

The nineteenth-century boulevards were generally part of large-scale city planning efforts and were designed to have many of the same characteristics as the earlier rampart boulevards: lines of trees, generous widths, separate pathways for vehicles and pedestrians, and an association with leisure and entertainment. But they were different in important ways. Rather than being isolated promenades, they were usually part of a broader boulevard system and integrated with their cities' street networks; they also tended to be straight and radial rather than circular or semicircular like the grands boulevards. Typically their purpose was to open up areas adjacent to the city for new urban development.

The physical form of the boulevard was also refined and modernized. Haussmann added paved roadway surfaces and raised curbs and developed three distinct types. Though there are no formal names for these types of boulevard, we may descriptively refer to them as the *boulevard street, the center-median boulevard,* and the *multiway boulevard.* The boulevard street is simply a wide street with generous, tree-lined sidewalks. The center-median boulevard has two roadways separated by a wide central tree-planted median; it also has tree-lined sidewalks. The multiway boulevard had three roadways, a wide one in the center and two narrower ones along each side, separated by tree-lined medians and sidewalks, also tree-lined.[7]

Many of the boulevards built in the mid- to late-nineteenth century were multiway boulevards, a form uniquely suited to the times. In the latter half of the nineteenth century traffic activity on city streets was changing rapidly. There were many more wheeled vehicles on the streets than before, and carriage makers were building newer, faster carriages. At the same time, there were more slow-moving commercial wagons that made frequent stops as well as many mounted riders. For most people, however, walking was still the principal form of transportation. By the 1880s, bicycles were added to the traffic mix, and, by the turn of the century, automobiles. The multiway boulevard, with its generous pedestrian spaces and separated vehicle roadways that could be designated for different types of vehicles, was wonderfully suited to handle this complex amalgam. It may also have been perceived as the most "modern" of the boulevard types—because the center roadway provided an unencumbered space for the new, fast-moving carriage traffic—and the grandest—because it could provide a central vehicle approach toward axially placed monumental structures or destinations.

To get an idea of how and why nineteenth-century boulevard systems were developed and to identify the differences that marked them in various cities, we will look closely at their configurations in Paris, Barcelona, and Brooklyn and consider more briefly a few other cities.

Names can cause some confusion. While many nineteenth-century streets with a boulevard form were *called* boulevards, others were designated *avenues,* while yet others, particularly in the United States, were called *parkways.* Moreover, streets lacking the attributes of the boulevard form were often named boulevards to bestow on them a sense of grandeur.

Paris

By the middle of the 1800s, the center of Paris was crowded and densely built. Most streets were narrow and without trees. The city's physical growth was constrained by an encircling customs wall that regulated the flow of goods in and out of the city.

When Napoleon III became emperor in 1852 he began reconstructing Paris to heighten the city's prestige and reinforce his own political power. His prefect of the Seine, Georges Eugene Haussmann, directed the work. The reconstruction, which included tearing down the customs wall and expanding the borders into the surrounding *faubourgs* (suburbs), had four physical components. Straight, wide streets called boulevards were built through the crowded city center and into the undeveloped outlying areas; at the same time, underground water and sewer systems were constructed beneath the new streets. New public parks were built throughout the city, existing parks were renovated, and an ambitious building program created new public buildings and marketplaces. The building program stimulated the economy, which had been in depression, providing public works employment and opening up new areas for development. The new boulevards improved public hygiene by opening up crowded areas with light and air and providing clean water; they facilitated traffic circulation by connecting the railroad stations with one another and with the center and by linking the center with outlying areas.[8]

The reconstruction was controversial at the time and remains so today. While it was taking place, it was at once widely acclaimed as a magnificent example of rationalized city planning and decried for its destruction of many historic buildings and disruption of residential neighborhoods, displacing many people, most of them poor. The wide boulevards themselves have often been criticized on the grounds that they were primarily for strategic military purposes—to facilitate artillery fire and make it difficult to erect barricades. Some have argued that many were deliberately cut through working-class districts to break up and encircle areas of political resistance. Similarly, others have seen in the baroque axial pattern of the boulevards a reflection of the authoritarian nature of Napoleon III and his government.

It is clear, however, that the boulevards were a response to the tastes and aspirations of a rising bourgeoisie and its need for improved living standards and status.[9] Modern critics favorably inclined to Haussmann's boulevards have pointed out their positive aspects. Marshall Berman calls them "the most spectacular urban innovation of the nineteenth century, and the decisive breakthrough in the modernization of the traditional city" because they "opened up the whole of the city, for the first time in its history, to all its inhabitants. Now, at last, it was possible to move not only within neighborhoods but through them. Now, after centuries of life as a cluster of isolated cells, Paris was becoming a unified physical and human space."[10] According to Berman, the boulevards created new economic, social, and aesthetic bases for bringing together enormous numbers of people.

What is incontestable is that the reconstruction greatly altered the physical form and social character of Paris. Fifty-seven miles of wide streets were built, 700 miles of sidewalk were added, and the number of trees along the streets was doubled. Public park space increased from less than 50 acres to more than 4,500 acres.[11] With the new boulevards came numerous architectural and social changes. Apartment buildings of a regulated six-story uniform height, and with uniform façade treatments, were built along many of the new

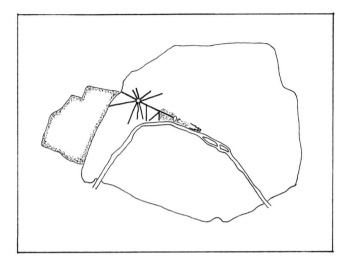

The Etoile Area Boulevards

boulevards, their ground floors occupied by cafes and restaurants. The people of the emerging bourgeoisie thronged to these establishments to eat, drink, and stroll along the boulevards. At night the brightly lit wide, tree-lined sidewalks were filled with a constant parade of people.

The widest and grandest of Haussmann's boulevards—almost all built in outlying areas—were of the multiway type. Their largest concentration was on the northwestern periphery of Paris around the Place d'Etoile and the Avenue des Champs Elysées. One, the Boulevard de Courcelles, was built adjacent to the reconstructed Parc Monceau on a stretch of land opened up by the razing of the customs wall. (We describe four of the present-day Etoile-area boulevards in Part One and consider the Boulevard de Courcelles in Part Four, "A Compendium of Boulevards.") The following discussion is intended to illustrate the context, layout, and original design characteristics of the Etoile boulevards.

Prior to construction of the new boulevards, northwest Paris was mostly open rural land with a scattering of mansions on large estates. A wide tree-lined road, the Avenue des Champs Elysées, ran through the area and ended at a high point of land called the Etoile; there stood the Arc de Triomphe, a massive arch built in 1806 to commemorate the first Napoleon's victories at Austerlitz. Napoleon III directed Haussmann to lay out a system of boulevards to encourage development of a fashionable residential area and to provide links between the city center and the Bois de Boulogne—a former royal hunting ground being converted into a public park.

Haussmann's redesign featured twelve boulevards radiating from the Etoile, an immense circular tree-lined *place*. Ten of the twelve symmetrical boulevards, including the redesigned Avenue des Champs Elysées, were multiway boulevards. Some of these boulevards apparently followed the lines of already-existing tree-lined roadways. Yet another new boulevard radiated from the Avenue des Champs Elysées; and two existing roadways that intersected the Avenue des Champs Elysées east of the Etoile at the Rond Point (a smaller circular *place*) were reconstructed as multiway boulevards.

The widest boulevard emanating from the Etoile was the first to be constructed. The Avenue de l'Impératrice, built in 1854, was originally called the Avenue Bois de Boulogne and is now the Avenue Foch. It was designed to be particularly impressive because it led directly to the new park. Three-quarters of a mile long and almost four hundred feet wide, it had a 52-foot wide center roadway bordered on each side by raised 39-foot-wide pathways, one reserved for pedestrians and the other for horse riders. Outside the paths were 100-foot-wide malls landscaped with grass and informal clusters of trees and shrubs. At the edge of each mall was a narrow roadway and sidewalk fronting elegant residences. To ensure an impressive street line, Haussmann imposed special building regulations requiring coordinated façade treatments, 32-foot setbacks, and uniform decorative cast-iron fences between front yards and sidewalks.[12] Travel along the Avenue de l'Impératrice offered dramatic views in both directions: the Arc de Triomphe to the east and the expanse of the Bois de Boulogne, punctuated by the Porte Dauphine to the west. The center roadway quickly became a fashionable place for carriage promenades.

None of the other boulevards were nearly as wide as the Avenue de l'Impératrice. Two, the Champs Elysées and the Avenue de la Grand Armée—which continues the line of the Champs Elysées beyond the Etoile—were approximately 230-feet wide; the others ranged

Les Champs Elysées about 1900

Drawn from a photograph in Jacques Hillairet, *Dictionnaire Historique des Rues de Paris* (Paris, Les Éditions de Minuit, 1985). Musée Carnavalet.

Les Champs-Elysées about 1900.

from 116- to 135-feet wide. The malls separating the roadways of these two boulevards were planted with formal lines of trees rather than with the informal landscaping of the Avenue de l'Impératrice.

The Avenue des Champs Elysées was first laid out in the seventeenth century by Andre le Notre as the visual extension of the axis of the central allée of the royal Tuileries gardens. Haussmann modernized its western section, which ran from Rond Point to the Etoile, into a multiway boulevard and rebuilt its eastern section, from the Tuileries to the Rond Point, where it passed through park areas with wide tree-lined sidewalks. The plan was to develop the western section as a mixed residential and commercial street. The 230-foot-wide multiway section had a central roadway of approximately 89 feet flanked by two 50-foot-wide medians with narrow side roadways and wide sidewalks. Each median was originally planted with two rows of trees and lined with light fixtures, while the sidewalks on each held an additional row of trees. (Later, probably during the 1950s when many Parisian streets were altered to handle more vehicular traffic, the center roadway was widened considerably and the medians were reduced to about ten feet wide.[13] In the early 1990s, the Avenue des Champs Elysées was again reconfigured, with widened sidewalks and an additional row of trees replacing the access roadways.)

The Avenue de la Grand Armée was configured in a similar fashion. Its center roadway was also widened during the twentieth century, and changes were made along the access roads to accommodate parking.

The design of the other, narrower boulevards—the Avenue Kléber, Avenue d'Iena, Avenue de Friedland, Avenue Hoche, Avenue Mac-Mahon, Avenue Carnot (which all radiate from the Etoile), and the Avenue George V, as well as the reconfigured Avenue Franklin Roosevelt and the Avenue Montaigne (which radiate from the Avenue des Champs Elysées)—was similar. Each had a center roadway approximately 42 to 48 feet wide, six- to ten-foot wide medians planted with one row of trees, narrow side roads, and wide sidewalks. (We refer to these streets by their modern names; some of their original names were different.) The central roadways of these streets were also widened in the 1950s to increase parking at the expense of the sidewalks.

As Haussmann and the emperor had anticipated, the areas surrounding the boulevards soon became fashionable neighborhoods; the boulevards were lined with fine six- or seven-story apartment buildings, with many shops, restaurants, and cafes on the ground floors. The wide center roadways of the Avenue de l'Impératrice and the Avenue des Champs Elysées became fashionable carriage promenades and popular places to stroll. The character of the two promenades was different, however, especially at night when the street lamps were lit and the cafes and restaurants along the Champs Elysées were full of color and gaiety. The Avenue de l'Impératrice, by comparison, was a quieter more elegant boulevard of stately townhouses.

Barcelona

By the mid-1800s Barcelona, like Paris, was densely built. Since the beginning of the century, the city's development as an important industrial center had produced continuous population growth. But the central government in Madrid had not allowed the city to expand beyond the old medieval walls. The wide cleared zone outside the walls was reserved for military purposes. The central government feared Barcelona's independent inclinations, associated with Catalonian nationalism, and wanted the cleared area available should an uprising need to be put down.

In 1854, however, the central government finally allowed Barcelona to take down its walls and expand the city. A competition to choose the expansion design was held. After much controversy—because the city government preferred a different plan—the central government selected a design by Ildefons Cerdà, an engineer and native of Barcelona who was in disfavor with local politicians.[14]

Like Haussmann's plan design for the northwestern part of Paris, Cerdà's plan for Barcelona's expansion used boulevards as major structural elements—though in a very different way. His design was large in conception. It called for an immense grid of square blocks and uniform streets covering over nine square kilometers—an expansion area more than eight times the size of the existing city. Superimposed over this grid was a system of wide connected thoroughfares, some aligned with the grid and others running diagonal to it; these thoroughfares connected important local and regional places or led toward them. They were designed as boulevards, with lines of trees and generous pedestrian areas bordering wide roadways. Three of the most prominent were multiway boulevards and had cross-sectional characteristics similar to those being built in Paris.

Cerdà envisioned Barcelona's expansion area as a suburban environment. He conceptualized the blocks accordingly and provided diagrams showing how they should be developed. The blocks were square and designed with bevelled corners on all sides, to open up the intersections to light and air. Most blocks were planned as purely residential areas and were to have buildings on only two or three sides; their interiors were to contain both private and communal gardens. The blocks were to be grouped into districts and would have their own institutions and city services, such as churches, schools, libraries, and medical clinics distributed in each district.

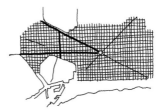

The Barcelona Boulevards

The boulevards, which would serve as district boundaries, were geared to commercial uses and had a more urban character than other streets. The boulevard side of all blocks would be lined with buildings, while other streets would have both built and open frontages alternating from block to block.[15]

Cerdà's expansion plan was thorough and sophisticated. Prompted by a concern for public health, he had been formulating his city planning ideas for some years. He had even undertaken, at his own expense, an extensive statistical study of working-class living conditions in Barcelona—one of the first such studies ever done. He had also prepared a comprehensive geographical survey of the land surrounding Barcelona. His plan was supported by written documentation presenting a detailed theory of urbanization and identifying circulation and hygiene as the most critical concerns of city planning. To Cerdà the boulevards were important critical elements of a comprehensive city plan.

The blocks and boulevards were laid out according to Cerdà's plan. As the expansion area developed, however, it was built up more densely than he had intended. Most blocks had buildings on all sides, typically six- and seven-story apartment buildings. The boulevards, as planned, developed as commercial streets.

Cerdà's three main multiway boulevards were the Passeig de Gràcia, Avinguda Diagonal, and Gran Via de les Corts Catalans. The Passeig de Gràcia began at the edge of the old city from a large new square called the Placa de Catalunya and ran in a northerly direction for nine blocks toward the important outlying suburb of Gràcia. Because it was laid out on the line of an existing rural highway, it was at a slight angle to the grid, which was aligned according to the cardinal compass points. The new boulevard widened the roadway of the existing road, which had been lined with six rows of trees and surrounded by a series of public gardens, and formalized its configuration. At 200-feet wide it was about 30 feet narrower than the Avenue des Champs Elysées; it featured a wide center roadway, wide medians, relatively narrow side roads, and wide sidewalks. (Although the dimensions of the individual cross-sectional elements are uncertain, Cerdà's drawings clearly describe the general multiway form.) Once built, land along the Passeig de Gràcia commanded the highest prices in the expansion area and was the first to be developed.[16] It soon became a locus for the traditional evening promenade, people dress up and stroll along the city streets before dinner.

The Avinguda Diagonal, as its name implies, runs diagonally across the grid. It intersected the northern end of the Passeig de Gràcia and pointed, at one end, toward the outlying suburb of Corts de Sarria and a vast open plain beyond and, in the other direction, toward the Mediterranean. The Gran Via de les Corts Catalans, which is aligned with the grid and runs between the old city and the expansion area, connected two important public open spaces: the mountain of Montjüic to the west and a new park to the east. At 165 feet wide, the Diagonal and the Gran Via were narrower than the Passeig de Gràcia but still much wider than other streets in the expansion area, which were a uniform 65-feet wide. In cross section these boulevards were similar to the Passeig de Gràcia, but with narrower center roadways.

The Passeig de Gràcia and other boulevards retained their original cross-sectional configurations well into the mid-twentieth century. After that they were modified somewhat to accommodate, in the case of the Passeig de Gràcia, more parking along the access roads and, in the case of the Diagonal and Gran Via, heavier traffic flows.

Beyond their central role in structuring Barcelona's citywide expansion, the boulevards gave local structure to surrounding neighborhoods, providing main shopping streets and boundary lines between the city's service districts. In addition, because of their prominent locations, great length, and orientation toward important outlying places, they furnished organization on a broader, regional scale.

Brooklyn

The first city in the United States to build a system of multiway boulevards was Brooklyn, New York. By 1860, Brooklyn was the third largest city in the United States—after New York City and Philadelphia—and had a population of 270,000. Originally a small agricultural town, it became increasingly urban in the 1810s and continued its rapid and ever-accelerating growth into the mid-nineteenth century. Located at the western end of Long Island across the river from the southern tip of Manhattan, by then it served as something of a bedroom community for New York City. Yet, with its growing industrial base and expanding downtown, it was also a substantial urban place in its own right. At the same time, the immense land area of King's County beyond the edge of Brooklyn remained largely rural and was occupied by independent farmers and small villages.[17]

The official city plan adopted in 1839, shortly after the city was incorporated, was functional and pragmatic. It consisted of several differently oriented rectangular street grids extending the original town-center grid and incorporating subsequent subdivisions. Several diagonal avenues were laid out along the intersections of various grids.[18]

In 1860 the city government decided to build a large public park similar to Central Park, then being laid out in rival Manhattan. A newly appointed Parks Commission selected a site for the new park at the undeveloped southern edge of the city and, in 1865, hired Olmsted, Vaux and Company to design it. Frederick Law Olmsted, the landscape architect for Central Park, was already a major figure in the developing parks movement. Calvert Vaux, his partner, was an architect and former partner of the landscape designer and influential editorialist Andrew Jackson Downing. Prospect Park, as it was called, was the focus of the firm's attention for over eight years, and Olmsted later considered it his masterpiece. It was planned as the centerpiece of a proposed park system that would include a number of multiway boulevards, which Olmsted and Vaux called *parkways.*

From the start, Olmsted and Vaux were concerned with street approaches to Prospect Park. They envisioned wide boulevards leading to the park entrances. Within a few years, their vision had grown to encompass a boulevard system on a scale never before imagined—larger by far than those created for Paris and Barcelona. Their 1868 parkway plan proposed an extensive system of parkways weaving throughout Brooklyn and extending out into the countryside. The system would connect Prospect Park with Central Park and other parks yet to be built and link up with parkways throughout the region. Overall, the proposed system covered an area of more than eighty square miles. The parkways were intended to structure new residential neighborhoods and serve as "linear" parks connecting residential areas to the larger parks.

To support the parkway plan, Olmsted and Vaux developed a theory associating the advance of civilization with changes in street patterns. The theory, which they expounded at length in a report to the park commissioners, divided city street patterns into five sequential historical stages. The first stage consisted of the narrow pedestrian streets of early villages and walled towns. In the second stage the same narrow streets had become filthy and congested as wagons and carts fought for space with pedestrians. In stage three, originating in the mid-eighteenth century, separate raised and curbed sidewalks for pedestrians were built on the sides of a central roadway for horses and carriages, while side gutters and sewers to some extent controlled human and animal filth. The streets of stage four were even further refined: the center roadway was divided into two by a raised and curbed landscaped mall for pedestrians. (They held Haussmann's central-median boulevards as the archetype of this form.) Olmsted and Vaux saw parkways, in which the central landscaped mall was

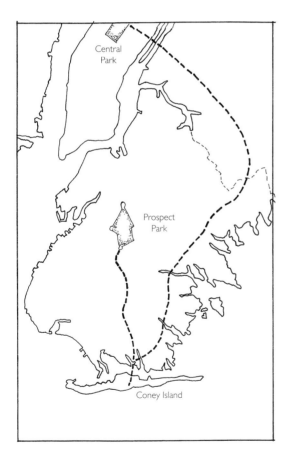
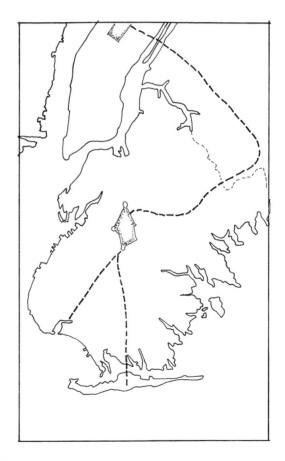

Olmsted's and Vaux's early ideas for a system of connected parkways

itself divided by a central roadway reserved for pleasure riding, as marking a fifth stage in the evolution and advancement of civilized town life.[19]

Their theory derived from their aesthetic convictions. As landscape architects, Olmsted and Vaux worked within the romantic landscape tradition that linked pastoral landscapes with artistic experience, well-being, and moral character. Their urban parks were designed to resemble secluded pastoral landscapes, offering views conducive to calm contemplation and recuperation from the stresses of urban life. They believed that such parks would refine the tastes of the lower classes and teach them a higher standard of morals. Conceptually, the parkways would extend these aesthetic benefits of parks, providing pathways to the parks that had similar aesthetic qualities. Moreover, people living near the parkways would gain these benefits as they went about their daily routines, even when they weren't traveling to a park. Though the parkways were designed for pleasure driving and promenades, they would also accommodate normal domestic functions by providing access to dwellings. Olmsted and Vaux described the parkway system as "a series of ways designed with the express reference to the pleasure with which they may be used for walking, riding, and the driving of carriages; for rest, recreation, refreshment, and social intercourse . . . so arranged that they will be conveniently accessible from every dwelling house. . . . [providing] access for the purposes of ordinary traffic to all the houses that front upon it, offering a special road for driving and riding without turning commercial vehicles from the right of way, and fur-

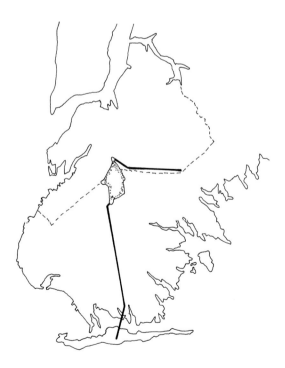

Eastern and Ocean Parkways

nishing ample public walks, with room for seats, and with borders of turf in which trees may grow of the most stately character."[20]

Olmsted and Vaux's cross-sectional design for the parkways was influenced by the European boulevards Olmsted had encountered in his travels. Their various writings mention the Avenue de l'Impératrice and the Avenue des Champs Elysées, among others. Yet the Americans wanted their boulevards to be less urban in form than the European boulevards and to have a more parklike and suburban character.

Though the metropolitan-scale parkway system envisioned by Olmsted and Vaux was never built, two parkways, Eastern Parkway and Ocean Parkway, were constructed between 1870 and 1874. Eastern Parkway began at Grand Army Plaza, a large, oval open space with symmetrically radiating streets that Olmsted and Vaux designed as the primary northern entrance to Prospect Park. The parkway extended eastward for two and a half miles to the city limits and was built along a low ridgeline. Until development surrounded it, it offered dramatic views in all directions: toward downtown Brooklyn, Manhattan, the Atlantic Ocean, and Long Island Sound. Ocean Parkway, built as the southern approach to Prospect Park, extended five and a half miles south to the beaches of Coney Island.

Both Eastern Parkway and Ocean Parkway were built with 210-foot-wide right-of-ways—about 20 feet narrower than the Avenue des Champs Elysées and Avenue Grand Armée and 10 feet wider than the Passeig de Gràcia. This was much wider than the typical Brooklyn street, which was then only 60- or 70-feet wide. Today the cross-sectional configuration of the parkways remains intact: broad central roadways flanked by wide raised malls,

Bicycle path on Ocean Parkway

Drawn from a photograph in *Annual Report for 1894*. New York City Parks Archive.

narrow access roads and sidewalks, with six rows of closely spaced trees, two on each median and one along each sidewalk edge. The uninterrupted rows of trees within grassy strips lend the boulevards a bucolic feel.

Olmsted and Vaux envisioned the parkways lined with single-family houses on large lots. The land bordering them was to be divided into "a series of lots adapted to be occupied by detached villas each in the midst of a small private garden." At the designers' urging, the city of Brooklyn imposed a number of development restrictions along the parkways. "Nuisance" uses (defined as any "manufactory, trade, business, or calling, which may be in any wise dangerous, noxious, or offensive, to the neighboring inhabitants") were forbidden, as was building structures other than stables and garages in the backyards of houses. A uniform building setback of 30 feet created front yards that owners were required to plant with greenery.[21]

To encourage development of a particularly fine residential neighborhood around Eastern Parkway, the first parkway built, Olmsted and Vaux designed a system of flanking service alleys and wide streets. Though this arrangement was partially implemented, it was later substantially dismantled.[22]

The two parkways were constructed through what was at the time open land. The city condemned the land and paid for the building and improvement of the roadway through tax assessments on adjacent property. This procedure was not without controversy, especially in the case of Ocean Parkway, which was built on land then wholly outside the Brooklyn city limits. Nonetheless, both parkways, including all the tree plantings, were completed in just a few years. However, the development Olmsted and Vaux had expected to happen in short order, especially along Eastern Parkway, did not occur. In fact, a series of economic crises and, in the case of Eastern Parkway, numerous land disputes related to takings associated with Prospect Park worked against any substantial development along the parkways for almost fifty years.[23]

During this time the tree-lined parkways were heavily used as horse and carriageways and, later, as cycling paths. The Parks Department, which had jurisdiction over the parkways, at various times implemented use restrictions. Early on, the center roadway was reserved for fast carriages and trotters, while slower carriages and delivery wagons were relegated to the side roads, and pedestrians used the medians. In the 1890s cycling paths were built on the medians but could be used only by registered cyclists; pedestrians were restricted to the sidewalks. When motorized vehicles came into common use in the 1910s and the use of horse-drawn carriages and bicycles waned, the center roadway became the realm of fast automobiles. One of the side access roads was reserved for slow service vehicles while the other was restricted to equestrians; pedestrians were allowed to mix with cyclists on the medians.[24]

Although streetcar lines were being built throughout Brooklyn at the time, and were expanded as late as the 1920s, none was built on either Eastern or Ocean Parkway. Olmsted and Vaux argued that streetcars and the commercialism that might accompany them would degrade the bucolic nature of the parkways, and the park commissioners adopted that view. In the 1910s a subway line was built beneath Eastern Parkway, with station entries located on the malls.

Substantial development finally came to Eastern Parkway in the 1910s and Ocean Parkway in the 1920s. Along Ocean Parkway the residences were single-family homes, much as the designers had envisaged; Eastern Parkway was more densely built with three- and four-story rowhouses and apartment buildings.

After Brooklyn, Olmsted and Vaux designed several other parkway systems, some of them with multiway boulevards, for a number of American cities, including Buffalo, Boston, and Louisville.

THE TWENTIETH CENTURY AND THE DEMISE OF MULTIWAY BOULEVARDS

Several large-scale boulevard systems were built in British and French colonial cities during the early twentieth century. The most notable are those in Melbourne—Royal Parade, Flemington Road, and St. Kilda's Road—which were built in the 1860s and 1870s; in New Delhi, India; and in Saigon, Indochina (now Ho Chi Minh City, South Vietnam).

In the United States, however, few multiway boulevards were built. They fell out of favor with traffic engineers grappling with ways to rationalize automobile traffic and speed its flow. American engineers developed new kinds of street and highway systems designed to separate fast-moving through traffic from slow local traffic and pedestrians and were particularly fascinated with the freeway, its split level intersections and the restricted access. The multiway boulevards designed to handle all types of traffic, including Olmsted and Vaux's suburban parkway version, were deemed old-fashioned, inadequate, and unsafe. Their original purpose as pleasure promenades was largely forgotten. The few multiway boulevards built in the United States after the turn of the century tended to emphasize through traffic over other uses, as did the few built in South America. The Avenida Nuevo de Julio in Buenos Aires, built in the 1930s and really more of an expressway than an urban street, is an example of the worst kind.

By the 1910s in the United States, the term *parkway* was no longer associated with streets of the multiway boulevard form. Instead, it designated highly landscaped, limited-access roadways extending out from cities into the surrounding countryside. The Westchester County Parkways built north of the New York City metropolitan area in the 1910s and 1920s were the first of this new type. Located mostly along river courses, they were designed not to connect parks with each other nor to spur suburban development but to open-up rural areas for scenic enjoyment by automobile drivers.

After the 1930s, when American engineers began building urban highway and arterial street systems on a large scale, many existing multiway boulevards were reconfigured; their central roadways were widened and, in some cases, turned into recessed limited-access expressways. An Olmsted-designed boulevard, Humboldt Parkway in Buffalo, suffered the latter fate. Its center roadway was depressed below grade and became a limited-access expressway.

The changing attitude toward street design that led to the demise of the multiway boulevard in the early twentieth century was embodied in a classification system for streets based on ideas of separation. The twentieth century reaction to the seeming chaos of the nineteenth-century cities was to try to impose order. Practitioners of the new professions of city planning and traffic engineering, which emerged late in the nineteenth century, came to see urban order as synonymous with functional separation. Increasingly, pedestrians and vehicles were separated from each other, as were various urban land uses. As early as 1916 American cities were zoned into separate land-use districts—residential, commercial, or industrial. Around the same time planners and engineers began separating streets into different classifications. According to Berman, "for most of our century, urban spaces have been systematically designed and organized to ensure that collisions and confrontations will not take place here."[25]

American planners first separated streets into different types based primarily on their land-use function. In a 1916 book Charles Mulford Robinson, an influential early city planner, argued against the practice of building city streets with a uniform width and form. He proposed that streets be classified into two types—*main traffic streets* and *minor residence streets*—and built according to different standards. Traffic streets should be commercial in nature and be straight, broad, and radial, whereas residential streets should be narrow and curvilinear. Within these classifications, he proposed, streets with different traffic and use functions would be articulated differently: traffic streets would be streetcar streets, fast-traffic streets, and slow-traffic streets; and residential streets would be classified as either high-class districts or those for humble homes.

A major difference between traffic streets and residence streets was their width. Robinson proposed a minimum width of 100 feet for traffic streets (with a minimum of 72 feet paved) and a maximum of 60 feet for residence streets (of which a maximum of 24 feet would be paved). Robinson, however, was no enemy of multiway boulevards. His illustrations suggest that he considered the advantages of boulevards as a street type that would organize different traffic flows, including streetcars, into different channels. But he neither advocated nor dismissed them.[26]

In the 1930s, shortly after the founding of the Institute of Traffic Engineers (ITE), traffic engineers developed a system of classifying streets based on a different idea of function. This method, called Functional Classification, became accepted practice and is still in use today. Functional Classification separates streets into different types according to the vehicle movement and property access functions they are supposed to perform. Basically, the method assigns specific movement and access functions to each street type. The two functions are inversely correlated; that is, the higher the movement function, the lower the access function. For instance, the classification assigned the highest movement function, freeways, is assigned no access function, while the classification assigned an unrestricted access function, local streets, is assigned virtually no movement function.

The inverse correlation of access and movement means that it is impossible to have a classification with both a high movement function and a high access function. The possibility of streets like multiway boulevards, which have both characteristics, is thus effectively excluded. Also, although both access and movement are considered in the classifications, it is clear that the emphasis—in terms of space and funding resources as well as design intentions—is on movement. This is reflected in the names of the classifications—freeways, expressways, arterials, collector streets, and local streets—as well as in the way the classifications are described. The ITE's *Traffic Engineering Handbook* characterizes each class of streets by "the nature and type of trips that take place, length of trips, and general traffic volume conditions."[27]

Functional Classification is defined in several engineering publications in very similar ways.[28] The following definitions represent a composite.

- *Freeways:* Divided highways that carry longer-distance major through traffic flows between important activity centers and have fully controlled access and no at-grade intersections.
- *Expressways:* Similar in function to freeways but may have only partial access control and may have at-grade intersections, although generally major intersections are graded separately.
- *Arterials:* Similar in function to freeways but with at-grade intersections and direct access to abutting property. (In practice, access is usually limited to intersections at one-half to one-mile intervals.)
- *Collector Streets:* Primarily provide links between local streets and arterial streets. They serve local through traffic but also directly serve abutting land uses.
- *Local Streets:* Primarily provide access to abutting land uses but also serve short local trips.

Traffic engineers have developed street-design standards for each functional classification based on criteria deemed appropriate for each. The criteria include access control, design speed criteria, design volume criteria, level of service criteria, and highway capacity criteria. The choice of criteria and the way in which they are applied to the classifications reflect the emphasis on vehicle movement, an orientation toward eliminating conflicts, and a basic philosophy of not questioning the preeminent needs of vehicular traffic. For instance, the *Traffic Engineering Handbook* recommends that some limitations on access be applied to *all* classifications, warning that "the quality of operation and safety of traffic flow is greatly affected by the type and manner of access control." In addition, the criteria for design speed, volume, level of service, and capacity recommend erring on the side of excess for all classifications—essentially overdesigning streets in terms of width and capacity in order to facilitate vehicular movement and accommodate possible future increases in traffic demand.[29]

If one sticks to the definitions of Functional Classification, a multiway boulevard is a combination of an arterial street and a local street. With this in mind, it is useful to look at design criteria for these classifications to see just how strongly this philosophy of street design discourages such a combination. *Residential Street Design and Traffic Control* states that on local streets "through movement may be possible but it is not encouraged by operational controls"; it also states that major streets "continue to perform some access functions, but these may be limited to parking restrictions to make the curb lane available for through movement in peak periods. In new subdivisions, individual lots may be laid out in such a fashion that none front the major street; this obviates the need for driveways and parking on the major streets."[30]

The street-design standards published by highway and traffic-engineering organizations are widely accepted as good roadbuilding practice and have been adopted by many cities. Generally these standards are the basis on which American streets are designed, or re-designed. Often they are the only criteria applied. This acceptance of engineering standards as the sole basis for street design has resulted in streets that are designed for cars and not for people. In traffic-engineering publications, street design is referred to as Roadway Geometric Design. A current edition of the *Traffic Engineering Handbook* describes the basic objectives of good geometric design to be: "to produce a highway that provides safe and efficient transportation which reflects the characteristics of drivers and vehicles that will use it, and that represents a reasonable trade-off in terms of its costs and other impacts."[31] These objectives express a concern for vehicles, safety, and efficiency but no direct concern for pedestrians or the environmental quality of streets. In the few places where pedestrians are discussed in the standards, the context is usually the need to separate them from traffic— either to protect them or to protect the traffic flow from the possible adverse effect of their presence.

The concern with pedestrian safety is responsible, but it may be overemphasized, and the approach of reducing conflicts by completely separating people and cars may be counter-productive. This is particularly troubling when one realizes that street standards appear to have been based on unproven assumptions and rationalizations about danger and safety rather than on actual data from studies of driver and pedestrian behavior on streets.[32]

The engineering orientation toward vehicles, movement, safety, and efficiency, which has also been advocated by two or three generations of city planners and architects[33] and gener-ally accepted by the public, has resulted in an extreme imbalance of power on what are sup-posed to be public streets.[34] Motorized vehicles have been given the right to dominate streets and thereby dominate public space, while pedestrians and people using nonmotor-ized vehicles have been significantly removed from streets and, thereby, from public space. In practice, this has meant that the power over street space has shifted from the people who live around a given street to the people who drive through it. The use value of the street for local people has been usurped for the use of outsiders who are just passing through.

A major lesson to be learned from the history of multiple roadway boulevards is their adaptability as a street form. Originally designed for completely different modes of trans-portation and land uses within a very different urban, political, and social context, the best multiway boulevards have succeeded, with minor alterations to adapt them to their mod-ern purposes, in accommodating today's radically different social scene.

To be sure, many design and planning professionals and social theorists have argued that it is time to rethink the concept of vehicle and pedestrian separation. There have been, and continue to be, other voices that command attention.[35] Yet overwhelmingly the voices of separateness continue to rule in regard to roadway location, size, and design in favor of sep-arate uses, separate lanes, separate functions, separateness. Professionals raised and nurtured under such a philosophy are accustomed to being listened to and followed. Certainly they are not challenged when they invoke the magic word, *safety,* and they are themselves perhaps unaware that their own standards and norms may not be based on real data and actual experience but on a professional dogma. Such professionals may be excused for perceiving multiway boulevards as dangerous, for at the present beginning of the new millennium ideas about separation of uses and Functional Classification, grown rigid in execution, have built considerable professional and bureaucratic constraints to the building of boulevards.

The present attitude is a far cry from the days when boulevards had their beginnings as promenades and places of recreation, days when it was taken for granted that streets were lively public spaces and could serve diverse uses. It remains to be seen whether multiway boulevards are indeed unsafe, or whether there are only particular conditions and designs that make them so. And, though the evolution of standards casts doubt on our ability to recreate in the present the best of the multiway boulevards of the past—if we choose to do so—we have not yet tested that hypothesis. These are the subject matters of Part Three.

Along St. Kilda Road

Drawn from a photograph in *Jack Cato, Melbourne* (Melbourne, Australia:
Georgian House PTY, Ltd., 1949).

Viale Angelico @ Via delle Milizie

We have seen that some of the best and most well-known streets in the world are multiway boulevards—among them the Passeig de Gràcia, Ocean and Eastern Parkways, and Avenue Montaigne. Other, lesser-known boulevards such as the Corso Isonzo and Via Cavour in Ferrara and a long section of Commonwealth Avenue in Boston are highly valued by the people who know and use them.

However, we have also noted that many transportation engineers consider multiway boulevards dangerous. If our own experience were limited to examples like the Grand Concourse, Queens Boulevard, or Avenida 9 de Julio in Buenos Aires we might agree with them. But what of all the others? Is there something inherently dangerous about this street type? American traffic-engineering wisdom, with its preoccupation with vehicles and their continuous movement, tends to view these streets as unsafe, primarily because of the complex intersections that result from their multiple roadways. This prevailing view has led to the gradual disappearance of direct references to boulevards, or to streets with side access ways, in the publications of the Association of State Highway and Transportation Officials (AASHTO) concerned with the geometric design of urban streets.[1] Further, while recent street-design guidelines do not specifically pronounce multiway boulevards unsafe, they do discourage some of their key features, such as multiple conflict points at intersections and trees that extend to the intersections. The attitude that streets with access roads are unsafe is revealed most often in conversation with professional street engineers and seems to be more an aspect of their professional culture than any specific misgiving about boulevards.

Our own informal experience and observations suggested that this street type is *not* unsafe. But we wanted to know more assuredly whether they are in fact safe, or unsafe. And, if multiway boulevards are relatively safe (or unsafe for that matter), are there particular physical design configurations and traffic-control arrangements that account for their safety or danger?

The two research questions discussed in this chapter are thus interrelated, in the sense that the answer to the first brings up the second. The first is about the relative safety of boulevards: our research hypothesis was that boulevards are not inherently less safe than normally configured streets. If this hypothesis is shown to be true, a second question arises: Are boulevards used by pedestrians and drivers in ways that negate the increased probability for accidents resulting from the many possible conflicting movements at intersections? Our hypothesis was that people adapt to the increased complexity of the environment by using more caution, and that the physical configuration of the street is important in facilitating this adaptation.

Investigating the question of safety involved comparing the accident records of existing multiway boulevards in the United States and Europe with those of nearby streets that carry comparable amounts of traffic. In this way we were able to control for the effects of urban context and socioeconomic variables. To arrive at a measure of safety, traffic counts and accident data for both the boulevards in question and control streets had to be obtained from local authorities and police departments in each city.

The difficulty of tracking down and then comparing accident and traffic-volume data has illuminated a matter of some importance concerning existing design standards and norms. Accident and volume data, particularly the former, are not easily found and assembled. Different cities and states keep the information in different places—here with the police, there with the state department of safety, for example. And there is no uniform way of keeping track of accidents; a type of accident reported in one city may not be included in the data for another. There are also different types of damage reporting. Cities reputed to have good data may not. Others do. No city, it seems, collects data on pedestrian volume in relation to traffic volume.

We wanted to be as comprehensive as possible. As long as money and time were available, we sought out information about any boulevard that came to our attention. For the most part, we visited them ourselves. In a few cases, colleagues were kind enough to bring or send us the information we were after. Ultimately, we were able to obtain data for eight multiway boulevards in the United States, eleven in Paris and Barcelona, and (for each one) a comparable nonboulevard nearby street.[2] The most significant comparisons of relative safety are between the boulevards and the nearby control streets (rather than between different cities).

Given the effort needed to retrieve and compile such data, a question arises: where are the data and analysis that led transportation engineers to the conclusion that multiway boulevards are unsafe, the data and analysis that back up the professionally promulgated standards and norms? We have yet to find them.

Accident data, vehicular volumes, and pedestrian counts are not by themselves enough to explain safety or the lack thereof. To understand how multiway boulevards work or don't work, and the relationship between their physical configurations and movement behavior on them, it is necessary to undertake detailed physical surveys. We selected for survey six multiway boulevards in the United States and six in Europe for which data were available. They represent a variety in terms of size, traffic volumes, and bordering uses. On these boulevards, pedestrian and driver behaviors were observed and recorded on videotape and by time-lapse photography. Detailed counts of movements were undertaken, and the physical components of the streets were measured.[3] Spending time on streets, walking on them, standing at intersections, counting, measuring, or just watching can be educational. In time, systematic patterns of behavior associated with certain physical configurations become evident.

MEASURES OF SAFETY

Many different measures of street safety are possible, and those chosen must be tailored to the data available. One measure of safety reflects the average number of accidents that occur over a year relative to the probability of accidents occurring, based on the sheer number of vehicles present on a street, as expressed by the average daily volume of traffic (ADT). For most of the U.S. boulevards studied, it was possible to assemble yearly accident counts for each intersection (ascribing accidents between intersections to the nearest intersection) and to determine a mean accident rate. The mean accident rate for each intersection, then, is the average number of accidents per year divided by the average daily vehicular volumes (divided by 1,000).

Table 3.1
Definitions

Mean accident rate (per intersection)	=	$\dfrac{\text{Mean accidents per year}}{\text{Average daily traffic}/1000}$
Pedestrian accident rate	=	$\dfrac{\text{Mean pedestrian accidents per year}}{\text{ADT}/1000}$
Weighted pedestrian accident rate	=	$\dfrac{\text{Pedestrian accident rate}}{\text{Pedestrians per hour}/1000}$

Because street safety is as much concerned with pedestrians as with vehicles—or should be—it was necessary to calculate a pedestrian accident rate too. One such measure of safety is the same as that for vehicles but uses the average annual number of pedestrian accidents as the numerator. A second pedestrian accident rate seeks to provide a weighting for the number of pedestrians present on the street. To do this, the calculated pedestrian accident rate is divided by the number of pedestrians observed in an hour (divided by 1,000).[4]

U.S. Boulevards

Analysis of the data strongly suggests that, as a group, the U.S. boulevards studied cannot be said to be less safe than comparable, normally configured streets. Some seem safer, some as safe, some less safe.

On the Grand Concourse, for example, the yearly average of accidents per intersection—20.94 divided by the 57.95-thousand vehicles that traveled on it daily in 1992—produces an accident rate of 0.36, significantly lower than the rates on its two parallel control streets, Jerome and Webster Avenues. Pedestrian accident rates are roughly similar for all three streets. However, the number of pedestrians on the Grand Concourse is significantly higher than on the comparison streets.

In Brooklyn, Ocean Parkway, despite having the highest daily traffic volume of all the boulevards studied, has an accident rate that is less than half that of its control street, Linden Boulevard. Eastern Parkway, however, has a somewhat higher accident rate and a significantly higher pedestrian accident rate than Linden Boulevard.[5] Queens Boulevard turns out to be the least safe of all the boulevards studied and does not compare well with ordinary streets. Indeed Queens Boulevard and the Grand Concourse are both noted in their localities for a high rate of pedestrian fatalities. Our view of this state of affairs, as we explain below, is that the high number of pedestrian accidents are the result of faulty boulevard design rather than of the boulevard configuration per se.

In Washington, D.C., the boulevard K Street was compared with Pennsylvania Avenue and Constitution Avenue, because these streets carry comparable amounts of traffic, and with I and L streets, which run parallel to it. Only L Street has an accident rate similar to K Street's; the other three streets are significantly safer than K. Again, we think this fact is a result of faulty boulevard design.

Table 3.2
Traffic Volumes and Accidents on Selected Boulevards and Control Streets in the United States

Streets	Volume (ADT/ 1000)	Accidents (yearly mean per intersection)	Accident rate (accident/ volume)	Pedestrian accidents (yearly mean per intersection)	Pedestrian accident rate (pedestrian accident/ volume)
New York City*					
Grand Concourse	57.950	20.94	0.36	4.88	0.06
Jerome	22.419	14.25	0.63	2.08	0.09
Webster	17.470	16.06	0.92	1.19	0.07
Queens Boulevard	37.654	36.99	0.98	2.14	0.06
Northern Avenue		14.94		0.68	
Eastern Parkway	61.000	42.38	0.69	3.65	0.06
Linden Boulevard	27.000	17.54	0.65	1.04	0.04
Ocean Parkway	74.000	27.30	0.37	1.20	0.02
Washington D.C.**					
K Street	51.850	18.20	0.35		
Pennsylvania Avenue	51.822	12.87	0.25		
Constitution. Avenue	58.100	15.33	0.26		
L Street	35.590	11.93	0.34		
I Street	34.600	8.88	0.26		
Louisville**					
Southern Parkway	17.211	8.00	0.47		
Third Street	16.503	14.97	0.93		
Chico***					
The Esplanade	24.800	4.83	0.19		
Mangrove Avenue	22.233	3.98	0.18		

Note: Street names in italics are boulevards
* Traffic volume data for New York are from the following sources: Grand Concourse and Queens Boulevard: NYC Dept. of Transportation; Grand Concourse Traffic Safety Study, Draft 12/92; and Queens Boulevard Traffic Safety Study (undated draft). Volume data for Jerome and Webster Avenues are estimated from traffic counts supplied by NYC Department of Transportation. Volume data for Eastern and Ocean Parkways and Linden Boulevard are estimated from counts performed by us, assuming a similar pattern of daily traffic on those streets as on Queens Boulevard and the Grand Concourse, for which we had data. Unfortunately, we have no volume data for Northern Avenue.

Accident information for all streets is from New York State Department of Transportation, Local Accident Surveillance Project. Data are generally for the period from 1/91 to 12/92. In fact we have been unable to reconcile major differences in number of accidents in this data with the NYPD accident data included in the Traffic Safety report; for comparison's sake we opted to use the Surveillance Project data that were available for all streets.
** Data for Washington D.C. were received from District of Columbia, Department of Public Works, Bureau of Traffic Services. Pedestrian accidents data were not available for Washington D.C. and Louisville. For Chico, they were so few as to be insignificant.
*** Traffic and Safety data for Louisville received from City of Louisville, Department of Public Works, Engineering and Architecture Division.
**** Traffic volume and accident data was received from City of Chico, Central Services, Department of Engineering.

In Louisville, Southern Parkway was found to be much safer than its control street. In Chico, the results are especially revealing. On The Esplanade, all possible movements are allowed at intersections, whereas on Mangrove Avenue, a parallel arterial street, all conflicts are supposedly eliminated by traffic signal arrangements. Despite this difference, their safety records are similar.

European Boulevards
Paris

Data from the Paris streets are not available in a form that makes it possible to easily compare them with American streets.[6] Moreover, major streets in Paris are generally much shorter than American streets and end in more complex intersections, often in roundabouts. Intersections with side streets also tend to be more complex, and rarely have angles of 90 degrees.

One of the best boulevards, Avenue Montaigne, has a daily traffic volume of about 9,300 cars; in only one section of the street, between Place Astrid and Rue du Boccador, 11 accidents were reported in a recent three-year period (a yearly average of 3.67).[7] It happens to be precisely the same section of the street where the access lane on one side of the street ends. Avenue Montaigne's comparison street, Avenue Victor Hugo, which carries an average of

Table 3.3

Traffic Volumes and Accidents: Avenue des Champs Elysées, Paris

Intersection	Volume (ADT/1000)	Accidents per year	Accident rate (accidents/ volume)	Pedestrian accidents per year	Pedestrian accident rate (pedestrian accidents/ volume)
Place de la Concorde	123.30	61.33	0.50	11.00	0.09
Avenue Dutuit	186.30	6.33	0.03	4.00	0.02
Place Clemenceau	98.60	21.00	0.21	2.67	0.03
Rond Point	101.30	19.33	0.19	5.67	0.06
Avenue Matignon	83.60	4.67	0.06	0.67	0.01
Rue Marbeuf	83.60	2.67	0.03	1.67	0.02
Pierre Charron	83.60	9.67	0.12	3.67	0.04
Rue Lincoln	83.60	4.33	0.05	3.00	0.04
Rue de Berri	83.60	6.00	0.07	1.67	0.02
Avenue George V	54.10	11.33	0.21	5.33	0.10
Rue Bassano	83.60	2.00	0.02	1.67	0.02
Rue Galilée	83.60	11.33	0.14	4.33	0.05
Rue Arene Houssaye	83.60	5.67	0.07	1.00	0.01
Rue de Presbourg	83.60	5.33	0.06	2.67	0.03
Place Charles de Gaulle	186.30	21.00	0.11	3.33	0.02
Average	83.46	10.67	**0.10**	2.91	0.03

15,200 cars per day and has two intersections, had 12 accidents at one of them and and 11 at the other (an average of 4.00 and 3.67 accidents per year, respectively).

Only in the case of the Avenue des Champs Elysées was it possible to reconstruct an analysis similar to the ones carried out for U.S. cities, because accident statistics are available for all intersections. Although the Avenue des Champs Elysées is no longer a multiple roadway boulevard (its access lanes having been dismantled and replaced by a sidewalk promenade), the accident data come from a time when it was still configured as a multiway boulevard. The Champs Elysées then had daily traffic volumes of about 84,000 vehicles and an average of 10.67 accidents per year per intersection, for an average accident rate of 0.10. This is a lower rate than most of the American boulevards studied, especially those in New York that are closest to it in terms of volume and capacity.[8] If, moreover, we consider that the four highest-ranking accident locations are such major traffic circles as the Place Charles de Gaulle or Rond Point, we see that the average accident rate for normal intersections is lower still. The pedestrian accident rate on the Champs Elysées also compares very well with that of New York's boulevards, especially if we bear in mind its much larger number of pedestrians.

Barcelona

Barcelona presents a different picture. Results indicate that its boulevards have traffic-accident rates that are higher than or similar to those of the control streets. But the picture becomes more nuanced when we consider pedestrian accident rates.

Table 3.4

Volume and Accident Statistics for Streets in Barcelona, Spain

Street	Volume (ADT/ 1000)	Accidents	Accidents per intersection	Accident rate (accidents per intersection/ volume)	Pedestrian accidents	Pedestrian accidents per intersection	Pedestrian accident rate (pedestrian accidents per intersection/ volume)
Passeig de Gràcia	39.87	172	17.2	0.43	44	4.4	0.11
Diagonal	101.26	317	16.7	0.17	47	2.5	0.02
Gran Via	66.34	367	16.7	0.25	79	3.6	0.05
Aragó	89.16	223	11.7	0.13	31	1.6	0.02
Balmes	52.00	126	11.5	0.22	23	2.1	0.04
Urgell	63.52	88	6.3	0.10	15	1.1	0.02

Note: Street names in italics are the boulevards.

Source: Municipality of Barcelona.

The overall pedestrian accident rate on the Passeig de Gràcia is significantly higher than it is on the Gran Via, the Diagonal, or the control streets. Pedestrian accidents there constitute 25 percent of all accidents, compared with only 15 to 18 percent on the other streets. The perspective changes, however, once we take into account the large number of pedestrians using the Passeig de Gràcia—3,270 pedestrians per hour. Its weighted pedestrian-accident rate is thus 0.034, as compared to 0.021 on Aragó (970 pedestrians per hour), 0.040 on Balmes (1,000 pedestrians per hour), and 0.042 on the Diagonal (480 pedestrians per hour).

RELATIVE SAFETY

Although the available data do not permit us to show a persistent pattern in which multiway boulevards are safer than "normally" configured streets, they also do not let us conclude that the contrary is true. Nor does the claim that boulevards are less safe specifically because of their complex intersections seem substantiated by the facts.

The so-called problematic cases—those in which the boulevards fare relatively worse than comparable streets in terms of their safety records—throw even more doubt on the logic of the safety argument against them. The main point of that line of reasoning is the contention that the complexity of movements and the multitude of potential conflict points at intersections make multiway boulevards unsafe. However, it is precisely in the two places where attempts have been made to resolve intersection complexity that boulevards seem to be less safe relative to their comparison streets than ordinary boulevards with complex intersections allowing all movements. On K-Street, long and detailed observations of traffic movement suggest that alterations made to the street in the name of safety have actually

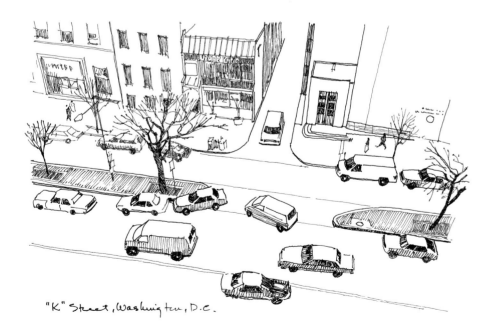

"K" Street, Washington, D.C.

proved damaging to both function and safety: breaks in the side medians (called *sleeves*) were introduced between intersections to allow movement between the access lanes and the central throughway; and many of the trees on the median were eliminated. Why did these changes make the street less safe? Because they eroded the demarcation between the access ways and the central throughway that is the basis for the usefulness and safety of boulevards. In Barcelona, too, conflict at intersections has been greatly reduced—by an overall pattern of traffic organization that relies on alternating one-way streets. The intersections along the Passeig de Gràcia are thus greatly simplified, and the number of conflict points is reduced relative to boulevards in other cities. Consequently, one would have expected less of a difference between its safety record and that of its comparison streets, rather than the reverse.

Perhaps an even more important finding that came from correlating observations of people's behavior with the accident statistics is that boulevards that have a significant amount of access road traffic also have a more problematic safety record. The Grand Concourse and Queens Boulevard are extreme examples of this phenomenon. Queens Boulevard's safety problems show up in its calculated accident rate. The Grand Concourse's are not as clearly evident in its accident rate, but local residents perceive the street as unsafe—and for good reasons.

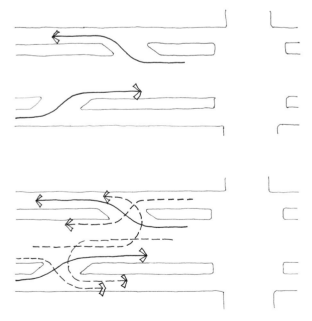

**Intended and actual traffic movements
at median sleeves on K Street**.

PHYSICAL FORM AND PEOPLE'S BEHAVIOR

This apparent paradox, that boulevards with less-complex intersections seem to have worse accident records than normally configured streets—and the observations regarding movement on the access ways—prompts a discussion of how people use boulevards in practice and how the physical configuration of the boulevard supports that use and helps people adapt to the complexities so as to negotiate them safely.

To illustrate how the physical design of boulevards affects behavior, let us look again at two of the boulevards in New York City: the Grand Concourse in the Bronx and Ocean Parkway in Brooklyn. The differences between them illustrate how boulevards can be designed to achieve usefulness and safety.

There are three major differences between these two boulevards. Two of them can be readily observed in the dimensions of the access roadway and the medians and the third in the way traffic on the access lanes is regulated. The access roadways on the Grand Concourse are wider and include two moving lanes of traffic and only one parking lane, whereas those on Ocean Parkway have one through lane and two parking lanes. Secondly, the medians on Ocean Parkway are wider, are planted more regularly and densely, and include such amenities as benches and a bike path. The third difference is that on the Grand Concourse the access roads are controlled by traffic lights, which allow swift through movement, while on Ocean Parkway they are controlled by stop signs at every intersection. The vehicular-movement diagrams show the impact of these differences in physical configuration and traf-

Table 3.5

A Comparison between Grand Concourse and Ocean Parkway

	Grand Concourse	Ocean Parkway
Physical Configuration		
Overall width of right-of-way (ft.)	175	210
Width of center roadway (ft.)	50	70
Moving lanes	4	6
Width of access streets (ft.)	35	25
Moving lanes on access streets	2	1
Parking lanes	1	2
Movement data		
Total car movement (vph)	2800	3592
Movement in access lanes (vph)	1292	244
Percentage of total in access lanes	46%	7%
Pedestrian movement (people per hour)		
Along boulevard	496	376
Crossing	864	252
On median	0	108

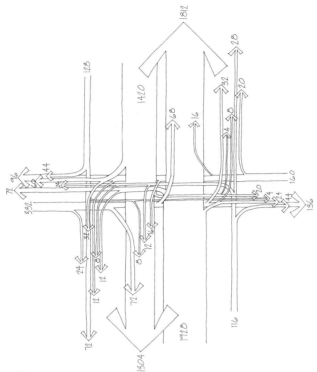

Ocean Parkway: traffic movements at Ditmas Street

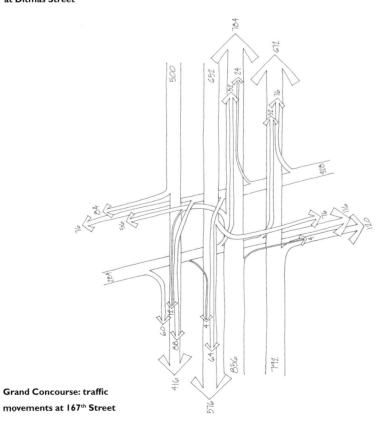

Grand Concourse: traffic movements at 167th Street

Pedestrian Realm on Ocean Parkway.

Access road lanes on Grand Concourse.

fic regulation on drivers' behavior. On the Grand Concourse 46 percent of all the vehicular movement occurs in the access lanes, compared to only 7 percent on Ocean Parkway. Moreover, speeds on the access lanes of the Grand Concourse nearly equal those on the central through lanes, while on Ocean Parkway vehicles on the access lanes go much more slowly, more in tune with the speed of pedestrian movement. Furthermore, on the Grand Concourse 84 percent of the cars entering an intersection on an access lane continue straight through, still on the access lane, compared to only 40 percent on Ocean Parkway; thus the access ways on Grand Concourse are more than twice as likely to be used for through movement as those on Ocean Parkway.

The second major difference in the way these streets are used is captured by their patterns of pedestrian movement. While there are more pedestrians on Grand Concourse than on Ocean Parkway, most of them only cross the street and are not likely to walk along it for any distance, whereas more people walk along Ocean Parkway than cross it. Even more significant is the heavy use of the medians on Ocean Parkway as places to walk and sit. The medians on the Grand Concourse are virtually unused.

These differences in movement and use patterns reflect a major difference in the impact of cars on the pedestrian environment. While Ocean Parkway carries 28 percent more traffic than Grand Concourse, a visitor to both streets would probably perceive the impact of cars and traffic on the pedestrian environment as much more significant on the Grand Concourse. Analysis of their accident data shows that while Ocean Parkway has an accident rate similar to that of the Grand Concourse, with regard to pedestrian accidents the parkway is

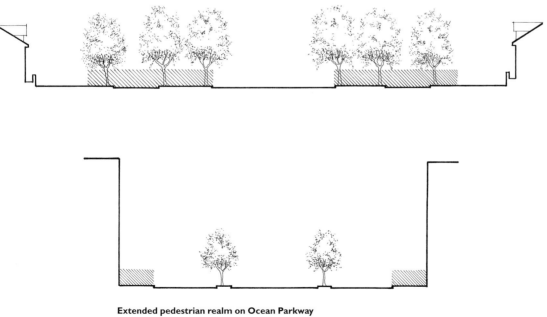

Extended pedestrian realm on Ocean Parkway
Pedestrian realm on Grand Concourse

three times safer. Moreover, detailed accident-location maps indicate that the majority of pedestrian accidents on the Grand Concourse occur on the access roads.

THE PEDESTRIAN REALM

Where does the difference between the two streets lie? Observations suggest that the key factor is the presence or lack of what we have come to call an extended pedestrian realm along the edges of the boulevard. This realm, which when it emerges stretches from the building frontage to the outside edge of the median, includes the sidewalk, the access roadway, and the planted median. Although it is not reserved solely for pedestrian use, its configuration encourages drivers within it to go very slowly and to respect pedestrians using the street. At the same time, its configuration encourages pedestrians to claim the access way as their own by walking along it or crossing it at will between the sidewalk and the median.

The study of varied boulevard types allows us to draw some conclusions about the necessary and conducive conditions for emergence of a pedestrian realm. They are:

- Uninterrupted median strips between the through lanes and the access lanes.
- A strong line of densely planted trees along the medians, continuing all the way to intersections.
- Relatively narrow access roadways that allow only one lane of traffic and are controlled by stop signs at every intersection.
- Placement on the medians of transit stops, kiosks, or benches—to encourage people to cross from the sidewalk to use them.
- Access ways that are further distinguished from the central throughway realm by a slight change of level and/or paving.

The first two conditions are necessary, for they define the boulevard configuration. Streets like the Grand Concourse or Shattuck Avenue in Berkeley, California, which have medians but do not have a regular line of trees, do not really work as boulevards, because the space of the street is not divided into three distinct areas by the trees. Observation of pedestrians' behavior on these streets shows that they seldom walk along the access way, even when cars there are moving slowly.

The third condition is most important for pedestrian safety because it helps maintain the integrity of the pedestrian realm. It is best clarified by a counterexample. The Diagonal and the Gran Via in Barcelona both have generous medians where people like to walk and linger, but their access ways have been turned into fast-moving trafficways by regulations that forbid parking on the lane next to the sidewalk. The result is that drivers are as likely to use them as throughways as they are the central lanes—and to travel on them just as fast. The situation is dangerous to pedestrians, who are drawn to cross the access way from the sidewalk to the median, often at midblock, only to be surprised by fast traffic. This may explain

Via Nomentana, Rome - The pedestrian realm.

why relatively more pedestrian accidents occur at midblock on the Diagonal and the Gran Via (35 percent of all pedestrian accidents) than on the Passeig de Gràcia (only 20 percent of pedestrian accidents).[9]

The fourth and fifth conditions, while not absolutely necessary for the establishment of a pedestrian realm, are good ways to reinforce its separate and slow-moving nature and encourage drivers to proceed more cautiously.

Together, the five conditions create a slow environment for drivers on a boulevard's access lanes. They must often wait for cars pulling in and out of parking spaces and must stop at every intersection. Double-parked delivery trucks often block the whole access way for a time. People walking along the roadway often cause drivers to move at a pedestrian pace. These factors discourage drivers from using the access lanes for through movement and establish a leisurely pace. In addition, the difficulty of negotiating intersections encourages everyone to take extra care at the point of highest conflict between drivers and pedestrians; this is particularly important for drivers coming out of the access lanes who, because of the stop signs, have the lowest movement priority.

The pedestrian realm is therefore an emergent product of physical design, the regulation of movement behavior by traffic lights and signs, and the patterns of use established by the behavior of pedestrians and drivers. Without the necessary physical configuration, or with the wrong kind of traffic regulation, the pedestrian realm fails to materialize in practice. In that case, the street may become more dangerous, particularly to pedestrians.

A clear demarcation between the access lanes and the central realm is also advantageous to through traffic. On city streets where building entrances and shops face the street and people need to get into and out of cars, taxis, and buses—and into and out of parking spaces at the curb—friction between through movement and access movement is inevitable and delays through traffic. Prohibiting parking in the curb lane does not help much, as deliveries and drop-offs still occur illegally. Observations of traffic movement in the central lanes of boulevards show that through traffic suffers less from disturbance than it does on normally configured streets and that there is less need for weaving between lanes to get around stopped or waiting vehicles. Thus the boulevard provides for both through movement and the access needs of a street, and it does so in a balanced way. This balance is reflected in the space given to each part of the street. On the best boulevards, the combined pedestrian realms account for about two-thirds of the street's width.

SUMMARY

Let us reiterate the answers to the two questions asked at the start of this chapter. The answer to the first is *no:* boulevards are not inherently more dangerous than ordinarily configured arterial streets. The data gathered from boulevards across the United States and in Europe do not support the prevailing professional view that they are.

The data we were able to obtain are not detailed enough with respect to the exact locations of accidents or their physical circumstances to let us say positively that boulevards function more safely than other types as major city streets. Indeed, the paucity of data—and the general lack of precision about these matters—is surprising; it also reinforces our belief that the original indictment of boulevards was not the result of careful studies of accidents and their causes but of reasoning from the statistical probability of conflicts at intersections.

Such reasoning, which equates the statistical probability of conflict between movements with the physical possibility of accidents, does not take into account people's ability to adapt their behavior in ways that ensure their personal safety. When a situation is complex, drivers and pedestrians use greater caution. Thus, eliminating conflicting movements and simplifying movement channels can have the paradoxical effect of creating more danger; drivers and pedestrians alike may believe the situation to be free from conflict when it is not. Adaptive behavior, however, requires an environment that provides clear information to drivers and pedestrians. A well-designed boulevard, separated into clear realms of fast movement and slow movement by the medians and the rows of trees and concentrating conflicting movements at the intersections, provides that information. Drivers in the center lanes can drive rapidly, safely, and directly without being impeded by the traffic and pedestrians in the access lanes, except at the intersections; there they can expect all kinds of movement. Pedestrians can venture into the access way—if they want to walk faster when the sidewalk is clogged, or if they want to cross to the median—without worrying about fast-moving vehicles. They are thus encouraged to cross the center roadway only at the intersections and are provided with pleasant surroundings for walking toward them.

The answer to the second question is *yes:* design matters. The main feature that makes boulevards safe and livable is the extent to which a clear pedestrian realm emerges between the buildings and medians. This realm is structured as a complex area where cars are allowed but pedestrians dominate. It allows access movements, through movements, and pedestrian comfort and safety to coexist on the same street, thus solving the conflict created in the twentieth-century by the growing disparity among the three needs. The multiway boulevard retains both traditional uses of the street—as a movement channel and a meeting place—without having to specialize in either one. The result is the immensely successful streets we have described.

Overly wide, built to standards, two-way access roadway in Fremont, California.

Chapter Two

PROFESSIONAL AND BUREAUCRATIC CONSTRAINTS

We have seen that multiway boulevards are not inherently more dangerous than other major traffic-carrying streets, a conclusion that would hardly surprise Parisians or Barcelonians, or people who regularly travel along Eastern and Ocean Parkways in Brooklyn or The Esplanade in Chico. On the other hand, residents who live near the Grand Concourse in the Bronx, or drivers who use Queens Boulevard, might require a lot of convincing. And the professionals? How might they respond to analyses showing multiway boulevards to be no more dangerous than other major traffic-carrying streets? And what of the codified standards and norms of practice that largely control the design of roadways in the United States—standards that originate with the professionals?

   We now return to one of our original questions: Can such boulevards be built today? Do today's standards and norms permit them? If the mayor and council of a U.S. city saw and liked a successful multiway boulevard in another city and concluded that the design would work well for one of their own streets, could they get it built? Would some of the positive attributes of the best boulevards be lost by following today's "rules of the road"? Even if it were not possible to build a street that exactly matched one of the model boulevards, could they build a *good* multiway boulevard?

STREET STANDARDS AND THEIR IMPACTS

The answers to these question are not as easy to find as you might think. To start with, we have seen that boulevards do not fit neatly into the prevailing functional categorization of streets found in the various manuals of traffic engineering. So another question arises: Which standards or guidelines are most applicable to boulevards? The prominence of multiway boulevards in cities where they exist, their width and their high traffic volumes, makes it seem natural to classify them as arterial streets. At the same time, the unlimited access to abutting property and the local nature of movement on the side access lanes make them more like local streets. However, as transportation professionals tend to think of boulevards as arterials, we shall look mostly at standards for arterial streets.[1]

   The more we observe and study multiway boulevards, the more apparent it becomes that no single standard or guideline, though it may be important, is necessarily critical to their ultimate success or failure. Many characteristics, when combined, account for the best boulevards. Standards, however, tend to deal with single elements—lane widths, for example, or intersection design—in isolation. Because of the complexity of multiway boulevards, it is necessary to look not only at the standards for individual elements but also to analyze their combined effect. Most important: standards for the various elements must be related to the roles they play in the overall street design. To simply say that it would not be possible to build Avenue Montaigne or another fine street today is not enough. We need a more detailed study of the way multiway boulevards work in order to understand the impacts of the prevailing standards and norms.

LANE WIDTH STANDARDS AND NORMS

Avenue Montaigne has a total right-of-way of 126 feet. There are three lanes for through traffic, two access lanes, at least three and sometimes four parking lanes, sidewalks, and medians. If rebuilt to American *minimum* roadway standards with no changes in the widths of sidewalks and medians, the avenue would need a right-of-way of 145 feet. *Desirable* standards would require 156 feet.[2] Those increases come to 15 percent and 24 percent, respectively. The amount of space presently devoted to vehicles—70 feet of combined roadway (or 80 feet where the access lane widens to allow more parking)—would increase to 99 feet using minimum standards, or 110 feet using desirable standards. Yet widening lanes to American standards would do little to increase the carrying capacity of the boulevard because the

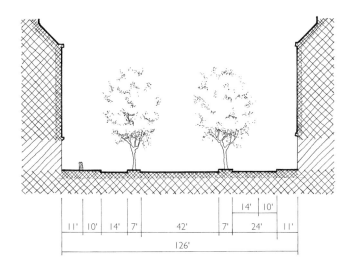

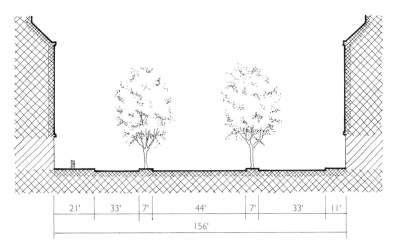

Avenue Montaigne: existing and hypothetical sections

Approximate scale: 1″ = 50′ or 1:600

center roadway would stay roughly the same; it would, however, encourage faster movement of cars on the access lanes where most of the increase in width would occur. Our observations of pedestrians' behavior on the access lanes of Avenue Montaigne has shown that they treat them as part of their realm and mingle freely with the cars. That is possible only if cars travel very slowly, which they do, in part because the access lanes are narrow. Moreover, on all the boulevards studied, pedestrians were observed crossing the access lanes to the median against a red light, so shortening the distance they had to cover to reach the other side of the street when the light changed. Widening the access lanes, and so allowing traffic to travel faster, would increase the danger to pedestrians making that crossing. The balance in the use of the street would shift from pedestrians' needs to those of drivers.

Clearly, required lane-width standards alone do not make boulevards impossible to design, though they might make them less safe. They also make it difficult to introduce boulevards where rights-of-way are limited. Using minimum standards, access lanes limited to one parking lane and one travel lane, and a center roadway limited to two through lanes in each direction, a boulevard could be built in a 124-foot right-of-way. Using so-called desirable standards and increasing the center roadway to three through lanes in each direction would expand the required right-of-way to 166 feet. In both cases, the pedestrian realm would be weakened by the wider access lanes, because they would allow traffic to move faster.

Applying desirable lane-width standards to the access roads on Ocean Parkway, which presently has two parking lanes and one moving lane, would result in a 36-foot wide roadway, instead of the 24-foot wide roadway that now exists. It is not hard to imagine how pedestrians and vehicles alike might alter their behavior.

Table 3.6

Comparison between U.S. Lane-Width Norms and Existing Lane-Widths on Avenue Montaigne

	American norms				Existing
	Design speed				
	Under 40 mph		Over 40 mph		
Lane Width	Minimum	Desirable	Minimum	Desirable	Avenue Montaigne
Curb/parking	11'	12'	11'	13'	6'–7' in access lanes 10' in center road
Curb travel	11'	12'	11'	13'	None 7'–9' in access road
Inside lane	10'	12'	11'	12'	10' in center road
Turn lane	10'	12'	11'	12'	None

Source: *Guidelines for Urban Major Street Design: A Recommended Practice*, 1984.

MEDIAN DESIGN

Applying the American recommended guidelines for the design of medians, a seemingly innocuous change, would seriously alter the Passeig de Gràcia, Avenue Montaigne, Ocean Parkway, and other fine boulevards. These guidelines address the questions of median widths and tree planting. The recommendation to limit the size of tree trunks to six inches in diameter would mean that most of the mature trees along the Passeig de Gràcia, Avenue Montaigne, and Ocean Parkway would have to be replaced.[3] It is hard to imagine these streets without the large trees separating the various traffic lanes and providing shade for pedestrians in summer while creating a canopied drive for drivers. The logic of removing large trees because they may contribute to fixed-object accidents is questionable. Moreover, their presence along the medians helps create a physical and psychological barrier that enhances pedestrians' sense of being safe from the speeding cars in the center. Clearly, removing them would further weaken the pedestrian realm.

The basis of the median widths recommended in standard professional publications are geometric calculations related to the ways medians facilitate or hinder traffic movement. The only consideration for pedestrians is how medians might function as pedestrian refuges.[4] However, on Avenue Montaigne and the Passeig de Gràcia, as well as on other boulevards, we have observed a much wider array of functions for the medians—first and foremost as locations for transit stops, promenades, kiosks, and newsstands. As we noted, Avenue Montaigne's medians are approximately 7.5-feet wide. On Passeig de Gràcia, medians are between 6 and 22 feet wide and accommodate a host of things—including

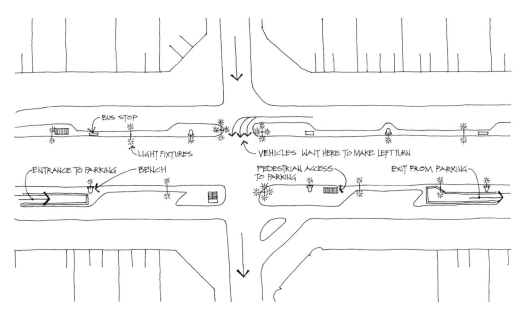

The many functions of the medians on the Passeig de Gràcia

benches, street lights, bus stops, and entrances to underground parking and the subway—which are on the wider portions of the medians. Near crosswalks at intersections the medians are widened, at the expense of a parking lane. This also provides a wider space for cars waiting to turn left from the access lanes.

INTERSECTION DESIGN

The common presumption that intersections on multiway boulevards are necessarily dangerous was one of our reasons for pursuing the inquiries that led to this book. It is true that boulevard intersections have many more possible points of conflict—places where traffic crosses other traffic moving in a different direction—than intersections of normally configured two-way streets. The familiar intersection of two two-way streets each two lanes wide has 16 major points of conflict. An Ocean Parkway intersection, where all movements are allowed, has 50 conflict points. An intersection on Passeig de Gràcia, which has one-way cross streets, has 33 such points. Professional wisdom says that the number of possible conflicts should be kept to a minimum.[5] It is not at all clear, however, that having more conflict points actually causes more accidents. Ocean Parkway has one of the highest traffic volumes of all the boulevards we studied; yet, in spite of its many conflict points, it does not have a bad safety record.

Recommended principles for intersection design generally include favoring the heaviest and fastest traffic flow. On the Passeig de Gràcia the heaviest flow is of pedestrians: 3,304 per hour versus 1,808 cars. On the Avenue Montaigne the pedestrian flow is 1,328 people per hour, compared to 1,653 cars. We see, therefore, that the heaviest movement flow is not

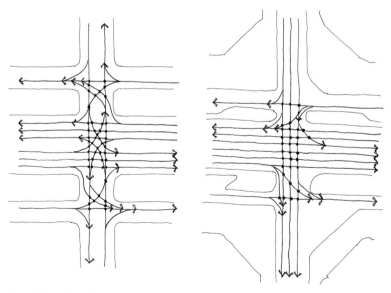

Potential conflict points: Ocean Parkway and Passeig de Gràcia

necessarily the fastest flow, and also that on some streets pedestrian flows are sizable. However, the principles of intersection design consider only vehicular traffic and do not take into account the existence of pedestrians and the possible ways that the two modes might interact. They assume the ideal of a single-function street and ignore the fact that in an urban area this ideal is probably neither attainable nor desirable. The Passeig de Gràcia and the Avenue Montaigne are prime examples of a very different approach to street planning, one in which pedestrians are recognized and welcomed and their needs are met.

The 1990 policy publication of the American Association of State Highway and Transportation Officials makes no distinction between major urban streets and expressways; they are both considered arterials. While the usefulness of frontage roads to facilitate access to adjoining property is acknowledged, that usefulness, according to the AASHTO, is overshadowed by the complexities they create at intersections. At intersections, the guide recommends a minimum separation of 150 feet between the right curb of the through lanes and the left curb of the frontage road.[6] Narrower separations (to a minimum of 8 feet) are acceptable, however, where frontage-road traffic is very light, where it is one-way only, or where some movements are prohibited at intersections. Thus, although one can still say that boulevards are possible under these norms, they are certainly not recommended or encouraged.

The Passeig de Gràcia and Avenue Montaigne employ two different solutions to the problem of boulevard intersection design. On the Passeig, the median width increases to 26 feet at intersections—providing room enough for cars wanting to turn left from the frontage roads to make a half-turn and wait for the light to change on the cross-street. They can then join the stream of cross traffic, either going straight to complete the left turn, or turning into the center lanes or the opposite frontage road to complete a U-turn. We have observed five or six cars waiting in this way without blocking the through movement on the access lane. This feature is aided by the one-way design of the cross streets, which enables cars to stack up across the whole width of the cross street. On Avenue Montaigne, the ac-

Street Venders at a Corner on "K" Street

News vending boxes on "K" Street.

cess lanes are raised slightly, by a one- to two-inch curb, and they turn inward slightly, toward the center of the intersections. The result is that priority for all kinds of turning movements clearly belongs to the cars in the center lanes, and drivers turning from the frontage roads use caution, somewhat like drivers entering the street from a driveway.

During our observations, we encountered no situation in which trees seemed to create a problem for drivers at intersections. Many other structures—for example, bus shelters and kiosks—are more obtrusive, bulkier, and more likely to obstruct sight lines. Yet they must be located near intersections for functional reasons. Parked and waiting cars can block the view, too, but also serve as warnings to drivers on the main street to slow down. At many intersections, especially on American streets, newspaper delivery boxes placed side by side provide a much more formidable barrier to sight for a driver sitting low in a car—and for

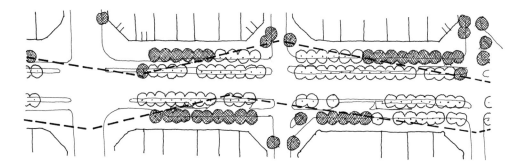

Effect of applying site distance norms to the Passeig de Gràcia

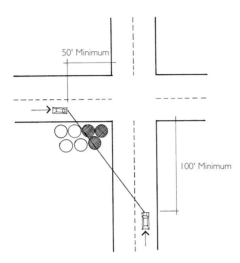

Site distances and tree removal

pedestrians moving into an intersection—than a row of densely planted trees. And news-paper boxes have none of the redeeming functional and aesthetic value of trees. Moreover, tree trunks at intersections are never more intrusive than the large-diameter poles that carry traffic signals and other paraphernalia, which seem to be standard equipment at all inter-sections of any significance.

Practical experience notwithstanding, the clear sight distances for a typical boulevard recommended by prevailing standards and norms—assuming speeds of 40 miles per hour and six lanes of traffic—are 520 feet for a passenger car and 680 feet for a truck.[7] Applica-tion of these sight distances to the Passeig de Gràcia would be disastrous. Many, many trees would have to be felled. This would destroy the street. Boulevards are characterized by rows of trees that run uninterrupted to the intersections, making them the strongest element in the definition and memorability of the street. Yet many U.S. municipal standards we have seen recommend keeping trees back a fixed distance from intersections—as much as 40, 50 feet, or more.

Where, we ask ourselves, might such standards for sight distances and setback distances have come from? They seem to defy the findings of field experience, and yet they are fre-quently one of the textbook problems given to student engineers.[8] The basic assumption of such exercises is that auto safety is positively correlated to sight distances and inversely re-lated to speed. That is, the greater the distance from which drivers approaching an inter-section can see vehicles at the intersection, and the more slowly they are traveling toward it, the better opportunity they will have to spot possible dangers and avoid accidents by stopping. Fine so far. From this assumption, therefore, the problem for the student is: As-suming a given speed on the boulevard (40 miles per hour seems to be the magic number), how far back from the intersection should a tree be planted in order to achieve the desired safe-sight distance? A table of required stopping distances at various speeds may accompany the question, or a diagram showing offending and nonoffending trees, to make the same point. One can easily imagine finding such a problem on an examination, replete with variations comparing accident prevention at different speeds. These are the sorts of problems that students generally answer correctly, especially if they have been asked them on earlier exams; the tables and diagrams are easily remembered.

The problems with such exercises are apparent. Why the 40 miles per hour speed assumption? What if there is a traffic light or stop signs? Isn't it reasonable to expect that drivers on the side streets will stop? Perhaps most strange of all are the trees in the accompanying illustrations: they are drawn as large cylinders with wide-spreading branches coming all the way to the ground. They are visually totally impermeable—bizarre trees indeed! The diagrams (and the logic) forget that a tree is really no different than a post or a pole or any of the hundreds of other minor visual intrusions—including people—that are a part of normal life.

PARKING

The design guidelines for major urban streets cite a number of reasons for strongly discouraging parking: reduction in street capacity, inappropriate use of public space, accidents associated with parking or parked vehicles, obstruction of fire-fighting apparatus, and impaired sight lines.[9]

Parking on the access lanes, however, performs an essential function on Passeig de Gràcia and the Avenue Montaigne, as well as on the better U.S. multiway boulevards. Avenue Montaigne has one or two parallel parking lanes. The Passeig de Gràcia has a variety of parking configurations. The parked cars separate moving cars and pedestrians. Drivers looking for a place to park slow the traffic on the access lanes.

These boulevards have a reasonable, though not overwhelming, amount of parking. They are readily accessible by public transportation and taxis, which run on special reserved lanes of the central roadway, allowing them to move faster than private cars. The result is a balance between cars and pedestrians, private and public transportation, that is conducive to a lively and pleasant street.

STANDARDS, NORMS, AND THE PEDESTRIAN REALM OF BOULEVARDS

If we examine a cross section of Avenue Montaigne, we see that the area devoted to pedestrians on the sidewalks and the medians consists of 44 percent of the total width of the street. On Passeig de Gràcia, it is 50 percent of the total width of the street. The lane widths on these two boulevards are substandard by American norms, especially in the access lanes. On Avenue Montaigne, as we have seen, some access lanes are 24-feet wide. To accommodate the uses it does under desirable lane-width norms in the United States, Avenue Montaigne would have to be 30 feet wider. Most of the widening would occur on the access lanes, which would be expanded to 36 feet (an increase of 50 percent). If we consider how Avenue

Montaigne really works, with the side access lanes as part of an extended pedestrian realm stretching from the buildings to the outer edge of the medians, we see that 67 percent of the width of this boulevard is geared to a pedestrian scale and speed. If the access lanes were widened, or parking on them were limited, drivers could go faster and would tend to use them more. Access roadways would then cease to operate as an extended pedestrian realm and become more a part of the motorists' realm. If that happened, the medians would become less useful to pedestrians because they would be separated from the sidewalks by fast-moving traffic. The delineation of the pedestrian realm would be further weakened by the removal of trees near intersections, and of all large trees on the medians—in order to "improve" sight lines—or by the construction of breaks in the medians to reduce the number of turning movements at intersections. As a result of applying the various guidelines and requirements, the area of the street devoted to the pedestrian would drop from 67 percent of the total to 25 percent, completely disturbing the balance between pedestrian and vehicular movement and between local and through traffic.

It is apparent that while existing standards and roadway-design guidelines, as well as design practices, do not make building multiway boulevards completely out of the question, they do make it extremely difficult. Perhaps more important, creating streets like the very best of these boulevards—the Avenue Montaigne or the Passeig de Gràcia or, in the United States, Ocean Parkway—becomes highly unlikely, well-nigh impossible. It must be noted that no single guideline actually does the damage on its own; it is their combined force that prevents us from designing and building good boulevards today. It is the pedestrian realm, the local-serving part of a multiway boulevard, that suffers the most from the application of prevailing standards.

But there is hope!

There is a somewhat discretionary character to the roadway-design standards found in the various professional handbooks and published guidelines, one that emerges in discussions with engineering professionals. Relatively few of the standards or guidelines are stated as *requirements.* They are *recommended* standards and guides. There are also fewer "thou shalt" admonitions in the state laws governing the design of highways and streets than you might expect. There may well be admonitions referring to the various published standards that make it near to impossible to attain federal or state funding for projects that do not conform to those standards. Yet a remarkable amount of discretion is left in the hands of local city engineers when it comes to building streets in their jurisdictions. Engineers may refer to a standard to justify doing something one way or rejecting another possibility, but in the end they have considerable design leeway, if they want to use it.

Today's ways of designing and building major roadways need not be tomorrow's way. The multiway boulevards in the United States and elsewhere, it is clear, deserve a second look. With that in mind, and based upon the research that constitutes the body of this book, it is appropriate to explore ways of redesigning existing boulevards that are not working well and designing new ones that meet the multiple needs of truly urban streets in urban communities. That is the subject matter of Part Five. First, however, we look at a large number of additional multiway boulevards from a wide variety of cities around the world.

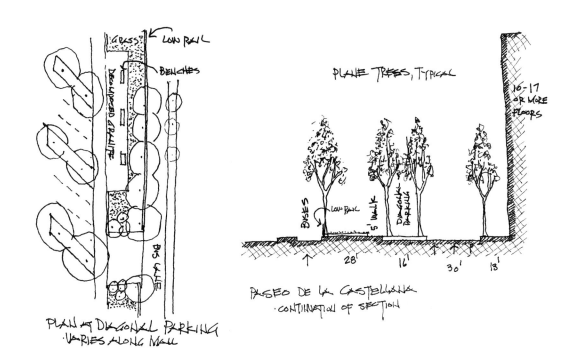

PLANE TREES, TYPICAL

10-17 OR MORE FLOORS

BUSES

LOW RAIL

5' WALK

DIAGONAL PARKING

28'   16'   30'   13'

GRASS   LOW RAIL

BENCHES

DECOMPOSED GRANITE

BIG TREE

PLAN AT DIAGONAL PARKING
·VARIES ALONG MALL

PASEO DE LA CASTELLANA
·CONTINUATION OF SECTION

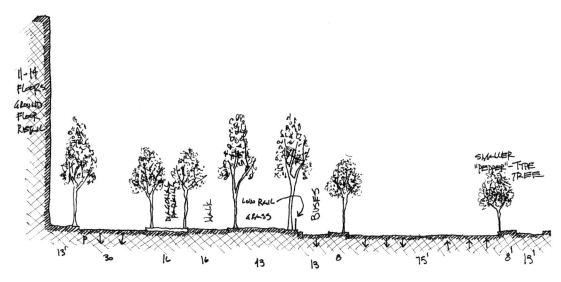

11-14 FLOORS
GROUND FLOOR RETAIL

DIAGONAL PARKING

WALK

LOW RAIL & GRASS

BUSES

SMALLER "PEPPER"-TYPE TREE

13'   30'   16'   16'   13'   13' 8'   75'   8' 13'

PASEO DE LA CASTELLANA

Aside from their surprising physical variety—large and small, long and short, curvilinear and straight—multiway boulevards are found the world over in a wide variety of land-use and socioeconomic contexts. In the end, they are either designed well or poorly. Decision makers at design and policy levels need to know as much as possible about them. The poorly designed ones may be as enlightening as those done well. In this part, therefore, we describe some of the amazing variety of multiway boulevards. In addition, based on our research findings, we have undertaken to show how one street, Queens Boulevard, could be reconfigured to transform it into a safe and even gracious asset to its New York borough—rather than the wide traffic river it has been for so many years. Case studies such as this one were instrumental in helping us develop the design guidelines for multiway boulevards presented in Part Five.

Overall, we chose forty-three multiway boulevards, to show a reasonable variety of physical characteristics, urban contexts, and geographic distribution. They include some of the best, some of the worst, and a lot of the in-betweens. There are certainly fine multiway boulevards we have missed, but there are enough here to give the reader a good sense of the situations that invite their use and of the variety of possible designs.

We tend to think of multiway boulevards as wide and elegant. Not all of them are. No sooner has one arrived at a general conclusion, born of experience and logic, that all multiway boulevards have at least four center lanes than one discovers San Francisco Boulevard in Sacramento; it has only one central lane in each direction and fits nicely into an overall right-of-way of 96 feet. The right-of-way of the Corso Isonzo in Ferrara, Italy, is even narrower, at about 88 feet, and has a central roadway only 30 feet wide. Pasteur Boulevard in Ho Chi Minh City, at approximately 62 feet wide, is the narrowest of all. These are all domestically scaled multiway boulevards, not grand avenues. Nor are the areas they pass through necessarily well-to-do. Like the larger boulevards, they are either principally residential or a mix of ground-floor shopping with commercial and residential uses above.

At the other extreme is the Avenida 9 de Julio in Buenos Aires. It is hard to imagine a boulevard with sixteen lanes in the center roadway—eight in each direction—but there they are, and the traffic races along them between the traffic lights. The boulevard's total right-of-way is 450 feet. Cristoforo Colombo in Rome, another raceway, has a right-of-way of 253 feet, but it seems much wider because the medians are not heavily planted and there is little to arrest the eyes along the roadway. Sunset Boulevard in San Francisco is an example of a multiway boulevard that is so wide and is so configured that it appears to be something else; its medians are so broad that they and the wide two-way access roads beyond them are disassociated from the central roadway.

The variety continues. There are short boulevards—San Francisco Boulevard is but five blocks long—and long ones like Queens Boulevard, which runs for five and a half miles. Commonwealth Avenue in Boston curves sensuously through its environment, while most multiway boulevards are straight. The Melbourne boulevards are famous as parkways and for the trolleys that run along them; some U.S. boulevards (Commonwealth) and Roman ones (Viale delle Milizie) also have trams. There are one-sided boulevards, such as Avenida Oswaldo Cruz in Rio de Janeiro and Boulevard Courcelles in Paris. On Paris's Boulevard Beaumarchais the side access roads have recently been combined with the pedestrian ways;

there are no curbs separating places to walk from places to drive and park—bollards serve that purpose.

For complexity, the intersection of two multiway boulevards in Rome takes the prize. The movement possibilities seem endless, all the more so because a streetcar line manages to turn from one of the boulevards onto the other amidst the rush of pedestrians, autos, buses, and motor scooters. And yet, the intersection seems to work well. On a more somber note, we have included a multiway boulevard without trees, Via della Conciliazione, also in Rome. Trees might or might not obscure the view of St. Peter's; nonetheless, they would certainly make what is now a daunting experience (walking along this boulevard) much more enjoyable.

Via Nomentana @ Via Trieste

ASIA

India

Ahmedabad

C. G. Road C. G. Road—Chimantal Girdharlal Road—is a major arterial route around the inner part of a relatively new section of Ahmedabad west of the Sabarimarti River. Though not in the center of the city, it is an important street, a lineal spine of a relatively well-to-do sector. One of only a few major streets taking traffic in a north-south direction on the western side of the city, it is the location of office buildings, upscale shopping, entertainment, and restaurants. Housing estates for the well-to-do are located either above commercial establishments on C. G. Road or just off it. It is a busy street at night.

In the early 1990s, not unlike many commercial streets in India, C. G. Road had a haphazard feel to it. New buildings intruded onto the public right-of-way, and sidewalks, where they existed, were often discontinuous. Vehicular parking was haphazard, in a very dusty environment. There were some trees—and the larger ones were a positive presence—but this was not a tree-lined street. There was a confusion of movement and modes of travel: pedestrians, automobiles, trucks, taxicabs, motor scooters (more of them than any other vehicle), scooter taxis, camel-, mule-, and human-drawn carts, and a few buses. It is easy to imagine the varying paces of so many different modes of travel. Any street redesign would want to keep all these travel types and paces in mind and to accommodate as many as possible, but not at the expense of the commerce and shopping along C. G. Road, and not at the expense of the activity of the people along it.

The Old C. G. Road, Ahmedabad.

The chief administrative officer and political leaders concluded in the mid-1990s that
C. G. Road could be a better street than it was. They decided to reconfigure it as a multiway boulevard. The first segment of approximately one mile long was completed in 1997.[1]
It is a very narrow boulevard with a total right-of-way of 100 feet. That narrowness is ac-
centuated because local driving habits require angle parking—not parallel parking—on
the side access roads.

- The high-volume central roadway has two 10-foot-wide lanes in each direction, separated by a low, three-foot, median (to prevent traffic on either side from claiming a third
  lane).
- The medians separating the center lanes from the access roads are exceedingly narrow, in
  places no wider than a raised curb. Trees are planted on the medians in the triangular
  spaces created in front of the angled parking spaces; medians are wider in the areas for
  motor scooter and bicycle parking.
- The access lanes are truly narrow; at 20.5 feet they provide only 12.5 feet for angled parking (most cars are compacts) and 8 feet for the one moving lane.
- The sidewalks, planted with another row of new trees, are 8 feet wide. Older trees have
  been kept, regardless of their location. Parking bays are simply built around them.
- The parking surface is slightly higher than the access-road travel lane, by about an inch.
  The sidewalks are two steps higher than the access lane, creating an informal lineal seating area. New pedestrian lights are along the walks.

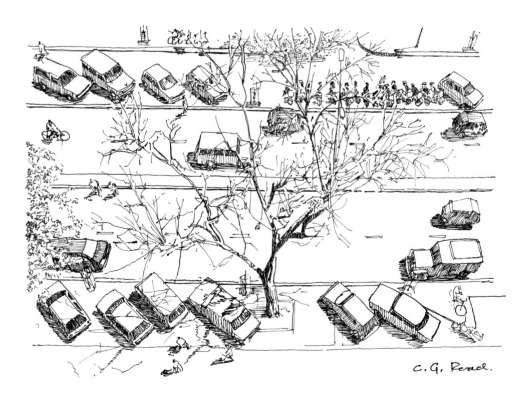

C. G. Road.

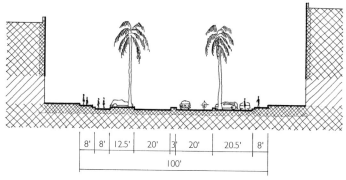

8'	8'	12.5'	20'	3'	20'	20.5'	8'

100'

C.G. Road: section

Approximate scale: 1″ = 50′ or 1:600

Along C.G. Road.

The Pedestrian Realm on C.G. Road.

- The access lanes and sidewalks are paved with bricks, while the central lanes for the faster traffic are asphalt.
- This is a multiway boulevard of small tolerances. The medians could certainly be wider, and the median trees (palms) could be larger than the spindly immature ones planted there; their future growth is chancy.
- Every indication is that extended pedestrian realms have been created. Vehicles, including motor scooters and bicycles, move slowly on the access lanes. The central lanes serve faster and heavier traffic. A camel-drawn cart is not exactly what we would expect to find in the "fast" lanes, but there is something wonderful about seeing it there.
- This is a street of quality, a multifunctional street serving diverse populations and uses.

New Delhi

One might well expect boulevards in a colonial capital, and New Delhi has them. This capital of the British Raj was designed not for walking but for the carriages of the city's administrators. Distances between destinations are usually long, and blocks can be large. Residents tend to go from place to place rather than travel along a route of possible stopping places. Millions may walk the streets, but by and large New Delhi is not an overly comfortable city for walking.

Unlike most multiway boulevards elsewhere, New Delhi's are not usually lined with buildings that face them directly or are open to them. Rather, consistent with development in much of urban India—except for the most westernized and intensely developed business districts—the boulevards are lined with walls, behind which are compounds that serve various uses. The pedestrian realms of the boulevards are not notable for an active street life nor for vehicular movement. Nevertheless, many people walk along them.

Another characteristic of many of these boulevards is that they have no sidewalks, or only very narrow ones at the outer edges of the pedestrian realm. The side access road may directly abut the defining wall of the street, or there may be a planted strip in between.

Differences between these and other boulevards notwithstanding, New Delhi's boulevards are generally pleasant places, particularly because large trees in the medians afford shade, very important under the summer sun of New Delhi.

The three multiway boulevards that follow, none of which are more than 124 feet wide, run in a line from the New Delhi railroad station to Connaught Plaza, to India Gate, and then to Humayan's Tomb.

Along Chelmsford Road

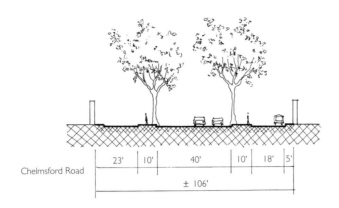

Chelmsford Road

| 23' | 10' | 40' | 10' | 18' | 5' |

± 106'

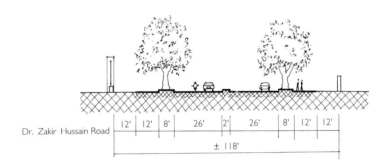

Dr. Zakir Hussain Road

| 12' | 12' | 8' | 26' | 2' | 26' | 8' | 12' | 12' |

± 118'

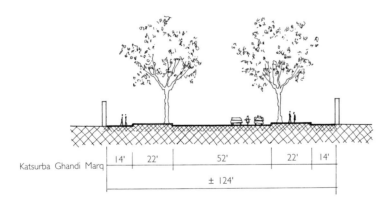

Katsurba Ghandi Marq

| 14' | 22' | 52' | 22' | 14' |

± 124'

Sections of three New Delhi Boulevards

Approximate scale: 1″ = 50′ or 1:600

Chelmsford Road

- This boulevard approximately 0.8 of a kilometer long connects the New Delhi railway station with Connaught Place.
- It is heavily used by buses, auto-rickshaws, bicycles, and pedestrians, although only pedestrians seem to use the side lanes.
- The medians are planted with either *jamun* or *ashupal* trees.
- High walls flank both sides.
- The side medians may have been installed after the trees matured because they are built around the trunks, half of which jut into the central roadway.
- Generally, this is a well-kept street.

Dr. Zakir Hussain Road

- This boulevard of approximately 2 kilometers connects India Gate to Humayun's Tomb.
- At its northern end, adjacent to the National Gallery of Modern Art, the side access lanes do not appear to be used by vehicles.
- Along another stretch of the road there is some vehicular traffic on the side access lanes, along with increased foot and bicycle traffic.
- The trees are the same as on the other boulevards, the jamun and ashupal.
- Vehicles move in both directions along the side access roads, although they are not designed as two-way streets.
- Medians are considerably wider near the southern end of the street—approximately 40 feet—to account for changes in topography.
- Too many signs obscure an otherwise pleasing scene.

Kasturba Gandhi Marg

- Approximately 1.8 kilometers long, it connects Connaught Place with India Gate.
- Medians are wide, at 22 feet, but many bus and taxi pullouts, 10 feet deep, are located in the medians.
- Very few drivers or pedestrians use the side access lanes, although in certain spots there is a concentration of pedestrian activity (usually around public restrooms).
- Nearer Connaught Place the old bungalows have long since been replaced by office buildings and hotels. Nearer India Gate, though, the bungalows, built for officials and bureaucrats and surrounded by large lawns, remain.
- This appears to be a "hanging-out" street for chauffeurs whose employers are otherwise occupied.
- The side access lanes abut the defining walls of the boulevard without benefit of sidewalks.
- Private front yards tend to be overgrown so that passersby cannot see inside.
- Trees on the median are a mixture of jamun and ashupal.

Chelmsford Road

Access Roadway on Dr. Zakir Hussain Road.

Along Access Roadway on Kasturba Gandhi Marg

Vietnam
Ho Chi Minh City

The French left the Vietnamese a significant collection of multiway boulevards. As a group, the Ho Chi Minh City boulevards demonstrate the adaptability of the road type and its ability to sort out many different types of movement, speeds of travel, and varieties of vehicle. One of them, Pasteur Boulevard, is among the narrowest we have encountered. Some extremely tall trees found on these boulevards reach as high as 120 feet.

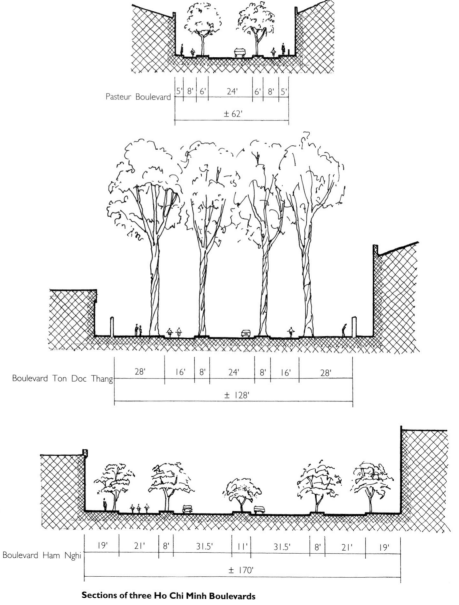

Pasteur Boulevard
| 5' | 8' | 6' | 24' | 6' | 8' | 5' |
± 62'

Boulevard Ton Doc Thang
| 28' | 16' | 8' | 24' | 8' | 16' | 28' |
± 128'

Boulevard Ham Nghi
| 19' | 21' | 8' | 31.5' | 11' | 31.5' | 8' | 21' | 19' |
± 170'

Sections of three Ho Chi Minh Boulevards
Approximate scale: 1″ = 50′ or 1:600

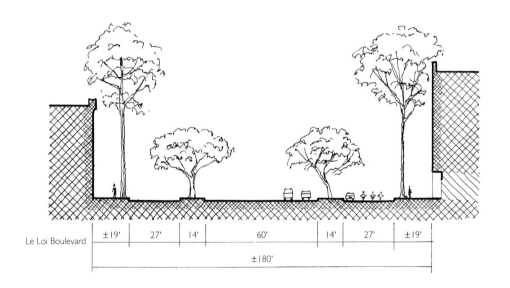

Le Loi Boulevard	±19'	27'	14'	60'	14'	27'	±19'
				±180'			

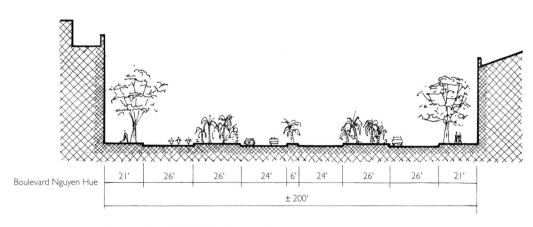

Boulevard Nguyen Hue	21'	26'	26'	24'	6'	24'	26'	26'	21'
					± 200'				

Sections of two Ho Chi Minh Boulevards

Approximate scale: 1″ = 50′ or 1:600

Pasteur Boulevard

Pasteur Boulevard

- This long and very narrow boulevard runs approximately three kilometers (1.8 miles) in a north-south direction through the downtown core and terminates at the Ben Nghe Canal.
- It is the only boulevard in Ho Chi Minh City to retain its French name, apparently because the Vietnamese so highly respect Dr. Pasteur.
- A one-way boulevard, it has one central lane reserved for autos and buses while the other is used only by scooters. Scooters and bicycles also use the side access lanes, although pedestrian uses predominate there.
- Various tree species are planted along the medians, but most are (in Vietnamese) either the Dau Con Roi (*Dipterocarpus alartus rex*) or the Bo Chet (*Leucoena leucace phala*). They are spaced roughly 28 feet apart. Their lower tree trunks, here as elsewhere in Vietnam, are painted white to be visible at night.
- Buildings along the street either abut the right-of-way directly or are set back behind fences or walls.
- At 62 feet wide, Pasteur Boulevard is the narrowest multiway boulevard we encountered.

Bicyclists on the access roadway on Boulevard Ton Duc Thang

Boulevard Ton Duc Thang

- In terms of its width, approximately 128 feet, this is a more "normal" boulevard than Pasteur Boulevard. Nonetheless, Boulevard Ton Duc Thang has but two central lanes and narrow side access lanes. The sidewalks and planted areas along the edges of the boulevard are quite wide, at 28 feet.
- Approximately two kilometers long (1.2 miles), it runs along the Saigon River, then turns north before becoming Dinh Tien Hoang.
- The tall trees that line the sidewalks and medians, the So Khi (in Vietnamese), are spaced about 40 feet apart.
- Free-standing walls define the right-of-way.
- Slow-moving traffic—bicycles, scooters, and peddle vehicles—use the access lanes, leaving the central lanes for automobiles.
- A traffic count taken at midday recorded 190 scooters and 32 autos in a fifteen-minute period.

Boulevard Ham Nghi

- A wide street, at approximately 170 feet, Boulevard Ham Nghi connects the Saigon River with the Ben Thanh Market.
- Though it is apparently less busy than some of the other boulevards, all of its dimensions are generous, particularly the central roadways, which are separated from each other by a tree-planted center median.
- This boulevard is approximately one kilometer (0.6 miles) long.

Le Loi Boulevard

Le Loi Boulevard

- Although only approximately one kilometer long (0.6 miles), this may be the most important stretch of street in the city, in terms of use and as a destination at the intersection with Boulevard Nguyen Hue. It also connects the Ben Thanh Market on the west with the Municipal Theater to the east.
- Its side access lanes are wide, at 27 feet, and heavily used by motor scooters: over 500 were counted in a fifteen-minute period during a weekday morning rush hour and many more on a Sunday night, when a pedestrian and scooter promenade regularly takes place.
- Sidewalks are dense with parked scooters, outdoor stalls, and tables.
- Telephone booths, trash receptacles, and trees are located on the medians.
- Sidewalk trees, the Dau Con Roi, are very tall—up to 120 feet—and spaced 18 to 26 feet apart. The Bo Chet trees on the median closely resemble the honey locust.
- Again, the adaptability of the street type is evident: Le Loi Boulevard carries many types of traffic and separates them from each other.

Boulevard Nguyen Hue

Boulevard Nguyen Hue

- Although a short boulevard, at approximately 0.8 kilometers (less than half a mile long), it is the widest of the Ho Chi Minh City boulevards studied. Its right-of-way is approximately 200 feet wide.
- It is well landscaped with Bo Chet trees on the sidewalks and groupings of low palms on the medians.

AUSTRALIA

Melbourne

Royal Parade, St. Kilda Road, Victoria Parade   It seems to be generally agreed that the "great" multiway boulevards radiating from the center of Melbourne to the north, east, and south are among the most memorable components of the city and provide a physical framework for understanding its structure.[2] Dating from the 1850s, they were part of a large-scale city expansion effort. All of them combine a major traffic-carrying function with grand and highly formalized designs.

- All have tram services that run on tracks in the center of each right-of-way. As such, they differ from most other multiway boulevards studied.
- All are wide, from 195 feet for Royal Parade to 225 feet for Victoria Parade.
- All have four rows of shade trees that run uninterrupted along them—for as long as three miles on St. Kilda Road. Clearly, the trees are the most compelling feature of these roadways.
- Royal Parade accommodates a bicycle lane on its 25-foot-wide access road as well as one moving and one parking lane.
- St. Kilda Road has wide side access lanes (30 feet) that permit two moving lanes as well as parking.
- Victoria Parade, the widest, is really an adaptation of the multiway boulevard form: the central lanes are for trams only, no autos. The medians are quite wide, at 43 feet, as are the side lanes, at 46 feet; the latter provide for three lanes of moving, and presumably fast, traffic plus a parking lane.
- Flemington Road, a fourth multiway boulevard, has access lanes wide enough to accommodate two moving lanes. It also has tram service in its central realm.
- Safety along these boulevards became an issue in the 1970s; it was concluded that through traffic on the access roads was the problem. Solutions considered at the time involved prohibiting certain movements through a variety of physical devices but not, apparently, reducing the traffic lanes on the access roads from two or three to one.[3]
- Today, Melbourne planners seem more concerned with "limiting traffic engineering measures to these streets, thereby maintaining their character."[4]
- Width of the tree-lined medians varies considerably, and none appear designed for major pedestrian use.
- Sidewalk areas are also generous, and all the boulevards but Victoria Parade have continuous planting strips along the curbs holding rows of trees.
- Many buildings along the boulevards are set some distance back from the right-of-way.

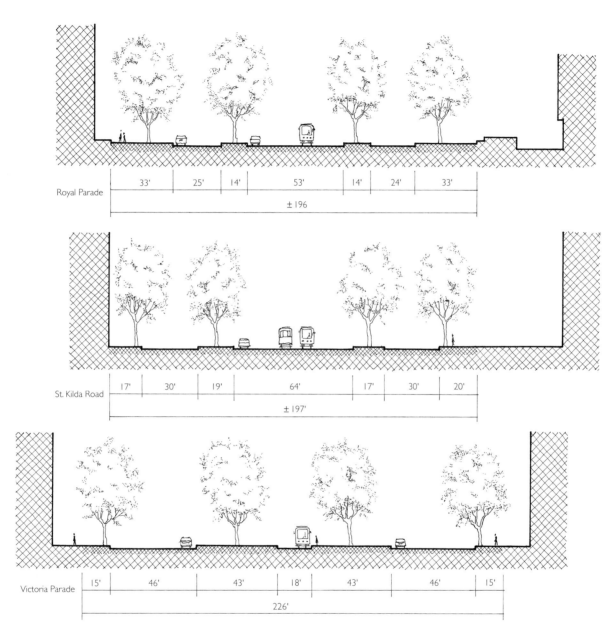

Royal Parade

| 33' | 25' | 14' | 53' | 14' | 24' | 33' |

±196

St. Kilda Road

| 17' | 30' | 19' | 64' | 17' | 30' | 20' |

±197'

Victoria Parade

| 15' | 46' | 43' | 18' | 43' | 46' | 15' |

226'

Melbourne, boulevard sections

Approximate scale: 1″ = 50′ or 1:600

EUROPE

France

L'Isle sur La Sorgue

Route to Fontaine de Vaucluse   A wonderful unexpected boulevard leads into and out of this elegant Provençal village, which is full of canals and tree-lined streets.

- It leaves the village center and heads in the direction of Fontaine de Vaucluse, a deep natural well that is the source of the waterways. It has a boulevard form for several long blocks, then turns into a narrow rural road lined along one side by an impressive row of plane trees that continue, unbroken, for many miles.
- The boulevard segment is delightful to behold, because of its narrow cross-section and the four rows of tall plane trees that line it.
- The center roadway is marked for one through lane in each direction, although it is wide enough to squeeze in four moving lanes when traffic is heavy.
- The narrow side lanes, which run between lines of trees spaced only 15 feet apart, are intended for bicycles only. Nonetheless, motorcyclists use them and a few drivers park cars there.
- Not many buildings front onto the street; instead there are mostly gardens surrounded by low walls and overhung with vegetation.

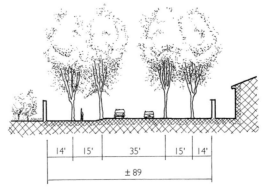

Route to Fontaine de Vaucluse

Approximate scale: 1″ = 50′ or 1:600

Isle Sur la Sorge, Provence
The pedestrian - bicycle realm

Paris

All (or at least most) of the Paris multiway boulevards have something special about them. We visit two of them here, because each has features that expand the normal possibilities of the street type. Boulevard Beaumarchais has a pedestrian realm where sidewalks are at the same level as access-way vehicles; Boulevard Courcelles, besides being a very elegant and beautiful boulevard, is one-sided, runs along a major park, and embraces a variety of parking and intersection arrangements.

Boulevard Beaumarchais

- Reconstructed in the 1980s from a street with broad sidewalks, it is now a multiway boulevard—of sorts!
- Boulevard Beaumarchais is one segment of the original Grands Boulevards—which were built on the raised ramparts of the city walls in the seventeenth century and have long since been lowered and integrated into the general city street system. Today they serve as an inner circumferential ring around the northern part of the city. From the Place de la Bastille, Boulevard Beaumarchais runs in a northwesterly direction for approximately 1,800 feet.
- A relatively narrow boulevard, at 116 feet, it is a major bus route and carries considerable vehicular traffic in its 52-foot central roadway.

Pedestrian Realm on Boulevard Beaumarchais

- The street is lined with six- and seven-story buildings with stores on the ground floor and, mostly, residential apartments above.
- Along each side a sidewalk, one moving lane, one parking lane, and a row of trees are all contained within a space of approximately 32 feet. The narrow six-foot-wide sidewalk is at the same level as everything else, separated from the moving lane by 18-inch high concrete bollards that are closely and regularly spaced. The real pedestrian realm is in fact the original sidewalk, on which vehicles too are allowed to travel and park.
- Because of the narrow sidewalks, pedestrians regularly flow into the access road's vehicular lane, even mothers with small children. The design seems to invite this behavior, with the single level implying a shared pedestrian and vehicle realm. Some pedestrians express discomfort with sharing space with moving vehicles, particularly when the cars are at their backs.
- In places, the considerable presence of vehicles in a relatively narrow space makes the pedestrian realm feel a bit like a linear parking lot.
- The access roads return to the center roadway well before the intersections, allowing the whole 32-foot width to be used as a sidewalk at those locations. There, glass-enclosed extensions from corner cafes encroach on the sidewalk, as do newspaper stands and kiosks.
- Benches and bus stops are located between the trees at the curb separating the median from the central lanes. The curb itself is higher than normal, designed to include an extra step.
- Problems aside, this street is a creative way of achieving multiple uses in a narrow pedestrian realm within the basic multiway boulevard form.

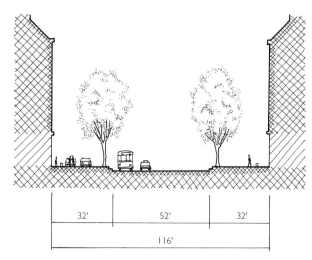

Boulevard Beaumarchais: section
Approximate scale: 1″ = 50′ or 1:600

Boulevard de Courcelles

- Running through a wealthy area in the northern part of Paris, it has a boulevard configuration for two long blocks where it approaches and passes the Parc Monceau. It occupies the site of the medieval customs wall that surrounded the city and was torn down by Haussmann in the mid-nineteenth century.
- The boulevard is lined with six-floor Empire-style buildings, most of them apartment houses. One block has buildings on both sides; the other has buildings along just one side, with the park on the other side. The first block contains shops at ground level. Across from the park residential uses continue to the ground floor, and the buildings there are particularly elegant.
- The park has no access road alongside it but, rather, a widened tree-lined sidewalk that provides a pleasant walking experience.
- The median and parking configurations of the two blocks are different. Adjacent to the park the one access road has diagonal parking between the median trees; the access roads on the other block contain parallel parking.
- The cross street that separates the two boulevard blocks comes in at an angle. This configuration emphasizes the corner buildings, which have been designed with angled facades that face the intersection. One of these buildings contains a flower shop, and its wares flowing out onto the wide sidewalk in front of the store's entrance create a beautiful display.
- Vehicles enter the side roads or exit from them a short distance before or after the intersection. The configuration of each corner varies substantially. One corner has a widened sidewalk bulb; at another, the access road entry extends to the intersection but is differentiated from the center roadway by an elongated, low (one-and-a-half-inch-high) raised paving—similar to that found on the Avenue Montaigne and other boulevards near the Etoile. This variety of access road/intersection solutions, occurring all at one intersection, might seem potentially confusing and therefore dangerous, but it works just fine.
- Although most of the shops along the street are fairly upscale, there is also an automobile repair shop. At this location in particular, double-parked cars and delivery vehicles frequently block the side access road.

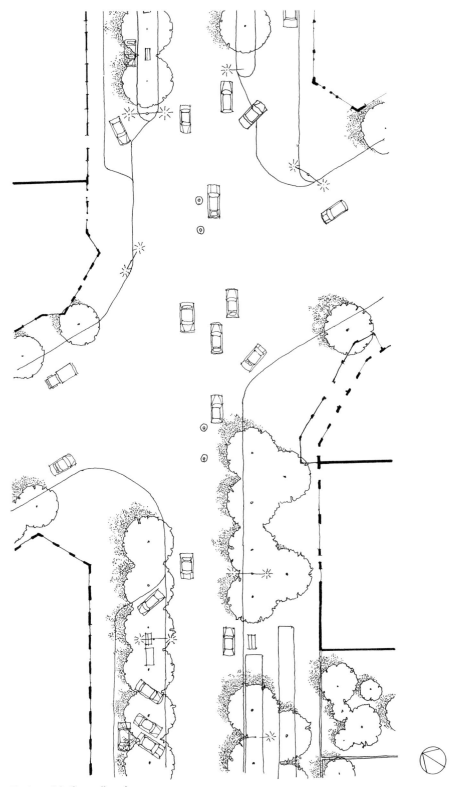

Boulevard de Courcelles: plan

Approximate scale: 1″ = 50′ or 1:600

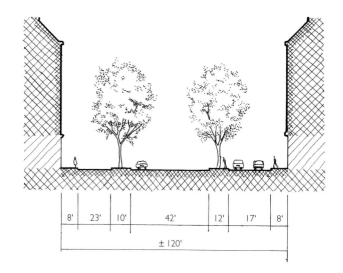

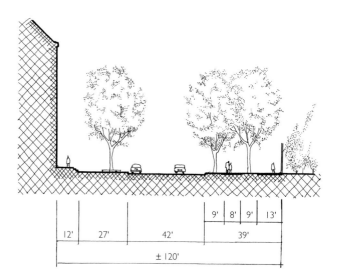

Boulevard de Courcelles: sections

Approximate scale: 1″ = 50′ or 1:600

Pedestrian Realm along Boulevard de Courcelles

Toulouse

Boulevard de Strasbourg and Boulevard d'Arcole   These two boulevards, part of a ring of major streets around the old city center, are of modest and similar widths, at about 120 feet, and have similar cross sections.

They both do exactly what many boulevards were intended to do: move and distribute large volumes of vehicular traffic around the city while serving as local service streets for the buildings that face them.

- A large section of one access lane along Boulevard de Strasbourg is the location of a street market on weekdays.
- Development along that boulevard is more intense in some areas—at major cross streets, for example—than at others. Most buildings are four floors in height. Compared to Boulevard de Strasbourg, Boulevard d'Arcole has fewer stores at street level; instead there are entrances to the dwelling units and offices above.
- These boulevards each have three rows of trees, rather than the usual two or four. In addition to the tall, 50-foot plane trees in the medians, one side access road on each boulevard has another row of trees in planting beds. There is angled parking between these trees on the 21–22-foot-wide access roads. Access roads of the same width on the other side of the boulevards have no trees and two parking lanes on either side of a narrow moving lane.
- Trees along Boulevard de Strasbourg are approximately 27 feet apart, while those on Boulevard d'Arcole are slightly closer together, at 23 to 25 feet.

Weekday Market Along Access Roadway
Boulevard de Strasbourg

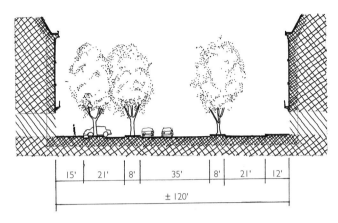

| 15' | 21' | 8' | 35' | 8' | 21' | 12' |

± 120'

Boulevard de Strasbourg: section

Approximate scale: 1″ = 50′ or 1:600

Along Boulevard D'Arcole

Italy

Ferrara

Not far west of the city center toward the old city walls and the train station is a largely residential quarter with at least six multiway boulevards, each different from the last and none of them particularly long or wide. We present four of them below. All except one, Via Cavour, are domestic in scale. They are all notable for their narrow access roads.

Ferrara Boulevards: street and building context

Approximate scale: 1″ = 400′ or 1:4,800

Via Cavour

- Via Cavour is the main city street between the historic city center and the railroad station. Development along its borders is varied. Buildings are of mixed age: "tall" eight-floor, relatively new buildings may be in the same block as two- to four-floor older villas; a small group of stores at the ground level of a post–World War II building may be followed by a 1904 Belle Epoque villa set back from the street, then by a more recent building with more stores and a set-back tall structure without stores. Approaching the city center, Via Cavour becomes a busy, more commercial street with many shops and sidewalk cafes.
- Buses use the central lanes, and there are waiting shelters on the medians. The otherwise regular line of trees spaced at 20 feet is sometimes interrupted at midblock (for kiosks) and at intersections, leaving large, uncomfortable gaps like the one at the Corso Isonzo intersection.
- The trees are lindens—very sweet smelling.
- Cyclists use the access roads.
- All traffic movements are permitted at intersections, but it is a regulated street—equipped with left-turn signal phases and the like. Drivers seem to obey the regulations.
- There are no trees on the sidewalks, though there are some benches. These unshaded areas can be uncomfortable to walk along on a hot summer day.

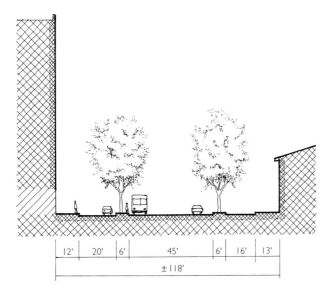

Via Cavour: section

Approximate scale: 1″ = 50′ or 1:600

Corso Vittorio Veneto

• Corso Vittorio Veneto is narrow and not very long (1,200 feet), something of a miniature grand avenue. Stately poplar trees 20 feet apart line the medians and lead to the formal monument at its end. The 30-foot-wide central roadway accommodates two lanes for traffic and two more for parking. One of the access lanes manages to fit two parking lanes and a moving lane into a width of only 18 feet. The narrow sidewalks, a bit more than 6 feet wide, are lined with two- and three-story villas, some set back from the walks. This is a delightful, domestic grand avenue.

central Roadway on Corso Vittorio Veneto

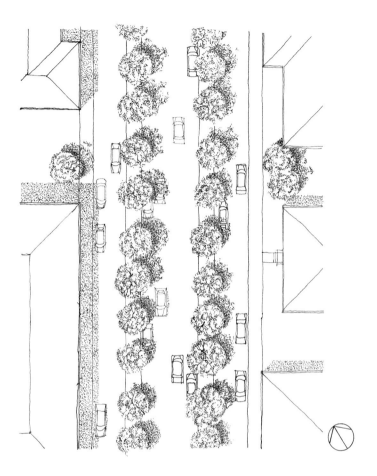

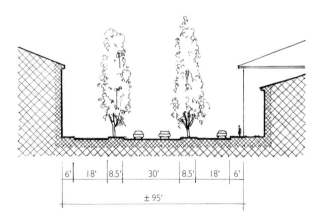

| 6' | 18' | 8.5' | 30' | 8.5' | 18' | 6' |

± 95'

Corso Vittorio Veneto: plan and section

Approximate scale: 1" = 50' or 1:600

Corso Isonzo

- Corso Isonzo is narrower, even, than Corso Vittorio Veneto. Everything about it is small: its 30-foot central roadway, 9-foot medians, and 5-foot sidewalks. The first block, immediately off of Via Cavour, is particularly inviting; its two- and three-story buildings 18 to 30 feet wide house apartments and a variety of ground-floor convenience shops serving the local area.

- There are large old plane trees that can rise 60 feet in height. Spaced 25 feet apart, they form a shade canopy over the street and impart a strong sense of definition.

- Farther along the street, away from Via Cavour, some of the buildings are newer and larger, up to seven floors, and present more varied facades to the street. One of the access roads widens to 20 feet to provide for two parking lanes.

- Overall, Corso Isonzo is a thoroughly delightful street that some local people don't recognize as a multiway boulevard.

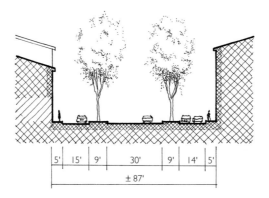

Corso Isonzo: section

Approximate scale: 1″ = 50′ or 1:600

A.J.

Along Corso Isonzo

Via IV Novembre

- Via IV Novembre replaced the old city walls, reminding us of the birth of the earliest Paris boulevards. It is a one-sided boulevard; the missing access road is replaced by a planted, sloping park strip that leads up to the top of the old brick city walls. The wall drops some 10 or 12 feet to a planted park strip away from Via IV Novembre.
- The side access lane is but 11 feet wide and is used mostly as a bicycle lane.
- The branches of trees planted 30 feet apart along the median and curb of the central roadway meet overhead. A third row of trees lines the top of the embankment.

Access Roadway on Via IV Novembre

Via IV Novembre: plan and section

Approximate scale: 1″ = 50′ or 1:600

Palermo, Sicily

Via della Libertà   Design and location make this the primary street of Palermo, the preferred location for political demonstrations as well as for genteel promenades on Sunday afternoon. The boulevard's importance to the city seems to be clearly recognized—witness the late–1990s renovations to paving and installation of new street furniture, streetlights, and bus shelters.

- Constructed in 1848–1850 as the centerpiece of late–nineteenth-century city expansion, it was a generator of new development; its spine continued the east-west axis of the city established earlier by the Spanish.[5]
- Approximately half a mile (700 meters) of Via della Libertà—from Piazza Politeama to the Piazza Croci—is a multiple roadway boulevard, after which it becomes a narrower street.
- A very wide pedestrian realm is created by generous medians that contain trees along the center-realm curbs, stone benches, lighting, dense shrubs, discount book-vending stalls (also along the center roadway), and bus stops.
- Large plane trees (30 feet apart), benches, and vending stalls reinforce the edges of the pedestrian realm. The center roadway is relatively narrow but carries four traffic lanes, two for buses and two (in one direction) for other vehicles.
- Sidewalks are narrow, as are the access streets, even though they have two parking lanes.
- Only one street crosses Via della Libertà in the segment where it is a multiway boulevard. Other cross streets stop at the median and turn onto the access lanes, creating long, uninterrupted medians; these are preferred places to walk, but they inhibit crossing movements from one side to another. Access lanes are locally oriented in scale and quality and almost completely separated from the central roadway.
- Buildings along the boulevard are architecturally mixed. Some are the original nineteenth-century neo-classical structures three to five stories tall and separated from the street by high fences and front yards. Their ground floors and some basements are used for shops and have offices above. Replacement buildings from the 1960s and 1970s, normally eight to ten floors high, are of a much lower architectural quality.

Via della libertà

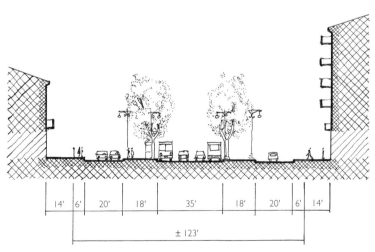

| 14' | 6' | 20' | 18' | 35' | 18' | 20' | 6' | 14' |

± 123'

Via della Libertà: plan and section

Approximate scale: 1″ = 50′ or 1:600

Rome

Rome, the "Eternal City," is chaotic. And so are some of its multiway boulevards, none more so than the three that intersect not far from the Vatican. The intersection almost compels the passerby to stop and look and try to figure out how it works.

The grand avenue to St. Peter's, the Via della Conciliazione, is relatively new, and most people would not think of it as a boulevard. Via Nomentana, by comparison with the others, is almost sedate.

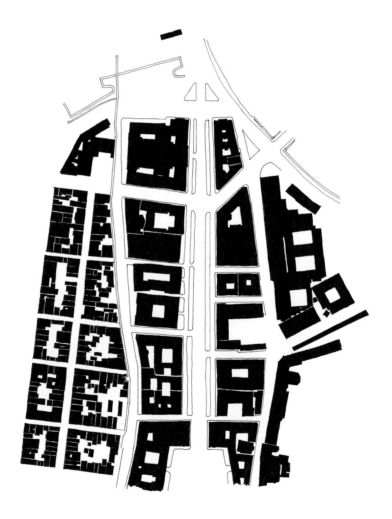

Via Delle Conciliazione: street and building context

Approximate scale: 1″ = 400′ or 1:4,800

Via della Conciliazione

- A famous, or infamous, street dating from 1929—the Fascist period in Italy—this boulevard runs from the Castel San Angelo and the Tiber River on the east to the Piazza San Pietro on the west. It aligns axially with Saint Peter's Cathedral.
- The street is slightly over a quarter of a mile long.
- It is without trees. Instead, on the medians, which vary from 14 to 18 feet in width, stand tall, monumental light standards, 25 to 30 high and approximately 95 feet apart.
- A major design feature of the street is its increasing width as it nears St. Peter's, an increase of approximately 20 feet in the central roadway alone, with increases in the medians and sidewalks as well. The right-of-way widens from approximately 120 feet to about 150 feet near the Piazza.
- The entrance to the Piazza is narrowed, at the very end, by symmetrical buildings on each side that replace the access roadways, leaving walkways that pass under the defining buildings through grand arcades.
- The central roadway has become a major staging area for tour buses.
- There is as much pedestrian traffic along the medians, which have benches, as along the sidewalks. Tourist-related religious goods are sold there informally.

Median on Via della Conciliazione

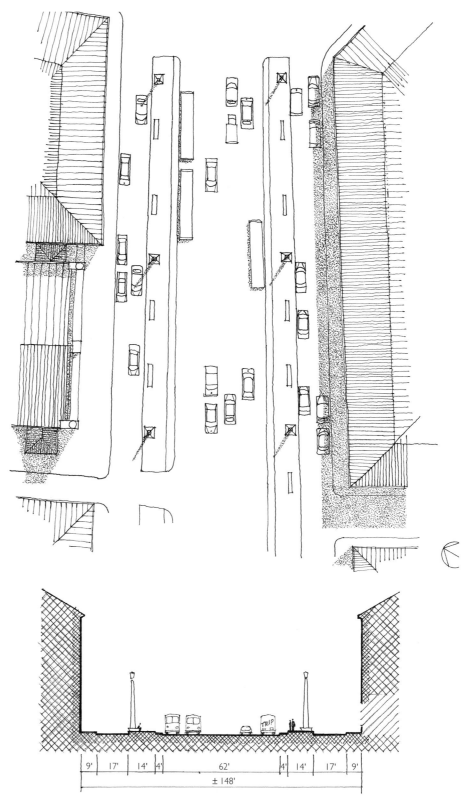

Via della Conciliazione: plan and section

Approximate scale: 1″ = 50′ or 1:600

- The medians are raised two to three steps above the roadways, giving pedestrians a superior position relative to autos but not to the tour buses.
- Buildings along the street are large and generally institutional in character. Stores, where they exist, tend to be restaurants or shops that sell religious artifacts. But even where there are stores there is no sense of light and transparency along the street, due to the formality and large scale of the buildings and the rather opaque nature of the windows.
- The Via della Conciliazione is not a particularly pleasant street to walk along. There is little of interest on the street itself, and it can be very hot in summer. The views toward the river are unresolved, without focus or strong orientation. The view to St. Peter's Cathedral is certainly compelling.

April 1996.   A.B.J.
Via della Conciliazione and St. Peter's

Via Nomentana

- A relatively long street that leads out of central Rome toward the northeast, the Via No-mentana is a multiway boulevard for about a mile.
- It is basically a residential boulevard, but one with a series of good-sized parks—once the grounds of private villas—spaced regularly along its length. Commercial sections are not intense and seem like spill-over extensions of commercial streets that intersect Nomentana, such as Viale Regina Margherita.
- Buildings along the street are from five to seven stories in height.
- Bus-taxi lanes along the medians are separated from the through traffic lanes in the center by a raised curb, but they are often used by other vehicles.
- Traffic in the central lanes at mid-morning is not substantially heavier than in the access lanes, the difference being motorbikes and scooters, which mostly travel in the center lanes.
- Right turns are legal only from the side lanes.
- Noise and air pollution are noticeable along the street.
- Some vehicles park on the median strips.
- People jaywalk quite regularly.
- Trees are London planes. Many have been removed, leaving stumps and giving the boule-vard a "moth-eaten" feeling, in places.
- In places, it is more pleasant to walk along the access lane than the sidewalk.
- Its problems notwithstanding, the street is pleasant as a place to walk during the day because of the light that filters through the tree branches and the feeling of being somewhat removed from the central traffic lanes.

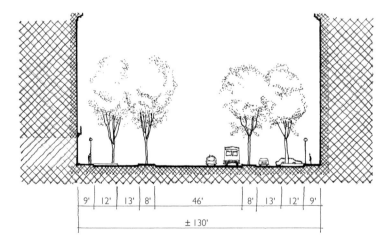

Via Nomentana: section
Approximate scale: 1″ = 50′ or 1:600

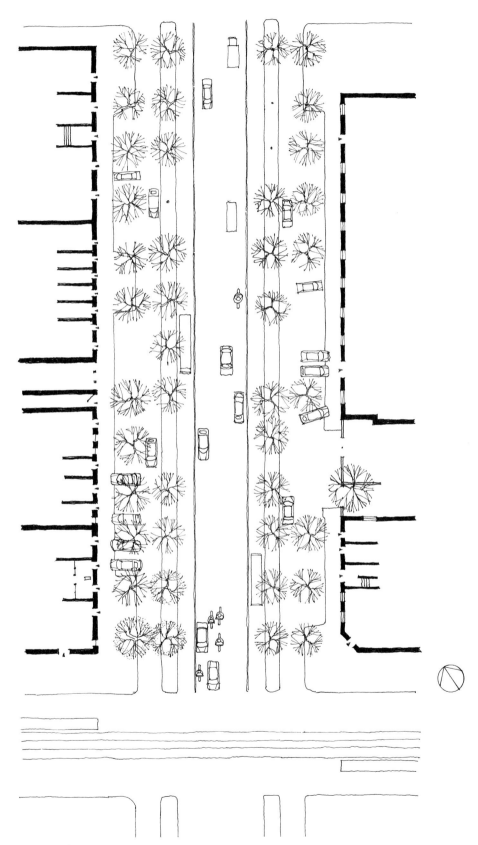

Via Nomentana: plan

Approximate scale: 1″ = 50′ or 1:600

Intersection of Three Boulevards: Viale delle Milizie and Via Ottaviano/Viale Angelico There is an immensely complicated intersection of three multiway boulevards in Rome that accommodates a large numbers of pedestrians, autos, trucks, motorbikes, streetcars, and buses. Essentially, eight separate vehicular traffic flows enter the intersection, each one presenting the driver with up to six choices. Some of the movements, though disallowed or discouraged, take place anyway, and other illegal movements, like U-turns, also occur. This is also a very active pedestrian area. There are access stairs to a subway station at two of the corners. Until 1998 a streetcar line turned at the intersection and ran on Via Ottaviano and Viale delle Milizie.

- Traffic lights slow traffic on access lanes, giving priority to the central lane.
- The design of Viale Angelico, which runs north toward the Foro Italico, is relatively new and includes a special bicycle lane, a rarely seen improvement in Rome.
- In a five-minute period on Viale delle Milizie, in one direction, we counted 59 motorbikes and motor scooters and 138 automobiles. This suggests that about 700 motorbikes and scooters use the street in an hour.
- Most of the trees are large London planes, with many trunks that exceed three feet in diameter. These very tall trees are generally planted about 32 feet apart.
- Lighting fixtures are located on the medians and sidewalks, and lamps hang on wires over the street.
- In spite of the diverse and complicated traffic movements permitted, and the overwhelming amounts of fast vehicular traffic in the central lanes, the side access lanes are nothing more than that: they accommodate parking, deliveries, slow-moving traffic, and pedestrians, who regularly walk in the access roads. Drivers enter and leave the side roads slowly and with caution.

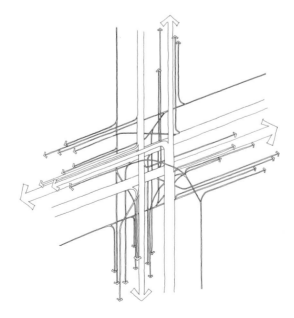

Traffic movements

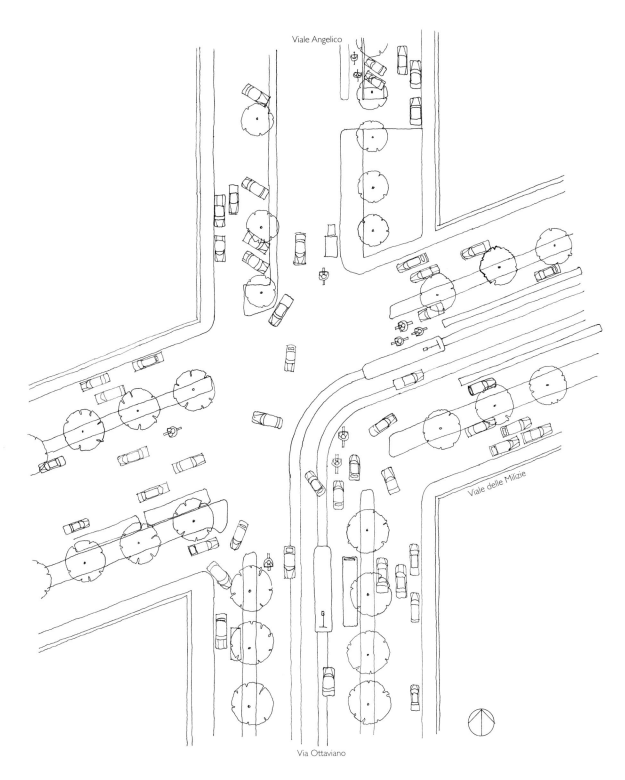

Viale Angelico

Viale delle Milizie

Via Ottaviano

Intersection of Viale delle Milizie and

Via Ottaviano/Viale Angelico

Approximate scale: 1″ = 50′ or 1:600

Portugal
Lisbon

The multiway boulevards of Lisbon embrace examples ranging from the best of this road type to be found anywhere to among the most problematic. The best of them, Avenida da Liberdade, is parklike in nature and is similar in many respects to the Madrid boulevards. The less-appealing ones, though they cater more to vehicles than to pedestrians, nonetheless have the potential to become fine streets.

Avenida da Liberdade

- The most important of the two major axes that structured the nineteenth-century expansion of the city northward from the historic center is approximately three-quarters of a mile long (1.2 kilometers) and runs between the Praca das Restauradores and the Praca Marques Pombal.
- Its relatively narrow central roadway of 48 feet accommodates five lanes of traffic, including dedicated bus and taxi lanes. The side access lanes are narrow and contain two parking lanes and one moving lane each within their 20-foot width.
- The standout features of this boulevard are its wide, parklike medians. Each is divided lineally into three parts: a central landscaped area 18 to 24 feet wide and planted with grass and exotic plants and featuring pools, statues, and access stairs to the subway; and two 27-foot wide walkways beautifully paved in small black and white stones.
- The medians on each block have four rows of trees planted at regular intervals of between 18 and 25 feet. Missing trees seem to be replaced.
- On one block, two cafés offer both inside and outside seating and occupy the paved part of the median near the access lane.
- Some cross streets have been closed, forcing traffic on them to enter the access lanes and turn right. These locations are used as bays for bus stops and added parking.
- Buildings along the Avenida are five to ten stories in height.
- Traffic counts indicate that drivers are two times more likely to use the center roadway than the access lanes. Most travel on access lanes is not through travel. At intersections there are traffic lights on both access roads and the central roadway. Left turns and U-turns can only be made from the access roads, thus requiring two light cycles.
- Pedestrians are more likely to walk along the sidewalks than within the medians, which are more suited to strolling. Pedestrians generally cross the boulevard at intersections. People walking along the medians tend to cross directly to the next median at intersections, rather than moving onto the sidewalk.
- Pedestrians cross the access roads at will, regardless of the traffic lights. Where side streets are blocked off from the central roadway there are pedestrian-activated traffic lights, but even at those locations people often jaywalk across the center.
- The dense canopy of trees that arches over the generous medians is the best feature of this boulevard. Perhaps because of its width, it feels more like a park than a street, and more like a boundary between neighborhoods than a center.

A median on Avenida da Liberdade

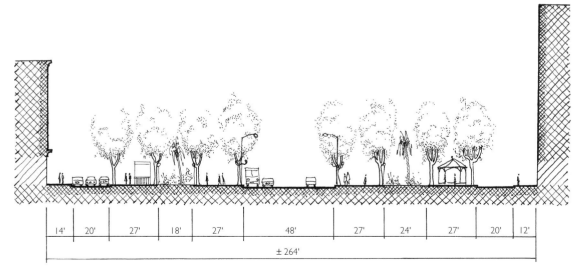

14'	20'	27'	18'	27'	48'	27'	24'	27'	20'	12'

± 264'

Avenida da Liberdade section

Approximate scale: 1″ = 50′ or 1:600

Avenida da Republica

- This avenue of approximately three-quarters of a mile is the third in a series of boulevards leading north from the city center to the Campo Grande park.
- Its wide central roadway of 69 feet is divided into two unequal parts: three lanes one way and four lanes in the other, each with a dedicated bus lane.
- The narrow access lanes have two moving lanes at many locations.
- Medians, though 20 feet wide, are used for diagonal parking, thereby reducing their attractiveness to pedestrians.
- The sidewalks are 15 feet wide and are also used for subway exits, kiosks, and, at some locations, parallel or diagonal parking.
- Trees in the medians tend to be small and are planted at 21- to 33-foot intervals. Because they stop 45 to 60 feet from the intersections, they do not form a consistent canopy to separate the central roadway from the pedestrian side streets.
- Four- and five-floor nineteenth-century buildings are being replaced with apartment and office buildings ten or more stories high.
- Despite being the same length as the Avenida da Liberdade, this boulevard seems much longer and daunting as a single walk.
- The overall impression is that of a central street through a well-to-do neighborhood, but one whose pedestrian realm leaves much to be desired. The farther north you travel, the more chaotic and car-dominated it becomes.

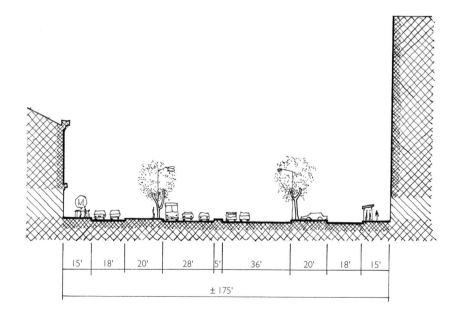

Avenida da Republica: section

Approximate scale: 1″ = 50′ or 1:600

Avenida 24 da Julio

- More of a multipurpose road separated into different realms of traffic than a multiway boulevard, the Avenida 24 da Julio runs for approximately one and a half miles (2.4 kilometers) along the riverfront.
- The central roadway has three lanes of traffic in each direction divided by a sparsely planted median. On the river side, two dedicated public transit lanes are separated from the central roadway by a median; closer to the river, a high security fence separates the narrow sidewalk from railway tracks.
- On the city side of the center roadway, a 33-foot-wide access road provides access to a mixture of warehouses—some of which have been converted into office space and night spots—and newer office buildings.
- Parking on the access road is diagonal but leaves plenty of space for fast movement.
- Tall trees are densely planted along the sidewalks in some blocks.
- As lonely and forlorn a street as this is, particularly on a Sunday, the renovation of warehouses into offices, restaurants, and clubs affords an opportunity to create a very pleasant working street. This could be done primarily by widening and reinforcing the medians and planting trees on them.

Spain
Barcelona

Avinguda de Roma

- This boulevard runs for ten blocks diagonally across the city grid from the main railroad station toward the city center.
- It is an asymmetrical multiway boulevard, with a 42-foot-wide median on one side and a 10-foot-wide median on the other. A railroad track originally ran along the wide median but was abandoned during the 1960s or 1970s when the wide median was reconfigured into a pedestrian promenade.
- In some locations the wider median takes on the character of a small neighborhood park; it is furnished with play equipment and fenced-off dog runs.
- The center roadway is one-way, carrying four lanes of through traffic away from the city center.
- Traffic on the access road adjacent to the wider median flows in the same direction as the central traffic, while on the other side it flows in the opposite direction.
- The boulevard is lined with newer seven-story apartment buildings for most of its length; there are some small ground-floor shops.
- The street has an unusual and attractive arrangement of trees: plane trees along the sidewalks, pines and poplars along the medians, and Magnolia grandifloras on the medians near the intersections.

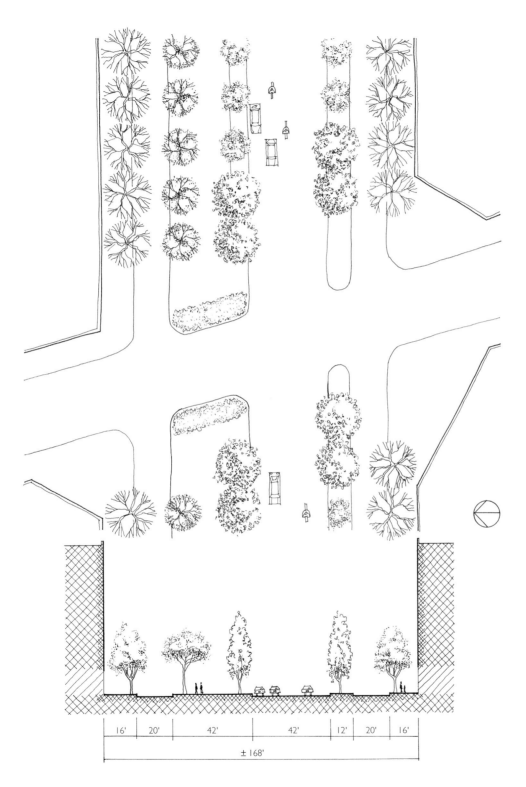

Avinguda de Roma: plan and section

Approximate scale: 1″ = 50′ or 1:600

| 16' | 20' | 42' | 42' | 12' | 20' | 16' |

± 168'

Madrid

Two multiway boulevards in Madrid illustrate the difference between earlier and later boulevards of this type. Both are designed to facilitate movement, but the older street, Paseo de Recoletos, has much more to do with the movement of pedestrians, their daily activities, and urban life. It is a major lineal open space for the city. The newer Avenida de la Ilustración is more for fast vehicular movement, and its integrating possibilities seem not to have been considered.

Avenida de la Ilustración

- This very wide boulevard of approximately 380 feet runs in the northern reaches of the city for about a mile and a half (2.6 kilometers) in an east-west direction. It starts from near the end of the Paseo de la Castellana and heads toward the Rio Manzanares and a major circumferential freeway. It is part of a major ring road designed as a motorway (the M–30)—except for this section, which runs through a highly populated neighborhood.

- Unlike the Paseo de Recoletos in central Madrid, it is more of a boundary between outlying neighborhoods than the spine of a larger urban system. In purely traffic terms, however, it may be rightly called a "spine."

- Intersections are distant from each other—from 1,000 feet to over 1,600 feet—and are designed as roundabouts, a much-used European intersection form. The distances between intersections encourage jaywalking and may be dangerous.

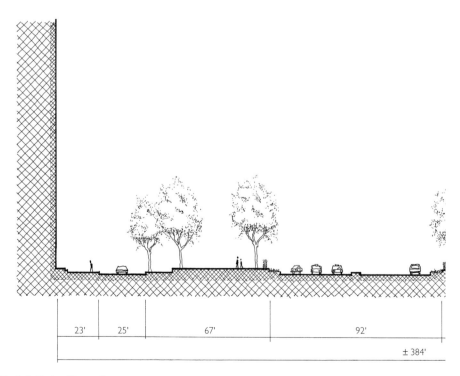

Avenida de la Ilustración: section

Approximate scale: 1″ = 50′ or 1:600

- The south access road is used increasingly for through traffic—perhaps vehicles making shorter trips than those in the center lanes but less local than those using the north side. The narrower north access road has one lane for traffic movement, compared to two lanes on the south side.
- Average vehicular speed is considerably slower on the north access road (30 kilometers per hour) than on the south access road (50 kilometers per hour) or in the central lanes (70 kilometers per hour).
- Given its great width and design, this boulevard might as easily be thought of as three streets rather than one. From one sidewalk or median it is not possible to see what is happening on the other side of the central roadway due to the intensity and speed of traffic in the center, the physical separation of the medians from the center by a continuous line of bushes, and the sheer distance from one side to the other.
- Each of the medians has three rows of trees and there are trees on the sidewalks as well.
- The medians have the appearance of rather simple, linear parkways and are used by almost as many pedestrians as the sidewalks.
- All in all, this is a somewhat formidable street.

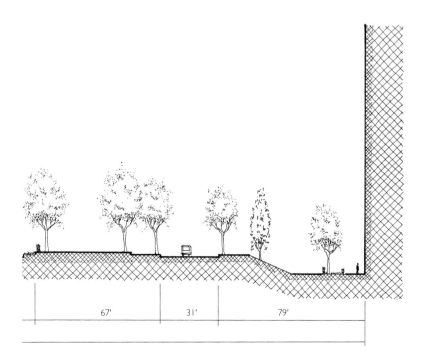

67'   31'   79'

Paseo de Recoletos/Paseo de la Castellana

- The central artery of Madrid, Paseo de la Castellana, extends approximately four miles as a boulevard through the central area of the city before becoming an expressway.
- In central Madrid it is a grand street known locally as the Paseo de Recoletos, and many important buildings, including the Prado Museum, front onto it.
- The boulevard section of the street is not consistent in design. Adjacent to the Prado it has a center median form, but elsewhere it has a multiway form that varies in its details from block to block.
- Some blocks are long and have wide intersections that are difficult to cross because they are configured as roundabouts. This feature means that for a pedestrian each block seems to be its own entity, although visually the street is a whole.
- The roundabouts at major intersections hold impressive fountains. Others are profusely planted.
- One block has asymmetrical medians—one three times as wide as the other. The wider one is lined with cafés that have outdoor seating. When activities such as book fairs take place along the medians, booths line both sides of the center walkway.
- The Paseo de Recoletos is on the route of many bus lines. There is a major regional bus terminal at the outer end of the boulevard, and some segments include special bus lanes at the median edge.
- Trees are a major presence along the street. Some blocks contain five or six continuous rows, others ten or eleven. Most are tall, closely spaced plane trees. Some, such as those lining the bus lanes, are smaller pepper-type trees.
- It is a pleasure to spend time on the medians or to walk along them, in spite of the traffic that flows by on both the center and side roadways.
- A minimum of three lanes run in each direction on the center roadway, plus bus lanes. The access roads generally have two moving lanes and one parking lane, and sometimes an additional lane of diagonal parking carved out of the median. Where this occurs, two lines of trees are planted at every third parking space.
- The height of buildings along the way varies from block to block; in some places they have five to seven stories and in others ten to seventeen stories.

Fountain and Book Fair Along Median at Paseo de Recoletos

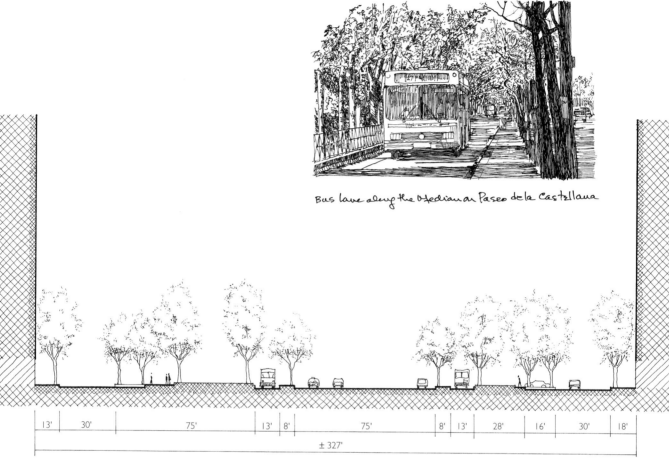

Bus lane along the Median on Paseo de la Castellana

13' | 30' | 75' | 13' | 8' | 75' | 8' | 13' | 28' | 16' | 30' | 18'

± 327'

Paseo de la Castellana: section

Approximate scale: 1″ = 50′ or 1:600

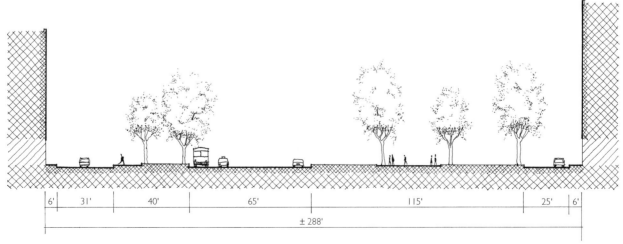

6' | 31' | 40' | 65' | 115' | 25' | 6'

± 288'

Paseo de Recoletos: section

Approximate scale: 1″ = 50′ or 1:600

SOUTH AMERICA

Argentina
Buenos Aires

Avenida 9 de Julio

- At almost 450 feet, this is the widest boulevard we encountered. A whole city block was taken down to build it in 1936–37.
- It is more of an expressway than a boulevard. More than 10,000 cars per hour were counted around noon on a weekday.
- The northerly section of the street carries an incredible eight through lanes in each direction in the center roadway and three through lanes on each access roadway, a total of twenty-two moving lanes. The southerly section carries five through lanes in each direction in the center, a total of sixteen moving lanes. At certain points one of the lanes on the access roads becomes a parking lane and is used by taxis waiting for fares.
- The extremely wide side medians are landscaped simply, with grassy areas bounded on either side by relatively narrow walks. The southern part of the street also has a wide central grass median.
- Huge billboards covering the top three or four floors of many of the buildings lining the street exhibit a scale more appropriate to a freeway than an urban street.
- It is a formidable street to cross as a pedestrian, and there are several underground passages intended to facilitate such crossings. Pedestrians have to move at a very fast pace to make it across the whole street on one light. Groups of people often fail to do so and must wait out a light cycle in a six-foot-wide space in the center while traffic whizzes by on both sides.

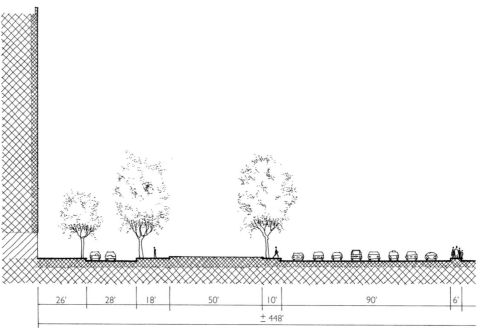

Avenida 9 Julio: section

Approximate scale: 1″ = 50′ or 1:600

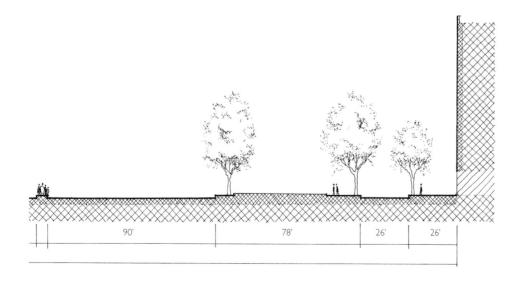

| 90' | 78' | 26' | 26' |

- Curiously enough, it can feel safer to jaywalk than to cross at an intersection. This is because there is a distinct traffic pulse. Signals for the whole length of the street are synchronized to turn red or green all at the same time. Thus traffic bunches up at the intersections waiting at red lights, leaving the length of the block clear. Jaywalking behind the waiting cars gives some sense of safety because traffic from the next intersection is somewhat distant. At intersection crosswalks, on the other hand, with so many lanes of traffic bearing down, pedestrians feel very vulnerable.

- Although there is commercial activity at street level, it seems somewhat tenuous, especially away from major intersections. Along some blocks there are many vacant buildings and properties for sale.

- There are some cafés, and although most offer sidewalk seating, we observed few people making use of them. Inside, people seem to sit far away from the door.

- Not many people walk along the medians or spend time on them. In spite of their width and the grass, the traffic moving all around is overwhelming. Moreover, the air is highly polluted and noise is constant.

- Infrastructure maintenance along the boulevard is not good. Sidewalks are rough, many benches are broken, and signage is generally old and worn. However, sidewalks are swept, and there is general cleanliness.

- Several of the prominent intersections feature fountains on the side medians. The intersection with Avenue Corrientes is also marked by a large obelisk standing in the middle of the center roadway.

- The dimensions of this boulevard exceed the limits of the multiway boulevard street form. It is simply too wide and carries too many lanes of traffic to function well as a city street. Likewise, the tremendous traffic noise keeps it from functioning well as a linear park.

Brazil

Rio de Janeiro

One might reasonably expect to find multiway boulevards curving along Rio de Janeiro's sensuous beaches. The street form could be adapted with ease, functionality, and beauty to waterfront development. Those we found, however, are not along the beach. Rather, one is in the center of a high-rise neighborhood; another borders the neighborhood; and a third is part of the central business district, an attempt at a grand statement that might better have been avoided.

Avenida Oswaldo Cruz

- A short street, it is only a single block long on the south side and three blocks long on the north side. It is situated in the Flamengo neighborhood and serves as a link between two major traffic roadways: the Praia do Flamengo and the Praia de Botafogo.
- A one-sided boulevard, with an access road on one side only.
- All traffic moves in the same direction. There are four lanes in the through roadway, one of which is used for parking and a bus stop.
- The access roadway is three lanes wide, with two of the lanes used for parking. Paradoxically, the moving lanes on the center roadway are narrower than those on the access lane, but the presence of parking lanes on both sides of the latter imply a slower-moving realm, and traffic generally does move slower there. Double parking and trucks stopped to load or unload are common.
- Traffic signals control both the center and the side roadways.
- The street is lined with high-rise apartment buildings from twelve to eighteen stories in height and built in an architectural style that suggests the 1950s.
- Sidewalks and the one median are lined with large and closely spaced trees, giving the street a human scale in spite of the tall buildings. Also, there are profuse plantings of tropical plants in the wide, set-back gardens in front of the apartment towers. The plantings, along with the delicate low ironwork railings that uniformly line both the gardens and the sidewalk planting strips, catch the eye and lend color and gracefulness to the environment. At street level, you feel part of an intimate street realm. On the north side of the street, where there is no access roadway to create a pedestrian realm, planting is intensified, with many small shrubs at the sidewalk edge between the trees, thus increasing the sense of protection and separation from fast-moving traffic.
- The tallest apartment buildings have above-ground parking structures so that signs of residential life—windows and the like—are removed from the street level. But the impact of this separation is mitigated by the copious trailing plants and vines that emerge from planter boxes at each parking level.

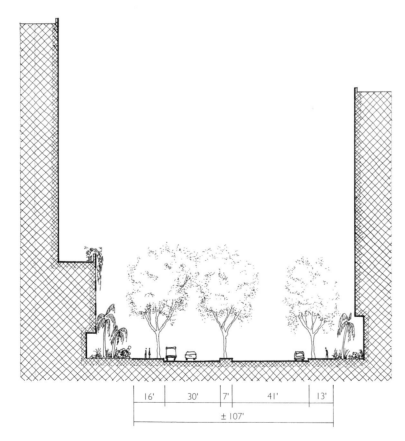

| 16' | 30' | 7' | 41' | 13' |

± 107'

Avenida Oswaldo Cruz: section

Approximate scale: 1" = 50' or 1:600

Praia do Flamengo

- This is a major traffic street running along the edge of the Flamengo neighborhood.
- Like Avenida Oswaldo Cruz, into which it feeds, this is a one-sided boulevard. The through roadway carries two-way traffic, three lanes in each direction. The access roadway has one lane of parking and one moving lane.
- Also like Oswaldo Cruz, the street is lined with high-rise apartment buildings twelve to fourteen stories high—but only on one side. The other side of the street opens onto a very wide linear park that lies between the neighborhood and Flamengo Beach. Although it contains some recreational areas, this park space is not very pedestrian friendly because a pair of expressways bisect it.
- Trees are not much of a presence on this boulevard. The palm trees on the side median are tall and slender and, at 45 feet, much too widely spaced. The other trees in the narrow center median and along the park side of the street are also widely spaced, and not very substantial.
- Unlike Avenida Oswaldo Cruz, the Praia do Flamengo conveys no sense of a pedestrian realm and very little sense of definition. There is not much detail to catch the eye at street level and no comfortable shaded place to walk when it is hot and sunny.

Avenida General Vargas

- Although apparently intended to be a grand boulevard like the Avenida 9 Julio in Buenos Aires, this street has a boulevard form for only three or four blocks, near its intersection with Rio's main street, the Rio Branco.
- There are many lanes of through traffic—four and sometimes five in each direction in the center roadway and four on each of the access roads. Parking is not allowed.
- At only 17-feet wide, the medians are narrow in relation to traffic roadways and do nothing to create an extended pedestrian realm. Small and widely spaced trees are but a minor presence.
- The street is lined with tall office buildings. Those at the intersection of Rio Branco are twenty-two floors high and of uniform design.
- The office buildings have arcades at the ground level that range from 18 to 27 feet deep. They substantially increase pedestrian space beyond the narrow 9-foot-wide sidewalks. At the corner of Rio Branco these arcades are filled with kiosks and hawkers. During the evening rush hour they fill with people hurrying to catch the buses that run on the access roads. For a brief time, the arcades take on the character of bus terminals.

Praia do Flamengo

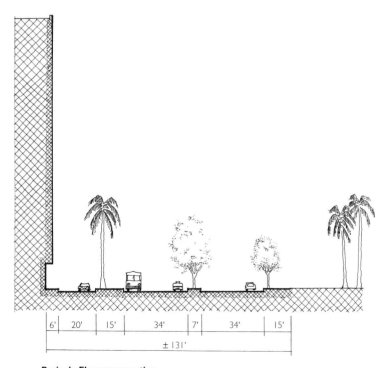

6' | 20' | 15' | 34' | 7' | 34' | 15'

± 131'

Praia do Flamengo: section

Approximate scale: 1″ = 50′ or 1:600

NORTH AMERICA

United States
Berkeley, California

Shattuck Avenue   Long the main street of downtown Berkeley—the location of department stores, offices, the main library, movies, banks, and a variety of other consumer establishments—the street declined as a major destination in the 1970s. New multistory housing units and commercial buildings suggest rejuvenation at the turn of the twenty-first century.

A major commuter rail line to San Francisco and Oakland, with a terminal in the downtown area, once ran along the street. The at-grade line was replaced by buses in the 1960s and by the underground Bay Area Rapid Transit (BART) service in the 1970s. Shattuck Avenue was designed and rebuilt as a multiway boulevard at the time of the BART construction.

- A wide street, at approximately 160 feet, it has broad access roads with angled parking; narrow, treeless medians (about 5 feet wide), and modest, 13-foot, sidewalks scattered with trees.
- Access roads begin and end well in advance of the intersections, leaving a wide "mini-plaza" at every corner.
- Because of the wide access lanes and the treeless medians, no pedestrian realm is created. The vehicular realm takes up approximately 130 feet of the right-of-way: very wide.
- Trees have little impact on the atmosphere of the street: those in the central median are widely spaced and have never grown large enough to be a presence, while those along the sidewalks are unevenly cared for and convey a sense of randomness—though there are newly planted, closely spaced trees in one or two locations along the street.
- Widening the medians and planting them with large, closely spaced trees—and either retaining existing angled parking or providing for two rows of parallel parking—would make a major positive difference in this street.

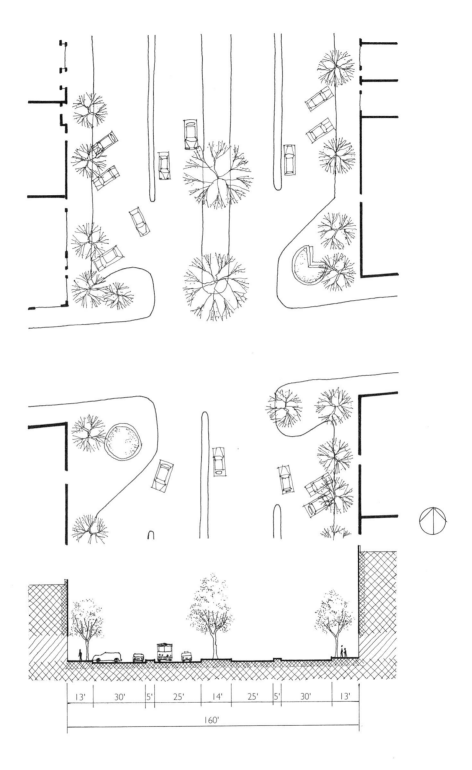

Shattuck Avenue: plan and section

Approximate scale: 1″ = 50′ or 1:600

Boston, Massachusetts

Commonwealth Avenue   An amazingly varied multiway boulevard that winds sensuously through southwestern Boston, Commonwealth Avenue varies in its cross-sectional configuration and width and in the arrangement of its elements.

- The avenue accommodates a main streetcar line, which is always separated from the vehicular lanes but changes locations within the right-of-way: for a long stretch it is on a center median, whereas for another fairly lengthy segment it runs between the central traffic lanes and one of the side access roads. The transition from a central to a side location is accommodated at an intersection.
- Forbidding fences along the streetcar lines may well discourage jaywalking and allow for speedy public transit, but they also create a division along the street that keeps it from being a unified whole, both visually and functionally.
- This is truly a grand boulevard in scale. With an overall width of approximately 200 feet, it is very American in feeling (as opposed to European)—more of a meandering parkway than a formal, axial passageway.
- For much of its length, three- to five-story residential buildings, mostly brick, line the access roads, many with modest setbacks from the sidewalks. Buildings tend to become smaller and less densely spaced farther from the city center and in areas where topography along the right-of-way is steep. Farther along, there are stretches of large single-family houses set well back from the street, but overall these do not characterize Commonwealth Avenue.
- Though a distinct, positive presence in its context and a pleasant street to drive along, there is an overall sense that this boulevard has not been well cared for. It could be much better.
- Movement possibilities are maximized at most intersections: drivers can pretty much do as they please.
- Access lanes vary greatly in width: from 20 feet where there is one moving lane and one parking lane; to 33 feet where there is one moving lane and angled parking, such as at the Harvard Road intersection shopping area; to 57 feet where there are two rows of angled parking flanking a moving lane, as at a major streetcar stop. Access roads with double angled parking are more like parking lots than streets and are not as attractive as those with a single row of angled parking, which are in turn less pleasant than those with one lane of parallel parking.
- At Chestnut Hill and Reservoir, the side access roads disappear, and the road becomes merely a central streetcar line flanked on either side by roadways with two moving and one parking lane.
- At Allston Street, 24-foot-wide access lanes provide for two traffic lanes and a single parking lane.
- Topography has dictated that in some locations the access lanes accommodate two-way traffic. At one point, the outbound access road disappears, and along another stretch it is quite a bit higher than the main road, separated from it by a wooded slope.

Commonwealth Avenue: street and building context

Approximate scale: 1" = 400' or 1:4,800

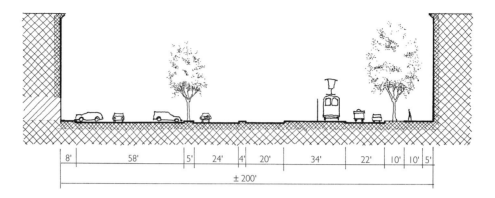

Commonwealth Avenue: section

Approximate scale: 1″ = 50′ or 1:600

Streetcar line on Commonwealth Avenue

- Overall, there is not much sense of a pedestrian realm on Commonwealth Avenue. What there is is limited to the sidewalks and the planting strips alongside them, which are sometimes 20 feet wide and contain large trees.
- Trees are much more of a presence along the sidewalks than along the medians. Their spacing varies greatly; in some segments they are as much as 45 to 60 feet apart. Some are tall enough that, even when spaced at 45-foot intervals, their crowns join overhead.
- The medians vary in width, depending on location and the width of the side access lanes and their parking configurations. The sensuous, winding character of the street, plus the constant wall of buildings and the narrow access roads at the outer locations help make up for the lack of trees in the medians. But at the few locations where there are median trees there is a distinct improvement.
- Some older trees along the medians suggest that there were once many more of them.
- There are lessons to be learned from this boulevard, both positive and negative—perhaps the most positive being the inherent flexibility and adaptability of the multiway boulevard street form.

Commonwealth Avenue

New York, New York

Queens Boulevard: Redesign for a Dangerous Boulevard   Queens Boulevard runs for about six miles in an east-west direction between the East River to the Van Wyck Expressway. It was built in the early 1900s to open up the then mostly rural Queens for suburban expansion. The street is lined for most of its length with five- and six-story apartment buildings, many with ground-floor stores and businesses. There are also concentrated areas of low-scale shopping and some strip development. Queens Boulevard is a very dangerous street.

- Traffic volumes in the mid 1990s were about 38,000 vehicles per day, based on New York City Department of Transportation information. They may, however, be as high as 60,000, according to observations and counts taken later. Queens Boulevard is both a main traffic route and a local focal point.
- A subway line runs under the street for part of its length, and a number of stops are under the street.
- It is also a main bus route. Buses run on the access roads, and bus stops and subway access stairs are located on the sidewalks.
- The center roadway has three lanes in each direction, which are separated by a 16-foot center median.
- Pedestrian activity is low in most areas but high in the concentrated commercial sections.
- Access roadways are wide and carry two moving lanes. There is almost as much traffic flow on them as in the center roadway, and it generally moves just as fast.
- Trees are not a strong presence.
- Aside from the sidewalks abutting the buildings, there is no significant pedestrian realm.

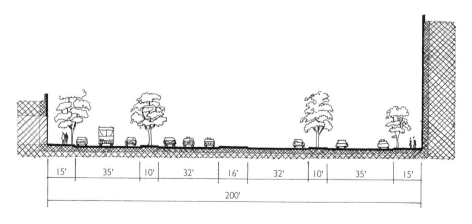

Queens Boulevard: existing section
Approximate scale: 1″ = 50′ or 1:600

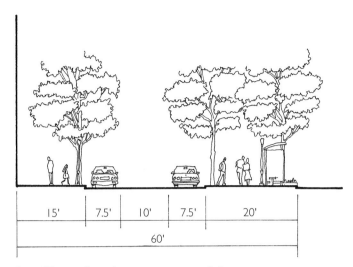

A possible reconfiguration to create an extended pedestrian realm on Queens Boulevard

Potential Redesign   Queens Boulevard would be a much safer and more pleasant street if it were reconfigured to create distinct pedestrian realms.

- There is an opportunity to provide community open space on widened medians. The 200-foot existing right-of-way means that there is plenty of room for generous pedestrian realms.
- Of the many excellent possibilities, the redesign illustrated here would involve the least intervention: the center roadway remains the same, but medians are widened and access roads are narrowed.
- The 20-foot-wide medians, planted with one or two rows of trees at 25-foot intervals, can be paved and provided with pedestrian-scale light fixtures and benches to encourage people to sit and walk along them. Raised planters line their outer edges to discourage midblock jaywalking. A long, high-backed bench would serve the same purpose.
- The access roads, narrowed to 25 feet wide, are reconfigured to provide only one traffic lane and two parallel parking lanes.
- Existing sidewalks remain but are planted with trees like those on the medians.
- The advantages of this design are that traffic on the access roads is slowed, four existing curb lines are kept intact, and a maximum amount of parking is provided. At the same time, generous pedestrian medians are provided.

Sacramento, California

San Francisco Boulevard   This modest, five-block-long residential boulevard located in a lower-middle-income neighborhood of Sacramento dates from 1910, when it was the centerpiece of a subdivision project: an early streetcar suburb.

- Modesty defines the street and the houses that line it: the central realm has but two lanes, one in each direction, and is 20 feet wide; side access roads 16.5 feet wide accommodate one parking lane and a movement lane; block lengths are short, at 200 feet; and the homes are one- and two-story bungalows set back 10 to 15 feet from sidewalks.
- Although narrow for a multiway boulevard, its 100-foot right-of-way is wider than most streets in the city.
- There are four houses on each block along the boulevard, and each one is bisected by an alley that terminates at the access road.
- The Phoenix date palms lining the medians are grand trees. They range from 40 to 50 feet in height and are spaced from 40 feet to 80 feet apart. It appears that some have died or been removed and not replaced. Nonetheless, these trees stand out and bring visual focus to the boulevard.
- Front lawns are well planted with a mixture of deciduous and evergreen trees and a variety of shrubbery.
- San Francisco Boulevard is a somewhat "special" street in its context: its design is part and parcel of a set of qualities that includes higher property values, better building maintenance than on surrounding streets, safety, a sense of community, and the residents' involvement in the comings and goings on their street.[6]
- Though located in an area that is clearly not upscale, San Francisco Boulevard is well known—witness a 1994 article in the *Sacramento Bee* that singles it out as a fine street, "a gem in the rough."

San Francisco Boulevard, Sacramento

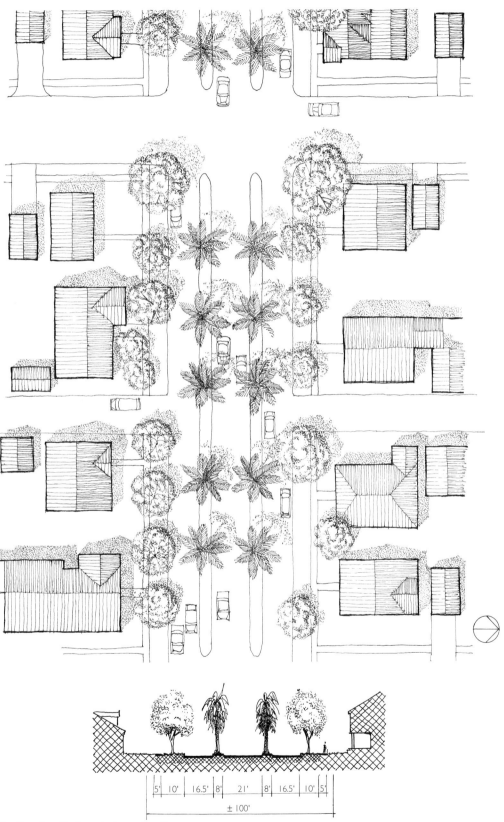

San Francisco Boulevard: plan and section

Approximate scale: 1″ = 50′ or 1:600

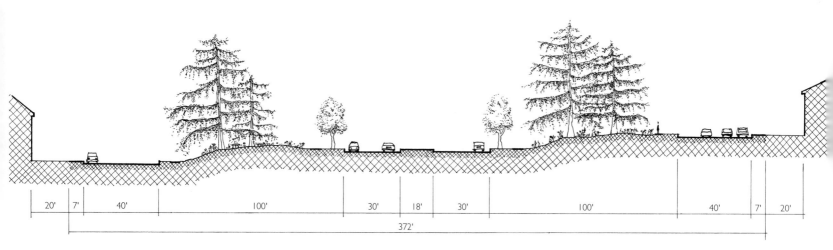

20'   7'   40'   100'   30'   18'   30'   100'   40'   7'   20'

372'

Sunset Boulevard: section

Approximate scale: 1″ = 50′ or 1:600

San Francisco, California

Sunset Boulevard

- A centerpiece of San Francisco's Sunset District, this boulevard runs for two and a quarter miles between Golden Gate Park and the southernmost limits of the city.
- The central roadway acts as a major commuter route through the west side of San Francisco, feeding traffic north and south. Vehicle traffic on the center lanes is fast and constant.
- Its particularly wide medians make it more like three separate streets than a single boulevard. In fact, the "access" roadways have different street names than the center and carry two-way traffic.
- The medians are landscaped in a picturesque manner, with grass and tall trees of a variety of deciduous and evergreen types; the medians function more as scenic viewing parks than as strolling places or neighborhood parks. A narrow sidewalk along the access road side of the medians and narrow dirt paths at the edge of the center lanes do provide linear walkways for pedestrians.
- Single-family bungalow row houses face onto the access roads. They are no different in character, lot size, or orientation than houses in surrounding neighborhoods.
- Topography varies along the length and width of the street. The boulevard climbs and descends several rises, and in some places one side is quite a bit lower than the other, with the grade change absorbed in the medians.
- Sunset Boulevard is a perfect example of how the multiway boulevard form evolved in America in the early twentieth century in the hands of traffic engineers.

Washington, D.C.

K Street

- An important east-west downtown commercial street running three blocks north of the White House, K Street is a multiway boulevard for eleven or twelve blocks along its central section and links Mount Vernon Square with Washington Circle.
- The street is lined with eight- to twelve-story office buildings and some apartment houses. Both large and small businesses occupy the ground floors.
- Appropriately wide sidewalks have a row of small trees at the curb line.
- The 48-foot central roadway squeezes in five lanes at intersections to provide for left turns.
- Side medians are planted sparsely with modest-sized trees 30 to 40 feet apart. These medians do not attract walkers; nor does it seem that they were meant to do so. Drivers moving into and out of the access roads are supposed to do so only at large midblock breaks (or "sleeves") in the median. Typical blocks contain two such breaks of 30 to 50 feet.
- No right turns are allowed from the center roadway, and vehicles on the access roads are not supposed to enter the center at intersections.
- By far the majority of traffic travels in the center roadway, typically over 70 percent. Much of the traffic on the access roads, as much as 60 percent, is getting ready to make a right-hand turn at an intersection.

Median "Sleeve" on K Street.

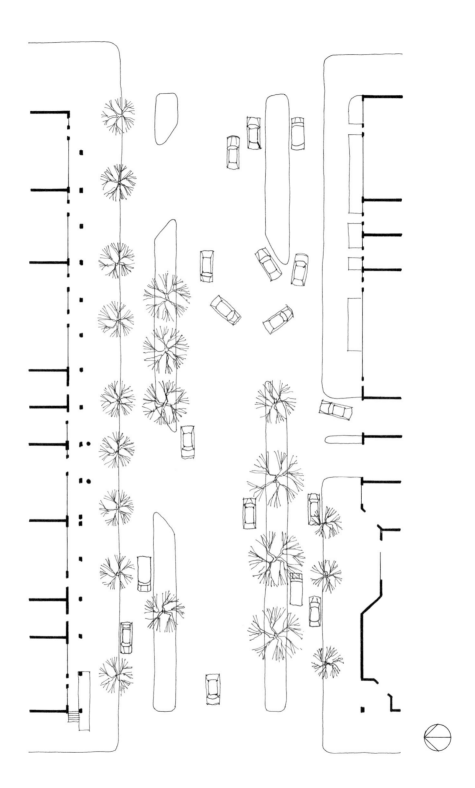

K Street: Plan

Approximate scale: 1″ = 50′ or 1:600

- Median breaks, though angled in one direction, often attract drivers making the opposite, presumably illegal, movement. These breaks, or sleeves, are also used to make illegal U-turns across the central roadway.
- Pedestrian volumes along the sidewalks and crossing the boulevard are high: 2,500 walked along the sidewalks and 1,940 crossed K Street in one hour on a very cold January Monday.
- Pedestrians regularly cross the access road to the median against the light, then wait until the light turns to cross the center roadway.
- This is a boulevard that could be much better than it is. It would be greatly improved by placing much more emphasis on the pedestrian realm—planting larger and closer trees on the medians, adding more facilities to attract pedestrians to the medians, and eliminating the sleeves. The answer lies in placing more emphasis on the wholeness of the street and somewhat less on its role as a carrier of vehicular traffic.

K Street @ 16th Street
From a photograph in AASHTO, 1957

Part Five BUILDING BOULEVARDS

Building Ocean Parkway, 1902
Drawn from a photograph in New York City Photo Archive.

Via Cavour

We have seen many existing multiway boulevards and observed the way they work. We think there is hope for both refurbishing old boulevards and building new ones.

To this end, design guidelines useful to the various people who may be involved in proposing, designing, planning, or approving boulevards have been prepared. The guidelines derive from our observations of their safety and usefulness and are nuanced by many discussions with professionals about boulevard design. These discussions have taken place both in informal conversations with close colleagues and in formal settings.

Preliminary to preparing the guidelines, it was decided to test professionals' reactions to emerging ideas through a series of case studies. A handful of streets in cities in the San Francisco Bay Area that have the potential to work as multiway boulevards were selected and boulevard redesigns were prepared for them. The streets represent a variety of contexts—a large-city major arterial street, a small-city commercial strip, a suburban commercial arterial strip, and a residential arterial street—and dimensions—ranging from 125 to 300 feet wide. Redesigns for two existing but poorly designed boulevards in New York City—the Grand Concourse and Queens Boulevard—were undertaken as well. (These reconfigurations are presented in Part One, Chapter 4 and Part Four.) The redesigns were then presented to transportation professionals in the cities where the streets are located. Reactions were mixed—some enthusiastic, some skeptical. We came to understand some of the common concerns professionals express when confronted with the idea of a multiway boulevard in their community, and we made sure to address these concerns in the guidelines. It also became clear that it is important to stress the wholeness of boulevards, because professionals and academics alike tend to focus on individual elements to the detriment of the whole.

The documentation and study of existing boulevards can provide analytical understanding of them, but applying that knowledge to other streets and generalizing it into general concepts is a different matter. It is of necessity a trial-and-error method in which a design is created, checked according to knowledge and experience, then improved and fine-tuned until it has the same "feel" as the successful boulevards studied. It is a procedure based on the adaptation of good real world models to new situations. By reflecting on the design process, via case studies, it was possible to identify issues and ways to address them in the preparation of design guidelines.

The guidelines that follow were made stronger through the case study process. The process also helped pinpoint the issues people desiring to build boulevards are likely to encounter. A discussion of these issues, and some further reflections on building boulevards, conclude this section.

Chapter One

DESIGN AND POLICY GUIDELINES

As we have come to know multiway boulevards, we have come to see them as part of an alternative paradigm for the design of city transportation systems, one that maintains access and multifunctionality at all street scales.

Much of the success of multiway boulevards hinges on two words: "appropriate design." Do them well and multiway boulevards can be great streets. Do them poorly and, like other ill-designed streets, they will cause problems. This chapter is concerned with doing them right.

The first purpose of these guidelines, therefore, is to create design standards and norms for multiway boulevards that recognize them as balanced multipurpose streets. The unique feature of the boulevard is its ability to accommodate many uses in a balanced way, not allowing any one use or mode of travel to dominate.

A second purpose is to establish a view of the boulevard as a complex whole that provides for diverse movement patterns, uses, activities, and social interactions. Social interaction and the existence of city streets as a social milieu are both the medium and the result of everyday activities.

Besides being a system in themselves, boulevards are also important parts of a larger system of city streets and spaces. Their location and design should take this into account: they can serve to actively enhance the organization and clarity of the street system in which they are embedded.

The guidelines have a broad aim. They are for use by urban designers, architects, city planners, landscape designers, traffic engineers, city officials in charge of street design and improvement, developers, citizen groups, and the general public. They are intended to serve as a tool for people looking at and analyzing the problems of existing streets or proposing new ones; and they can direct attention to the changes needed to improve the arterial streets of our cities.

ORGANIZATION OF THE GUIDELINES

Boulevards are integrated wholes. One must beware of reducing them to a series of issues for which specific guideline dimensions and solutions are given, losing the vision of a whole street and the ways in which its different aspects interact. We present here, therefore, a series of qualities that are crucial to the construction of a good boulevard. But as important as each of them is, the connections and the relationships *among* those qualities are even more important. The solution to any particular problem, the achievement of any one quality in the design of a boulevard, has to amplify and reinforce earlier decisions and, in turn, be respected and strengthened by subsequent decisions.

To make the design task easier the guidelines are organized into sixteen sections. The first two sections deal with the location of boulevards within a city, their roles, and the nature of the surrounding development that makes them a sensible option. Sections 3 to 6 deal with questions of the overall design of boulevards, their major parts, and the contribution that each part makes. Sections 7 to 14 deal with particular and crucial design aspects of the various elements. The final two sections discuss optional enhancements for boulevards that can also help deal with particular problems.

HOW TO USE THE GUIDELINES

The use of the guidelines depends on the context of the desired intervention. They can be used to design new boulevards in a new town or new development, to renovate an existing boulevard that was faultily designed or has deteriorated, or to transform an existing wide street into a boulevard. The guidelines could also be used to make small incremental improvements to existing streets.

The guidelines set forth in the first eight numbered sections, taken together, encompass the basics of boulevard design. They create the sense of the boulevard as an integrated whole and thus should be read, no matter what particular design issue is being considered. Readers can then turn their attention to a specific problem without losing the sense of the whole street.

1. The Location, Context, and Uses of Boulevards

Multiway boulevards have a paradoxical nature, which is perhaps one reason why they are not always well regarded. They are at once normal and extraordinary. The uses they accommodate, the buildings that line them, and the traffic that travels on them are the stuff of normal everyday life. And yet the combination of these elements, and the sheer space and amenities they provide, make them spectacular, unique, and memorable—when they work well.

Eastern Parkway in Winter.

In the United States opportunities for boulevards exist in at least seven distinct contexts:

1. *Existing boulevards dating from the late nineteenth century and early twentieth century.* Existing boulevards may not be functioning well due to neglect or to misguided reengineering intended to make them carry more through traffic or to make them less complex. Often trees have been removed, carelessly. Some of these boulevards were not well designed in the first place.

2. *Existing inner-city major streets.* Such streets are usually located immediately outside the original urban core and connect it with outlying residential areas. Historically these streets may have been the transportation spines of the first wave of suburbanization that extended from the 1920s until immediately after World War II. They often form part of the major physical structure of the city and may have had their roadways widened at some point at the expense of sidewalks—to facilitate traffic flow. Current traffic volumes may be high, or may have slacked off from earlier times.

3. *Existing "strip development" streets.* Generally these are country roads that, as suburbanization progressed around them, were gradually turned into auto-based commercial streets in the late 1940s and early 1950s. These streets are characterized by low-density commercial uses, often set behind parking lots. Shops are generally too far apart to allow for pedestrian movement between them. Often these streets are used and occupied by people with relatively lesser means than those they originally catered to, people who have a greater need for public transit and pedestrian access. Transformation of the housing patterns along these streets or in their vicinity—from single-family owner-occupied to multifamily, rental, condominium, or elderly housing, all of which tend to raise residential density—is also common.

4. *Existing expressways and freeways.* These limited-access roadways often create strong dividing lines in cities. If a city desires to reduce or eliminate such divisions, redesign of the right-of-way into a boulevard is an option.

5. *Existing suburban residential arterials.* Some of the early suburbs were built with arterial expressways that had a cross section similar to that of boulevards but featured wide lanes, two-way frontage roads, and sparsely planted medians. Falling land values along some of these streets may have created difficulties. Their wide two-way access streets fail to create a comfortable pedestrian environment, and the medians rarely act as true buffers between abutting properties and the grind and noise of fast traffic on the center roadway. Redesign may improve land values and, at the same time, turn the excess space along these streets into a usable neighborhood amenity.

6. *Existing suburban commercial arterials.* These streets were designed according to the standards of modern traffic engineering. Some are changing in ways that make certain boulevard features relevant and promising. There may, for example, be an increase in pedestrian and bicycle traffic, a result of the extension of mass transit systems into suburban areas. The changing economics of housing may also be making multiunit development more probable along such streets or in their vicinity. The suburbanization of work may be creating a demand for nearby services such as small cafés and lunch spots

that require a street-based exposure to be economically viable. A boulevard street could address these multiple challenges.

7. *Major traffic streets in new urban or suburban developments.* It is likely that some streets in new developments will need to carry more traffic than others. Boulevards offer better solutions to such needs than standard arterials or expressways.

It is significant that boulevards exist, and have a potential to exist, in such very different contexts. The fact attests to the versatility of this street form, its ability to change and adapt as the area around it changes.

Guidelines for Choosing the Location of a Boulevard

- Boulevards are appropriate where there is a need to carry both through traffic and local traffic, where there is good reason for the through traffic to move faster than the local traffic, and/or where there is real or potential conflict between the two traffic types.

- They are appropriate for streets that, by virtue of their size and/or location, can become significant elements in the city. They have a potential to become special places.

- Boulevards are appropriate where there is either a significant volume of pedestrians who need to cross the street or a potential desire to do so. Commercial streets, streets with high residential density, streets that incorporate public transit, or streets with a significant presence of public institutions are examples.

2. Buildings that Face the Street

Boulevards do not make sense where buildings do not face the street. In fact, the major differences between boulevards and ordinary arterial streets are that on boulevards access to the abutting properties is not limited and there is no stipulated distance between intersections. On arterial streets, on the other hand, accepted standards recommend that distances be-

Boulevard de Courcelles, Paris

tween intersections be as great as possible and discourage direct access to abutting property, suggesting instead that access be provided from side streets. These standards result in large stretches of development that turn their backs on the main roadway.

Building frontage on streets, besides contributing to pedestrian accessibility and safety, renders the structure of the city more visible for people driving through it. On predominantly residential boulevards it makes smaller areas of commercial development feasible, because visibility makes their connection to the urban fabric immediately evident and stores need not conglomerate in large malls to attract customers.

Today, noise-level regulations at times mandate sound walls along streets with heavy traffic. On boulevards, medians and access lanes distance the abutting buildings from the noise and air pollution generated in the center through lanes; moreover, the generally improved pedestrian environment can effectively reduce the psychological impact of traffic. Uses that are less adversely impacted by traffic and that profit from the added visibility—such as multifamily apartment houses or office buildings with shops on the ground floor—are particularly appropriate along boulevards, although single-family housing can work as well.

Entrances on the street

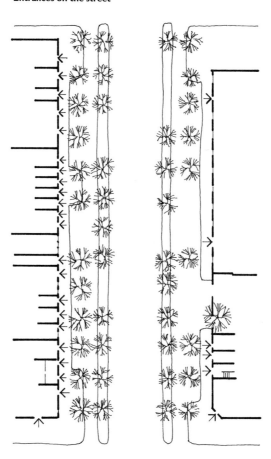

Guidelines for Buildings that Face the Street

- Wherever possible, buildings should face streets and have direct pedestrian access from sidewalks.[1] A boulevard configuration can help abate the negative impacts of through traffic on buildings and neighborhoods that face a busy traffic artery. On existing arterials where buildings face away from the street, permitting the construction of new buildings to face the street may generate opportunities for conversion of parking lots into more useful development.

- When a boulevard borders a public park or a major institution like a museum or civic center and parking is not desired, it can be one-sided, with an access street only on the side with ordinary buildings. A widened pedestrian promenade might front on the park or public institution, reinforcing its importance.[2]

- If only one side of the street has street-facing buildings and the other has a commercial development surrounded by parking lots, a one-sided boulevard with a pedestrian promenade along the parking lot frontage can be constructed to mitigate the impact of the open parking lot. In time, the latter could be replaced by buildings facing the street and an access roadway.

3. Boulevard Realms and Overall Size

Multiway boulevards are made up of two realms: a through-going realm and a pedestrian realm. The central roadway is devoted to relatively fast through-going traffic and may include a median separating the opposing traffic streams. On the outer sides of this roadway, and separating it from the abutting buildings, are pedestrian realms, which include a continuous tree-lined median, a narrow access roadway, and the sidewalk. People and vehicles in these realms move slowly, at a pedestrian pace. These parts of the boulevard are mainly

Ocean Parkway, Saturday Morning

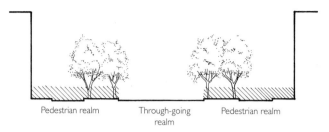

Boulevard realms

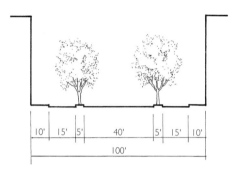

Hypothetical minimum width boulevard

intended to provide access to the buildings along the street and to accommodate slow, local traffic.

The tree-planted median can be of varying widths. Its function is to form a boundary for the pedestrian realm, protecting it from the central roadway's fast-moving traffic. It is the interface between the local pedestrian realm and the through-going center realm.

Generally on a good boulevard the distribution of the right-of-way between the pedestrian realms and the through-going realm is at least equal: at least half, and probably up to two-thirds of the width is devoted to medians, access roads, and sidewalks.[3] (Table 5.1 illustrates the overall widths and realm widths of several existing boulevards and some hypothetical redesigns.)

One hundred feet would seem the absolute minimum right-of-way required for a boulevard carrying substantial through traffic.[4] With this width, a hypothetical configuration would include four central lanes each 10.5 feet wide; access ways 16 feet wide, allowing for one passing and one parking lane; two medians 5 feet wide; and sidewalks 8 feet wide. This configuration is very tight indeed. A right-of-way of 125 to 140 feet would be much easier to work with and can be found in many cities. Of course, boulevards can be built narrower than 100 feet if the central roadway carries fewer than four lanes, an unusual but not at all unknown arrangement.

Table 5.1

Width of Boulevard Realms

Street	Overall width (feet)	Pedestrian realm (feet)	Through-going central realm (feet)	Pedestrian/ center realm (ratio)	Pedestrian realm/ total/ overall width (ratio)
Avenue. de la Grand Armée, Paris	230	70 + 70	89	0.70	0.61
Avenue Montaigne, Paris	126	42 + 42	42	1.00	0.67
Passeig de Gràcia, Barcelona	200	70 + 70	60	1.17	0.70
The Diagonal, Barcelona	165	57.5 + 57.5	50	1.15	0.70
Ocean Parkway, Brooklyn,	210	70 + 70	70	1.00	0.67
K Street, Washington, D.C.	150	51 + 51	48	1.06	0.68
The Esplanade, Chico, Calif.	165	40 + 63	64	0.62 and 0.98	0.62
Geary Boulevard, San Francisco, redesign	125	33 + 33	60	0.55	0.53
West Capitol Avenue, Sacramento, redesign	134	42 + 42	50	0.84	0.63
Grand Concourse, The Bronx,	172	20 + 20	135	0.15	0.23
redesign	172	61 + 61	50	1.22	0.71

Is there a maximum width for boulevards? This is a harder, and perhaps also less critical question, because there are many economic pressures that work to limit rights-of-way. Experience suggests that boulevards can function well up to an overall width of about 230 feet (Ocean and Eastern Parkways in Brooklyn are 210 feet wide; Avenue de la Grand Armée in Paris is 230 feet wide). There are some concerns that may make it difficult for wider boulevards to be successful. A good boulevard shouldn't have access roadways much wider than 25 feet, which can handsomely accommodate one moving and two parking lanes. Wider access roads create the possibility of two lanes of moving traffic or increased speeds, which would erode the slower character of the pedestrian realm. Other possibilities for widening the street are in the central roadway, the sidewalks, or the medians. In order to maintain balance between the realms, widening would have to occur in both, leading to potential problems. Very wide sidewalks need to have significant pedestrian traffic to enliven the street and make it pleasant for walking. Few locations attract that many pedestrians—the Passeig de Gracia in Barcelona comes to mind as an exception. If medians are very wide, then the perception of the street as one entity breaks down and it becomes three different streets.

Very wide center realms and many fast-moving traffic lanes make pedestrian crossings difficult and hazardous. On commercial streets, opposite sides of the street then become independent of each other in their support of shops and businesses. Avenida 9 de Julio in Buenos Aires is such a street. Not many overly wide streets are well enough located or have enough prestige and staying power to handle this problem without negatively affecting businesses.

Guidelines for Boulevards' Overall Size and Realms

The following are the key points concerning overall size and the relative dimensions of each realm:

- A right-of-way of 100 feet is the feasible minimum for a boulevard design, assuming four lanes of travel in the central roadway.
- Right-of-way dimensions of between 125 and 230 feet allow for more flexibility in the design of a boulevard, more generous pedestrian realms, and more capacity in the central roadway. This configuration permits more flexibility in meeting the requirements of many travel modes.
- The establishment of a strong pedestrian realm is of primary importance to the creation of a well-functioning, safe boulevard. A balance between the central and side realms is critical. On the best boulevards, the pedestrian realm is never less than 50 percent of the total width of the right-of-way, and often approaches 70 percent.

4. The Through-going Central Realm

The boulevard's function as a carrier of relatively rapid and nonlocal traffic is just as important as its provision of local and pedestrian access. Multiway boulevards form connections over the city as a whole and allow for easier and calmer through-travel than on city streets that give direct access to abutting property—because the center lanes of multiway boulevards are less subject to interference from parking and from service vehicles.

A minimum of two lanes is needed to serve substantial amounts of traffic in one direction. Three lanes in each direction allow for more flexibility in traffic arrangements and for

Central Realm on Ocean Parkway

Paris: standard bollard for
traffic diversion and a
pedestrian haven

the possibility of devoting an entire lane to public transport vehicles. If there are more than six lanes in the central roadway, a boulevard may become too wide and hinder pedestrian crossings.

The arrangement of traffic in the center roadway can vary: traffic may run symmetrically in two directions; it may move in one direction only, perhaps with one lane for public transit in the other direction; or it may have some other asymmetric arrangement.

Parking on the center-realm side of the medians should be discouraged—although it occurs on some boulevards, particularly in Paris. It reduces the benefits gained from the access road, namely facilitating uninterrupted traffic flow. Parking in the center can also overwhelm the median as a part of the pedestrian realm, surrounding it with cars and making it impossible to dedicate the lane next to the median to public transit.

Guidelines for Design of the Center Realm

- The overall width of the center realm should be determined by balancing considerations of available right-of-way, traffic capacity desired, and need for safe street-crossing by pedestrians.
- A width of 50 feet can accommodate two lanes in each direction and an alternating left-turn lane, albeit somewhat tightly. A width of 70 feet accommodates three lanes in each direction and a left-turn lane.
- Public transit is best accommodated in the center roadway, to facilitate speed and accommodate large vehicle size. The curb lane can be somewhat wider than the other lanes to accommodate transit vehicles (see section 9).
- It is advisable to provide a refuge for pedestrians in the center of the boulevard; even a simple bollard—as is often used in Paris streets—is sufficient. A refuge becomes especially necessary if there are more than three lanes in each direction.

Corso Isonzo-Ferrara

ABJ

5. The Pedestrian Realm

Establishment of a pedestrian realm extending from the building frontage to the edge of the median along the central roadway is key to a successful and safe boulevard. The pedestrian realm includes the access roadway, which should be designed so that movement will be slow and drivers will respect the presence of pedestrians.

An extended pedestrian realm is absolutely necessary to creating a balance between the use of the boulevard as a major through-going road and its local residential or commercial purposes. It provides space for parking, slow vehicles, and pedestrian movement; it makes street crossings shorter and easier; it provides the city and local inhabitants with an open-space amenity; and it buffers abutting properties from the pollution, noise, and psychological impact of heavy traffic.

A half-hearted attempt to create a pedestrian realm may be less safe for pedestrians than a conventional street design. On boulevards where the pedestrian realm is violated by allowing fast and through movement of cars on the access way, the rate of pedestrian accidents is likely to be higher than on other normally configured streets. On boulevards where a slow-moving realm is created but physical definition is lacking—such as when there is no strong row of trees on the median—the side realms are less effective as pedestrian-dominated spaces and there is a sense that through traffic dominates.

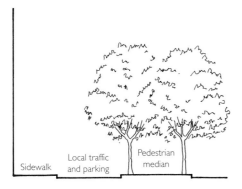

Elements of the pedestrian realm

Guidelines for the Establishment of a Pedestrian Realm

- The edge of the pedestrian realm should be defined strongly by a continuous median, planted with at least one uninterrupted, closely spaced line of trees.
- It is very critical to allow parking on the access road. The friction caused by cars moving in and out of parking spaces and looking for space to park slows traffic on the access way and discourages drivers in search of speed from moving into the pedestrian realm. Parking is also necessary to give access to buildings on the street.
- It is important to have only one travel lane in the pedestrian realm. Having two lanes allows for faster speeds and may offer nonlocal traffic an attractive opportunity to bypass heavy traffic on the central roadway, at least for a block or so. This may result in increased danger for pedestrians, as the example of the Grand Concourse suggests. Street designers should also be wary of providing too much parking, because an empty parking lane might be used as a moving lane.
- Access to the pedestrian realm by vehicles is best achieved at intersections. Breaks in the median to allow vehicle access at midblock locations (as on Avenue Marceau in Paris and K Street in Washington, D.C.), though intended to eliminate conflicts at the intersections, may in reality create more conflict points with through traffic. They also disturb the continuity of pedestrian use of the median.

The pedestrian realm can be reinforced by certain design features.

- Pedestrian amenities on the medians—transit stops and subway entrances, kiosks, benches, fountains, or flower stands—encourage many crossings between the sidewalk and the median, thereby increasing pedestrian domination of the access roadway.
- Lighting on medians and/or sidewalks should be designed for pedestrians: closely spaced (approximately 50 feet apart), low in height, and preferably warm in color.
- Sidewalks can be relatively narrow. On boulevards with limited rights-of-way sidewalks can be as narrow as five feet. Although this is usually insufficient for ordinary streets (where the sidewalk is the only space reserved for pedestrians), on boulevards it can be

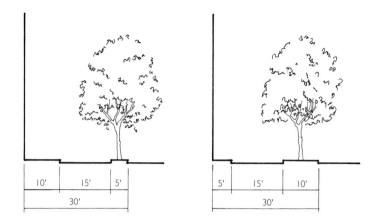

Hypothetical minimum width pedestrian realm

adequate because people can also walk in the access way and on the median when pedestrian traffic is heavy.

- The slow-moving nature of the access road can be articulated by a slight change in elevation from the center realm and a different, perhaps rougher, surface material.

6. Continuous, Tree-lined Medians

On boulevards, continuous medians bound the center roadway and the pedestrian realms, separating them and joining them together at the same time. Medians are the most flexible element of boulevard design, and to a great extent their design determines the form and character of the boulevard.

Their primary function is to define and protect the pedestrian realm from the central through traffic. A complementary function is to shield the through traffic from interference by parking and access uses. Observation suggests that driving in the center realm of a boule-

Ocean Parkway Median

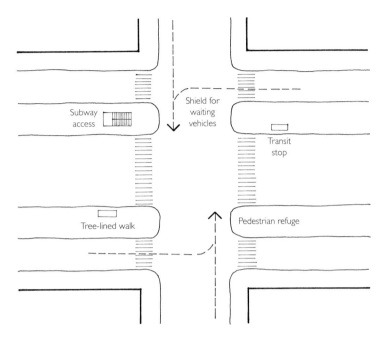

Various functions of the medians

vard is smoother and involves fewer swerving motions in and out of lanes to negotiate traffic than on ordinary streets.

The medians also create a space where passages from one realm to the other can take place: they allow pedestrians to board or disembark from buses, and they can momentarily shield cars trying to move from one realm to the other while waiting for an opportunity to merge into traffic.

A boulevard, like any arterial street, is a formidable barrier to cross. Breaking down the scale of the street enables crossing movements to proceed in two or even three stages: to the edge of the median, across the center realm, and across the second pedestrian realm. Waiting pedestrians and cars can use the median as a shield from traffic. Almost universally, pedestrians cross from the sidewalk to the median without regard for the light if the access road is free—which it often is—and then wait to cross the center roadway with the light. The ability to cross this way is particularly helpful for older people and those who cannot move quickly.

Guidelines for the Design of a Continuous Median

- Depending on the width of the boulevard, medians may range from 5 to 50 feet wide, depending to a large extent on the width of the overall right-of-way. In narrow rights-of-way, medians tend to be minimal; in wider ones, they are more generous.
- The most important element in the median, its defining characteristic, is the line or lines of trees: closely spaced, uninterrupted, and reaching all the way to the intersection.
- Medians should also contain attractions to encourage pedestrian use.

- If there are buses or streetcars on the boulevard, stops should be located on the medians, as should subway access points.
- Most good boulevards have many regularly spaced benches on the medians.
- Pedestrian-scaled street lights, at intervals not greater than 50 feet, are a staple of boulevard medians.
- In places where the median is wide enough, and actively used, water fountains, kiosks, public toilets, café seating, and flower stands can add to its beauty and usefulness.
- Medians may be paved or not, and trees may be set in continuous planting strips or in tree wells, depending on the expected volume and type of pedestrian use. Wider medians designed to be used as promenades are usually partly paved.

7. Rows of Trees and Tree Spacing

Trees are indispensable components of boulevard design. They are perhaps *the* defining characteristic of all boulevards and fulfill three functions.

To start with, they give definition to the various boulevard realms. The median trees mark the boundaries between the central, fast-moving-vehicle realm and the slower pedestrian realms. It is extremely difficult to create a strongly defined, extended pedestrian realm with a treeless median. Trees also break down the visual scale of wide rights-of-way. Observers consistently underestimate the width of boulevards that have strong rows of trees and overestimate the width of arterial streets without them.

Trees create a pleasant environment for pedestrians and drivers alike. They provide shade in summer and help eliminate glare and sharp contrasts. They are delightful to look at; the eye is held by the play of light among leaves and branches. A tree canopy over the pedes-

Avenue Grand Armée, Paris

trian realm affords a very different feel from that of the central realm. Finally, the lines of trees become a clear urban element that helps people orient themselves in the city as a whole. The boulevard becomes a memorable street that helps people find their way around in the city.[5]

Trees are an investment and need frequent maintenance. In Paris, trees are constantly being replanted to maintain the close spacing of 15 to 25 feet typical of its boulevards. Severe pruning of trees on the Passeig de Gràcia in Barcelona recently left it bereft of the dense canopy that was one of the street's major assets. Old pictures of K Street in Washington, D.C. show a remarkably better street, before most of its trees were cut down some time in the fifties.

Guidelines for the Design of Tree Rows

- It is important that trees be closely spaced and that they continue all the way to the intersection. They should have a maximum spacing of 35 feet—25 feet is better. A minimum spacing as low as 12 feet apart is possible, depending on the species. Spacing should be close enough to allow branches to form a continuous overhead canopy.
- Trees do not have to be all the same species: an alternating pattern of two or three species can work.
- Deciduous trees are generally preferable. They provide shade in the summer yet allow sun into the street in winter. In warm climates their shade-giving function is paramount.
- To have a visual connection across the street, and to maintain the integrity of the street as one whole, trees that have dense foliage below eye level should not be used.
- Trees can be arranged in various ways.
  —In medians 5 to 10 feet wide, trees are best planted in the center of the median, to allow for growing space.
  —In medians 10 to 20 feet wide with one row of trees, they may be best placed closer to the center roadway so that most of the median's width is protected from fast traffic. It is also possible to plant two rows of trees in a staggered pattern.
  —On medians wider than 20 feet, two rows of trees probably make the most sense. While freer arrangements are possible with the interior row of trees, it is important to keep the defining line of trees at the edge of the pedestrian realm constant. Experience suggests that a simple, rhythmical planting arrangement is more effective than complex ones in achieving the grace and pleasantness characteristic of the best boulevards.

8. Public Transport

Multiway boulevards are a natural location for public transportation. Public transportation benefits a boulevard by encouraging pedestrians to use the street. At the same time, boulevards benefit public transportation lines, which require easy pedestrian access and cause frequent street crossings.

If a subway or light rail system already exists, or is contemplated, it can usually be accommodated within a boulevard's right-of-way. High-volume surface transit can be

The Esplanade, Chico

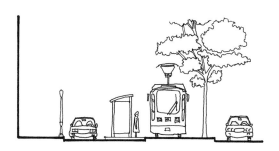

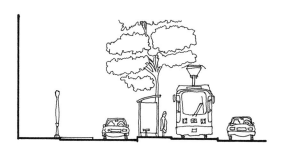

Possible configurations for light rail on a median

achieved by including dedicated transit lanes. Designs to facilitate quick embarkation and wheelchair access generally place transit stops on the medians.[6]

Recently the high-density land-use potential of such public transportation corridors has also come into focus.[7] There is a good fit between high-density urban corridors and public transportation corridors, both of which can be accommodated with grace on boulevards.[8]

Guidelines for the Incorporation of Public Transport

If buses are used, they should travel in the central roadway rather than in the access roadway. Curb lanes may become designated bus lanes.

- If light-rail is incorporated into the street, it can run on the curb lane of the center roadway or, if the city desires to separate it from cars, on the median, toward the center edge. Given a wide enough right-of-way, light rail can run in dedicated lanes in the center of the street.
- Locating transit stops on the medians will encourage pedestrian use of the medians.
- Where a subway system exists, or is contemplated, it is desirable to place entrances on the medians.

9. Parking

Parking on the access roads is an essential part of an extended pedestrian realm. Even though existing street standards and guidelines discourage parking along major streets, there are a number of reasons why parking is important on boulevards, and other streets as well.[9] Parking on boulevards slows traffic on the access lane as cars pull in and out and drivers slow down to look for spaces. Generally, the presence of on-street parking increases the number of pedestrians moving along a street. On-street parking also increases access to abutting

Side Access Road - Eastern Parkway

buildings. It encourages street-oriented commercial development and may help small businesses succeed as they have to provide and pay for less parking on their own premises.

Moreover, parked vehicles act as a physical barrier between pedestrians and moving cars and thus provide a sense of safety. They create an interface between cars and pedestrians that enlivens street activity. Goods being unloaded from parked trucks and people lingering to talk before one of them gets in a car and drives off are normal everyday scenes repeatedly observed on good boulevards.

However important parking may be, it should not dominate the pedestrian realm but should be balanced with other pedestrian uses. In Paris, for example, a third lane of parking is added to some boulevards along the curb of the center roadway. Besides negating the benefits of an unhindered central roadway, this extra parking creates a parking lot feel, diminishing the pedestrian nature of the median.

Guidelines for Parking

- Access ways can include one or two rows of parallel parking, depending on available space.
- Parking lanes should be narrow. A lane width of 6 or 7 feet is possible and sufficient; 8 or 9 feet is the maximum. Greater widths contribute to a wider travel lane, which may encourage speeding.
- If a boulevard's design includes a wide median and there is a demand for more spaces, an angled parking lane can be incorporated into the median.
- Where an access way has two parking lanes, pedestrians may be helped by widening either the median or the sidewalk at intersections. The presence of such a bulb or "neck" makes it easier for pedestrians to cross to the median, and it slows cars that are entering or leaving the access way.
- If more parking is needed near a boulevard, consider providing it in underground parking garages beneath the central roadway, with entries and exits for cars from the access road and from the medians for pedestrians. However, these access points should not disrupt the pedestrian character of these spaces.

10. Lane Widths

The ability to implement boulevards in limited space (between 100 feet and 140 feet) depends on accepting narrow lanes—7 to 9 feet in the access way, 9 to 11 feet in the center roadway. Research shows that narrow lanes work well in boulevards and that they may increase pedestrian safety by making crossing the street easier and slowing cars on the access ways.[10] Further, it is more difficult to achieve an extended pedestrian realm when access lanes are wider (12 or 13 feet). For this reason we have specified maximum as well as minimum widths.

A concern, of course, is access for emergency vehicles, particularly fire trucks, and garbage and recycling trucks. This issue sometimes comes up in relation to narrow access lanes, but the problem is less acute than it seems. The width of most access ways is not less than that of many normal residential streets, which fire trucks can, of course, enter. They could also operate from the center roadway across a narrow median without overly increasing distances to the buildings. Even if general standards for emergency vehicle access prescribe excessive lane widths, it is worth investigating whether there is room for flexibility. Often there is.[11]

Lane widths on the access roadway and center roadway should be governed by different criteria. The access roadways function as local streets and should be designed with constricted widths to induce traffic to go slow. In the center roadway it is appropriate for lanes to be wider—but not so wide as to encourage speeding and prevent pedestrians from easily crossing the street.

Guidelines for Lane Width

- Travel lanes on the access roads can be as narrow as 7 feet and as wide as 11 feet, while parking lanes should be between 6 and 9 feet wide. However, where the access road is configured with two parking lanes its overall width should not exceed 24 feet.
- In the center roadway, the travel lane at the median curb should be a minimum of 9 feet and a maximum of 13 feet wide (where this lane is dedicated to public transit).
- Inside lanes of the central roadway can range from 9.5 feet to 12 feet wide. Wider lanes may encourage speeding.
- Left-turn lanes in the center (if used) can be 9.5 to 12 feet wide.

11. Bicycle Lanes

Boulevards easily accommodate bicycle travel. There is a growing movement to create separate lanes for bicycles on city streets. It is fueled by two considerations: the recognition that cyclists are endangered by cars when they share a lane with them and that bicycles present a danger to pedestrians when they share a path with them.

Ho Chi Minh City : Ton Duc Thang

Two types of bicycle travel, however, need to be distinguished: bicycling for local movement, either by adults or children, and bicycling for commuting or sport. The first type involves running errands, play and leisure, or visits to local destinations. Riders generally go slow and travel only short distances. The second type of bicyclist goes faster and may travel for long distances. The two types of movement have different characteristics and may be accommodated in different ways on boulevards.

Guidelines for Bicycles on Boulevards

- Local bicycle traffic can easily be incorporated on the access roadway within the pedestrian realm. Observation teaches that cyclists use the realm very much as pedestrians do—disregarding the direction of the automobile traffic—and that they do so with safety.
- Designated bicycle lanes for faster-moving commuter bicycles can be incorporated into a wide median on a designated path or as a narrow first lane in the center roadway, next to the median.

Bicycle Path on Ocean Parkway

12. Distribution of Pedestrian Space between Sidewalk and Median

The best boulevards are energized by a certain tightness of conditions. Boulevards cannot be built in rights-of-way of 100 feet to 140 feet without making the sidewalks, traffic lanes, and medians quite narrow. This is not necessarily a problem. As the sidewalk becomes congested with people, those wishing to walk faster feel comfortable walking in the access way. Once on the access way, people tend to stay there. This also happens when a sidewalk is obstructed by café seating, a street vendor, or an occasional front stoop. Other people coming into the boulevard, seeing the access way used in that fashion, follow the example. It becomes a shared space.

On wider boulevards, the street designer is faced with a choice: should the extra space in the pedestrian realm be used to make the sidewalk wider or the median wider?

The two spaces are different in their intent and function. Sidewalks afford visual and physical access to abutting buildings. They can provide space for strolling, but they also accommodate purposeful movement. The median, however, is more wholly geared to strolling and lingering, although it too may invite purposeful longer-distance walking.

Therefore, adding more width to either space produces different results. Overly wide sidewalks may be counterproductive. Unless they are full of people, they may look desolate and uninviting. Wide medians, on the other hand, may provide more attractive strolling places, especially if a second line of trees can be incorporated.

In cities where utility lines run beneath sidewalks, narrow sidewalks may be perceived as a problem. In fact, a boulevard configuration allows expanded space for underground utility lines, which can be placed under the entire width of the pedestrian realm without hindering through traffic when repairs are necessary.

Sidewalk/Median arrangements

Narow sidewalk/wide median vs. wide sidewalk/narrow median

Guidelines for Distribution of Pedestrian Space

- It is better for sidewalks to be slightly congested with pedestrian traffic than to appear empty and desolate. Narrow sidewalks are generally not a problem on boulevards because pedestrian traffic can easily spill onto the access way and the median.
- If the dimensions of the right-of-way are wide enough to support either a wide median or a wide sidewalk, consider making the sidewalk narrow and the median wide.

13. Intersection Design

When intersections are complex and there are many choices of movement, drivers act with caution. Well-designed intersections do not predetermine all the movements that drivers and pedestrians will attempt; nor do they separate all the possible movements from each other. Boulevard intersections should be designed to help people negotiate potential conflicts in consonance with an easily understood set of priorities, and pedestrian safety, in mind. Because they understand that boulevard intersections are complex, most drivers approach them with caution, particularly when going into or out of the main traffic flow on the center roadway.

Guidelines for Intersection Design

- All turning and weaving movements can be allowed at boulevard intersections unless there is a compelling reason to prohibit them. The presumption should be to allow them.
- Priority is given first to center through traffic, then to crossing traffic, then to movement on the access road.
- Turning radii and the configuration of medians are determined primarily to allow pedestrians easier crossing of intersections. Ease of turning for cars and large vehicles are secondary considerations.

Intersection configurations

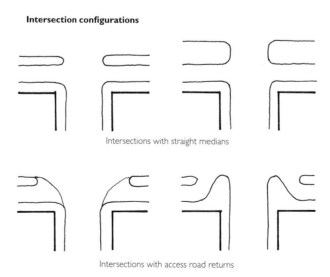

Intersections with straight medians

Intersections with access road returns

Many different physical configurations are possible for boulevard intersections, depending on the width of the medians and the character of the street.

- The most straightforward intersection arrangement has straight medians that extend more or less the same distance into the intersection as the sidewalk edge. Crosswalks across the boulevard are then interrupted by the medians, reinforcing the pedestrian nature of the medians. (Curb cuts can be installed there for disabled access.) This arrangement is appropriate for both wide and narrow medians. Parking lanes along the access roadway may end short of the intersection to allow for a widened sidewalk or bulb—making it easier to cross the access road.
- Access roads may be designed with entries to and exits from the central roadway just before and just after intersections, as on Shattuck Avenue in Berkeley. An advantage of this design is that intersections are simplified, as there is only one roadway crossing the intersecting street. However, there are disadvantages. When traffic in the center is heavy, merging into the center is difficult and left turns from the access roads may not be possible. The arrangement forces local traffic to enter through-going traffic at every block, disrupting the natural pace of the access ways, and perhaps that of the center. Moreover, it shortens the medians near every intersection, interrupting the continuity of the tree lines and pedestrian paths.
- Medians may be designed to end a short distance from intersections and be connected to sidewalks at this point by a slight curb lip, as on most Paris boulevards. This arrangement increases the sense of difference between the pedestrian realm and the center roadway, giving the access road an aura of separateness. The curving edge of the access way and the slight shortening of the medians compel drivers to leave the access road at an angle, making it easier for them to see the intentions of drivers in the center. The arrangement also makes it easier for drivers coming out of the access way to go in any direction. On the other hand, the set-back medians provide less shelter for pedestrians crossing the center roadway.

14. Traffic Controls

Traffic controls should reinforce traffic priorities. For drivers and pedestrians alike, traffic controls on boulevards should enhance the ability to achieve their aims. Drivers need to travel relatively fast on the center roadway, turn easily into cross streets, and move into the access lane when they reach their boulevard destination. Drivers from cross streets may wish to turn onto the access way or the central roadway in either direction or simply cross the boulevard without conflict. Drivers on access ways may want to rejoin traffic on the center roadway in the same direction or the opposing one, enter the cross street in either direction, or continue to drive on the access way for another block. All of these movements can be safely accommodated with the help of traffic controls that acknowledge the existence of potential conflicts but provide clear and safe ways of negotiating them.

Intersection Controls on The Esplanade

Traffic Control Guidelines

- As a rule, through traffic on the center roadway is given first priority, then traffic on cross streets, and lastly traffic on the access ways. To facilitate boulevard through-movement at intersections, the central lanes are either uncontrolled or controlled with a traffic light.
- On some boulevards, like The Esplanade in Chico, every second intersection is signalized. At unsignalized intersections, both the cross street and access way should be controlled by stop signs, so that while traffic coming from the center roadway proceeds without stopping, traffic on the cross street and access ways has to make sure the way is clear before proceeding. At signalized intersections, only the center roadway and cross

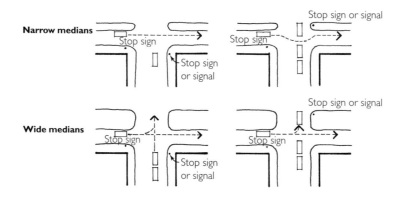

street are controlled by signals, while the access lane is controlled by a stop sign. The location of stop signs and traffic signals generally depends on the width of the medians.

- On boulevards with narrow medians, the stop sign or signal controlling the cross street
  may be at the sidewalk edge or on the median. When the control is on the sidewalk (i.e.,
  before the intersection), the intersection remains clear of waiting cars and drivers on the
  access road can continue across it. When, however, the cross-street control is on the median, the intersection may be partially blocked by waiting cars. Observation informs us,
  however, that in the latter situation the access way usually remains passable because drivers on the cross street leave a gap in the roadway or go out of their way to back up, leaving room for a car to pass.

- On wide-median boulevards with signalized intersections, the cross-street signal is usually placed at the sidewalk edge. Access-road drivers wishing to enter or cross the center
  can then move into a waiting position in the protected space provided by the wide median. At intersections where the cross-street traffic is controlled by a stop sign, it is
  placed at the outer edge of the median, which increases visibility for drivers waiting to
  enter or cross the center. Sight lines are not blocked by median trees, as they might be if
  traffic were held back at the sidewalk. Access-road drivers wishing to turn left under
  these controls must make two stops, along the access road and then at the median. This
  arrangement emphasizes the change in roadway function between side and center.

- Placing the stop sign or traffic light at the sidewalk edge on wide-median boulevards allows for generous pedestrian crosswalks in line with the medians, emphasizing the continuity of the median and encouraging people to walk or cycle along them. This feature
  may be most appropriate where medians are intended to serve as promenades or where
  they contain a bike lane. At times, merging or crossing cars may block the crosswalk, but
  only momentarily, and pedestrians can usually negotiate around them just fine.

- On some boulevards the access roads are controlled by signals with the same timing as
  those in the central roadway. This arrangement runs counter to the intended function of
  the access roads, diluting their slow, local nature.

- If cross streets are one-way, the control situation is greatly simplified: left turns from the
  access way and right turns from the center roadway are only possible in one direction.
  Left-turning vehicles from the access way or right-turning vehicles from the central
  roadway, can easily merge into the stream of crossing traffic.

15. Discouraging Jaywalking

Long blocks or the existence of many businesses on both sides of the street can create an unsafe situation in which jaywalking is frequent. The reason why people jaywalk, despite the
danger involved, is that on signalized streets, particularly when traffic is not heavy, traffic
flows with a rhythm, leaving the street empty of cars for short periods. At such times pedestrians may feel it is safe to cross.

On some streets high fences are erected in the center to discourage this behavior. These
are disruptive visually, create a sense of separation between one side of the street and the
other, and are often disregarded or vandalized by people still intent on crossing. It is possible to discourage jaywalking without defacing the street but, rather, adding to its livabil-

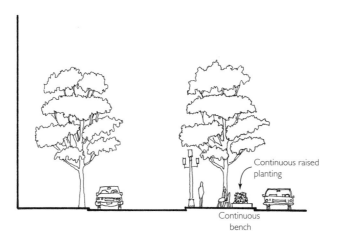

Continuous raised
planting

Continuous
bench

Median barriers to jaywalking

ity and usefulness. Continuous benches or dense planting along the median can form a barrier to jaywalking while enhancing the protection of the pedestrian realm from the central roadway.

Guidelines for Discouraging Jaywalking

- Run benches or planters without interruption between intersections on the side of the median closer to the central roadway. Benches should face inward, toward the access road.
- Plants must be tall enough and dense enough to discourage walking through them.
- When raised planting beds are used, their walls can double as seating ledges.

Avenue George V : Raised access lane

16. Differentiating the Roadways

Establishing a strong boundary between the pedestrian realm and the through-going realm is essential to a successful boulevard. This is accomplished primarily by tree-lined medians, but additional design details that differentiate the roadways and require drivers to moderate their speed on the access roads can reinforce the boundary.

Guidelines for Differentiating the Roadways

- A design detail that increases the definition of the pedestrian realm is a slight rise (about one inch) at the entrance to the access way. This is especially useful in tight conditions where some extra protection of the pedestrian realm is helpful. The small break in paving makes cars slow down on entering the pedestrian realm and makes them cautious on leaving it. It creates a sensation on the access way that is somewhat akin to what drivers feel leaving a driveway and entering a street. Drivers seem to understand that it is their responsibility to use caution when entering the street and to defer to pedestrians while they are on it.

- Use of a different paving material on the access roadway and the center roadway can also differentiate them. If the access-roadway material looks similar to the material used on the sidewalks and medians, it clearly suggests that all three are part of a single realm.

- Another version of the same idea is to slightly raise the surface of walkways that cross the access roads, perhaps by using a different paving material, such as brick, to mark them.

These arrangements, and possibly some others, follow the basic principle of establishing a strong boundary for the pedestrian realm, protecting it by clear definition and by requiring cars to move slowly as they move into it.

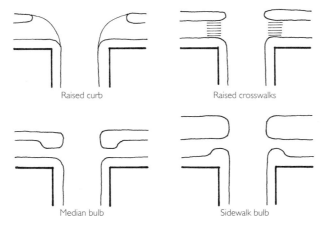

Raised curb   Raised crosswalks

Median bulb   Sidewalk bulb

Possibilities for differentiating the roadways

Chapter Two

CONCLUSIONS

The point of departure for this book was a contradiction between personal experiences of multiway boulevards as great streets alive with many people and activities, relaxed, without a sense of danger, and extraordinary places to walk, and the general conception held mostly by transportation professionals that they are unsafe or remnants of a bygone age. Given this contradiction, we started with two basic inquiries, soon to be joined by a third: Are multiway boulevards indeed unsafe, as contended? Would it be possible today to emulate a much-admired boulevard, a justly famous one, if we wanted to? And—perhaps more important than the second question—Are multiway boulevards useful today, or could they be?

To be sure, advocacy was and is a part of our inquiries. At the start, multiway boulevards seemed to us to be among the best of urban streets, when designed well. Almost 150 years after they first became widely used, they still seem to fulfill all the functions expected of them with grace and beauty. We suspected that multiway boulevards were getting a "bum rap" and that they were an appropriate street type for contemporary cities. We wanted to set the record straight and, if our intuition proved correct, to advocate their use in appropriate urban settings. In addition, the many design natures of these streets and something of their histories is worth knowing for anyone interested in the evolution and complexity of cities— whether multiway boulevards are reintroduced or not.

The research and findings go beyond the simple exploration and presentation of a street type. Along the way it became necessary to confront a larger issue: the so-called functional classification of streets as a generally accepted basis for street design. For truly urban settlements that are dense, diverse, and complex we need a different way to approach street design. Just as it is necessary, in order to create a lively city, to have multidimensional urban areas of mixed use, so it is possible and desirable to have streets that accommodate pedestrians as well as vehicles, traffic of different speeds, and local as well as through traffic. The challenge is to design them so that these different users can work well together.

Professional and bureaucratic constraints—determined in part by years of adherence to a belief system that embraces largeness in everything associated with street design as well as separation of traffic types—are not easy to change. They are embedded in professionally promulgated standards and norms that have in turn become, in effect, commandments to the insurance industry.[1] A different way of looking at street design is required, one that involves a perception of wholeness. Street design is more than numbers and speed of vehicles; the behavior of pedestrians and drivers and their multiple, often conflicting, needs are critical components.

As we write these words, some eight years after embarking on our research of boulevards, we are hopeful. New approaches to thinking about streets are emerging. So there is reason to be optimistic in regard to the future of multiway boulevards. Indeed, we end our discussion with a description of a newly designed and voter-approved San Francisco boulevard to show the possibilities. But first, let us reiterate what we have found.

SAFETY AND THE PEDESTRIAN REALM

Multiway boulevards are not more dangerous than normally configured streets carrying similar amounts of traffic. This is no unimportant finding. Multiway boulevards have long been considered dangerous, largely because of the multiplicity of possible conflict points at intersections. But available data do not show that there is anything inherently dangerous about them as a street type. If anything, research suggests that conclusions about their safety are not based on a rigorous analysis that included on-site observation.

Design is extremely critical to matters of safety. Overwhelmingly, safety on multiroadway boulevards is associated with an extended pedestrian realm. Within this realm the overall pace of movement is dictated by pedestrians. It is a slow pace. Regulations, such as those that give priority for movement to the central lanes and to the intersecting streets, are also important, but basic design is crucial. On the best boulevards, the combined widths of the two pedestrian realms, one on each side of the central through lanes, constitute at least 50 percent or more of the overall street width.

USEFULNESS

Multiway boulevards deserve attention because of their existing and potential contributions to good urban environments. If limited-access, limited-purpose roadways—freeways for the most part—were ever appropriate solutions for the intracity movement of vehicles, it is hard to see how great cities such as London and Curitiba, Brazil, have managed without them, or how San Francisco has reduced its freeway mileage in recent years. In any case, freeways are less likely to be built in the future. They are extraordinarily expensive and space-consuming. Because of their limited-access nature, they almost always create barriers within cities, dividing what is on one side of them from what is on the other. When they become congested, they force traffic onto local streets ill-suited to handling it. Citizen groups in the twenty-first century are more likely than earlier residents to resist efforts to build new freeways in or near their neighborhoods. At the same time, many American urbanites have come to understand that the specialness of where they live relates to the complexity, density, and multiplicity of nearby land uses. The period of large single-use areas has passed, or is passing.

It is more than appropriate to look to public streets to serve multiple uses as well. Not all streets can or should do so, but some can and must. Multiway boulevards, when located properly and designed appropriately, are particularly well suited to both multiple modes and paces of travel and diverse abutting land use. Most pointedly, these streets can handle large volumes of through traffic at the same time as they provide for local travel and direct access to abutting properties. And, unlike freeways or expressways, these roadways can integrate rather than divide neighborhoods.

Multiway boulevards are necessarily wider than most streets. For this reason, there will never be many of them relative to other street types. At the same time, because their very size and nature make them prominent, they offer splendid opportunities to structure urban development in positive ways. They are easy to recognize and to remember and so can serve as positive landmarks in a city.

BUILDABILITY

It would not be impossible to build a new finely scaled multiway boulevard in the United States today, but neither is it likely. We fear for the futures of Eastern Parkway and Ocean Parkway in Brooklyn, despite the fact that they have been declared historic landscapes. Today's standards and norms for roadways, if not geared to prohibit them outright, are seriously stacked against multiway boulevards. It is more likely that the Grand Concourse and Queens Boulevard will be cleansed of their remaining complexities to achieve traffic-movement objectives than that they will be modestly changed and lovingly planted to serve complex, diverse functions.

To a considerable extent, multiway boulevards were put in jeopardy by the ascendancy of the functional classification approach to highway and street design and the seemingly ever-larger street dimensions associated with speed and presumed safety for vehicles. Because multiway boulevards serve multiple purposes and uses it has become difficult to consider and deal with them under the prevailing design orthodoxy. At the same time, ever-wider lane widths (even for slow-moving traffic), wider parking lanes, larger turning radii at corners, a seeming abhorrence of trees, and professionally promulgated norms and guidelines (if not legally established standards) make it even more difficult to retain these streets, let alone build new ones. These standards and norms are basically antiurban in concept and reality, whereas multiway boulevards are the very opposite.

Bias has a lot to do with professional views of multiway boulevards—and, worse yet, with their prospects. The abstract logic of accepted intersection design—that the more possible conflict points there are the more dangerous the roadway will be—seems to be treated as gospel, without testing or extensive observation. We were surprised to find so little observational research about this issue—really almost none—being used as a basis for today's street design guidelines. When presenting our research findings to faculty and students of transportation engineering, we were surprised that our audiences seemed to accept this lack of evidence.

As noted earlier, part of the research that went into preparing the guidelines presented in the preceding chapter involved a series of boulevard design and redesign case studies intended to test professional reactions.[2] In every community where these case study designs were prepared and presented, questions were raised, usually during the last half of the ensuing discussion, about the probable political, social, or bureaucratic constraints to implementing them. It is relatively easy to "pass the buck" and therefore avoid endorsing or rejecting boulevard proposals. During these meetings a professional might be convinced of the strength of a new boulevard proposal but mention that another agency, at the same or higher level, would be the stumbling block or would have to be convinced. The most frequently named "others" were fire departments at the local level and state or federal funding agencies. In the end, though, the reviewers held that it is mostly the elected officials and bureaucratic bosses—not the local professionals who would carry out the policy—who would have to be convinced. This is a telling observation and no minor stumbling block. Boulevards, because of their multifunctional nature, need the cooperation of many different agencies and departments, as well as the support of the local community, if they are to become reality.

Fear of lawsuits and liability is an extraordinarily strong concern of local professionals and may be more responsible than any other reason for their reluctance to consider new approaches to roadway design, especially if proposed new guidelines cast doubt on existing standards and norms. Existing standards provide a fall-back position of some strength and general acceptance, regardless of their appropriateness. Casting doubt on them—at the same time designing guidelines that run counter to generations of standards that increase space for autos and trucks—may be looking for trouble. Professionals, like others, tend to develop vested interests in the ways they have been working and the standards and norms that have governed their decisions and designs. We all like to think that we have been doing things right, albeit in a very imperfect world. Given that very human way of thinking, local professionals' very cautious responses to proposals to redesign local roads as multiway boulevards are to be expected.

Once again, today's standards do not have to be tomorrow's. Professionals in some places, very much including transportation engineers, are rethinking existing standards for a variety of reasons. The Portland, Oregon, Cheap and Skinny Streets program is noteworthy.[3] Faced with the problem of improving unfinished rights-of-way at prices residents can afford and would pay for, the Portland Office of Transportation Engineering and Development designed "skinny" streets, roadways as narrow as 18 feet, and proved to local agencies that they can handle fire equipment. *Making Choices* is a set of advisory guidelines for the design of streets in the province of Ontario. It is intended as a philosophical introduction to an approach to standards that is one alternative to conventional street design.[4] Dutch-inspired Woonerf designs, 30-kilometer-per-hour traffic zones, and traffic-calming methods pioneered in Europe are finding increasing acceptance in the United States. Projects and guidelines of the New Urbanism movement are generally associated with street designs that depart from conventions of the past fifty or more years, and guidelines have been created by the Institute of Transportation Engineers especially for "neo-traditional" development. Most important, perhaps, is a recent guidelines book produced by the metropolitan authorities of Portland called *Creating Livable Streets;* it is aimed at making the region's major traffic-carrying streets more livable and uses the concept of the pedestrian realm. There need not be an adversarial relationship between traffic engineering professionals and those who might propose new multiway boulevards.

THE ELUSIVENESS OF WHOLENESS

As has been noted or alluded to often in this book, no one or two specific qualities make the best boulevards work well or are singularly responsible for increasing or decreasing safety. Rather it is a combination of characteristics, some having to do with design and some with regulations working together that—sometimes counterintuitively—account for the best boulevards. The slow speeds that characterize narrow side access roads mean that vehicles approach intersections slowly and carefully, which makes the multiple and complex turning movements that may be allowed at intersections safer. Similarly, knowing that the intersections are complex induces slower, more careful travel on them by those on the side streets and the access roads. In all likelihood, the slowness of the access lanes and the complexity at intersections inhibit through traffic from using them. The slow lanes encourage jaywalking, or even strolling along them, which in turn encourages drivers to be cautious. Closely planted trees on medians are part of what sets the pedestrian realm apart from the central traffic-way, providing a pleasant walking space in the pedestrian realm as well as clearly defining the driving space of the center. There are interdependencies amidst interdependencies.

Professionals and lay people alike seem to have difficulty accepting or grasping the interrelatedness of the parts of multiway boulevards. It is easy for them to see and isolate individual elements of a boulevard proposal as unsafe—potential conflicts involving turning vehicles, medians not wide enough to "store" turning vehicles, lack of provision for double-parking of delivery trucks, close tree-spacing and tree rows that continue all the way to the intersections, and the like. They may propose solutions that would presumably make the individual element work better—or simply conclude that the design is faulty. Most proposals meant to correct what are seen as design faults, however, would result in larger space requirements or in movement restrictions at intersections; they are thus likely to be counterproductive of the very qualities that characterize the best boulevards. It is remarkably easy, as well, for boulevard designers to get caught up in discussions of these isolated issues. In general, professionals' responses to boulevard proposals are noteworthy for their inability to perceive and discuss an interrelated whole. A focus on details and an emphasis on the smooth functioning of particular traffic movements is inconsistent with the logic associated with the ways that good boulevards work in the real world.

Seeing is believing, and experience counts! When reviewers, professional or otherwise, can relate a proposal to a successful design they have actually experienced, they tend to be more accepting of it, even if it runs counter to existing norms. The wholeness of one's experience, recalled or of the moment, takes ascendancy over piecemeal analysis.

A NEW BOULEVARD

San Francisco's streets are more noted for steepness and the spectacular views they offer than for the grandness of their design qualities. Nonetheless, its people led a "revolt" in the mid-1960s—the first such in the United States—to stop freeway construction along the waterfront, through a central part of the city toward Golden Gate Park, and, ultimately, to the Golden Gate Bridge. As a result, for years, there were a number of stub-ended, double-decked, elevated freeways that went nowhere. By the mid-1970s, the city's Planning Department had concluded that the waterfront freeway along the Embarcadero could be replaced by an at-grade roadway; and though there were no funds on the horizon to take that

Central Freeway over Octavia Street.

freeway down, it became the policy of the city to do so. The equally unfinished Central Freeway was not to be extended, though no replacement designs were prepared.

Fortune, or misfortune, depending on how events are viewed, intervened. The 1989 Loma Prieta earthquake showed the freeway stubs to be hazardous and presented city and highway officials with alternatives: retrofit the two freeways or take them down. Then, however, there were federal emergency funds to help pay for the work. The Embarcadero freeway is no more, having been replaced by a surface roadway similar to the Planning Department's earlier design. It pays to have plans ready to take advantage of opportunities.

There were no at-hand alternative designs for the Central Freeway, but neighborhood activists and many others opposed a retrofit, calling instead for an at-grade solution to handling the large traffic volumes destined for western neighborhoods: the Sunset and Richmond districts. What remained of the Central Freeway (part of it came down soon after the earthquake) was a classic overhead structure, noisy and close to buildings; it created dark streets and intersections below and divided the Hayes Valley neighborhood for five blocks. To live in close proximity to a freeway, literally in its shadow, is to know its disruptiveness— all the more so where residents can see a nearby neighborhood knitting itself together in the blocks near where ramps have come down. Traffic studies carried out in the 1990s show that

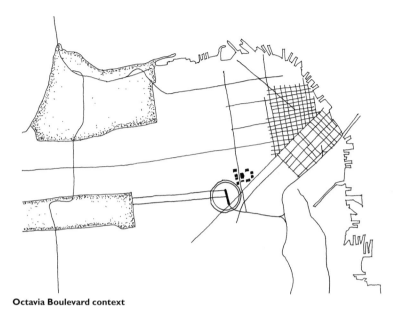

Octavia Boulevard context

traffic through the area could function without undue delay if the freeway in Hayes Valley is removed, coming to ground south of the city's main thoroughfare, Market Street. Nonetheless, a ballot measure in favor of rebuilding the Central Freeway over Market Street was passed in 1997. This was repealed in 1998 by a second vote favoring an at-grade boulevard through the neighborhood. But such a boulevard had not been designed.

Octavia Boulevard, designed by the authors with staff of the San Francisco Department of Public Works, is a response to the voters' mandate of 1998. It is designed to do precisely what a good multiway boulevard is supposed to do: carry large amounts of traffic with reasonable dispatch through the Hayes Valley neighborhood, at the same time catering to local needs for access to abutting property and safe space for slow-moving vehicles, pedestrians, and cyclists. It is accommodated in a right-of-way of approximately 123 feet, significantly narrower than the space consumed by the freeway it will replace. The unused right-of-way is reserved for new abutting uses, particularly housing, that will face onto the boulevard—a very important part of the design.

The design starts, on its western edge, with an existing sidewalk that provides access to residences. This 15-foot walk will have new trees to supplement the few that exist. Next comes a narrow access road 18 feet wide for one moving and one parking lane, then a 9-foot-wide median with London plane trees spaced 20 feet apart, new pedestrian lighting, benches, and flowering shrubs. Cyclists will use the access roads. The central realm for the faster traffic has two lanes in each direction and a central median planted with groups of Lombardy poplars. The eastern pedestrian realm of median, access road, and sidewalk is largely the same as that on the western side.

Essentially, this is a very simple design. The boulevard runs for only four blocks between Market and Fell Streets. Movements at two of the intersections are made relatively easy because the intersecting streets are one way. Four minor intersecting streets stop at the access lanes, simplifying their integration with the boulevard. The problem of how to end the

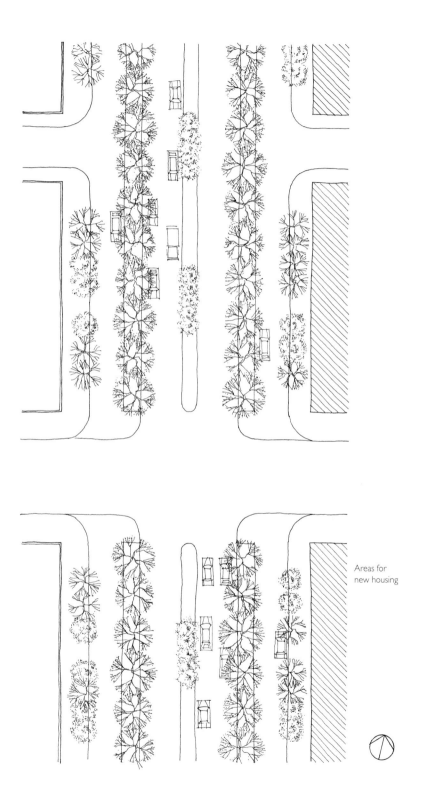

Areas for
new housing

Octavia Boulevard: plan

Approximate scale: 1″ = 50′ or 1:600

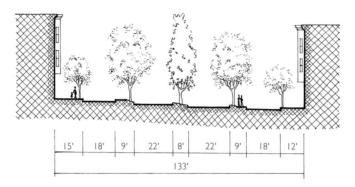

Octavia Boulevard: section
Approximate scale: 1" = 50' or 1:600

boulevard and fit it into San Francisco's grid street pattern was solved with ease: a one-block-long public park tentatively named Hayes Green will take the place of the central lanes. It can be a memory to an unfortunate freeway interlude.

The boulevard's design was not without controversy within the design team. As might be expected, the urban designers and the public works engineers did not always see eye to eye, but they were willing to listen to each other. Differences surfaced exactly where expected: the width of the access lanes, turning radii at corners, locations of crosswalks, tree locations in relation to corners, tree-spacing in relation to parking meters, and permitted turning movements. Real world examples—that is, specific situations that could be shown to work without compromising safety or function—were often the keys to resolving the problems. The design participants agreed to forward to citizen meetings for discussion only designs that they could all sign off on despite their differences. In the end, alternative versions of the design were presented: one in which the side access road went straight to the intersecting streets and one in which there are breaks in the median before and after each intersection.[5] The urban designers preferred the first version, and so did the citizen groups.

San Francisco is a feisty city. In 1999 the pro-freeway forces put another measure on the ballot to rebuild the freeway, which was countered by another, pro-boulevard measure by the anti-freeway people. This time, however, there were specific images and designs that voters could reference in making their decisions. They voted for the multiway boulevard!

Access Road and Median design for Octavia Boulevard
(from a drawing by Norman Kondy)

Would that we could report unequivocal success—that Octavia Boulevard is now complete, or at least under construction. Not the case! The state highway people, Caltrans, must first take down the offending freeway and bring what remains to ground level south of the Hayes Valley neighborhood. Those people at Caltrans don't like to lose. Nobody does. Their part of the project, which must precede the building of the boulevard, may not be their highest priority. But progress is being made, and it *will* happen.

BOULEVARDS ARE GREAT STREETS

Boulevards are great streets when they are well designed, well built, and well maintained. They capture the imagination because they are grand and worldly. They are optimistic statements about the power and the magic of urban places, of cities. They have long since evolved beyond their authoritarian origins.

Streets like The Esplanade in Chico, the Passeig de Gràcia in Barcelona, and Ocean Parkway in Brooklyn speak simultaneously of the grandeur of cities and the ordinary day-to-day life of the people inhabiting them. It is the unique balance between the needs of through travel—reflecting the needs of the city as a whole—and the needs of automobile and pedestrian access—reflecting the needs of the local community—that enables them to be pleasant settings for everyday living.

It remains to be seen whether boulevards can be built in today's pluralist and often-fragmented American cities. Because of their significant locations and multifunctional roles, boulevards, by their nature, involve many different people. Therefore, to convert a street into a boulevard, or to effectively redesign an existing boulevard, many different agencies at the city, state, and possibly federal level would have to cooperate. Changes would also touch many citizens: residents of surrounding neighborhoods as well as commuters and business interests that depend on the street's capacity to move traffic through the city. In today's cities, which often lack strong and cohesive political leadership, multiway boulevards would have to be accepted and understood by the many people with a say in their introduction or redesign—and that is not an easy proposition.

Involved citizens and professionals alike note regularly that what is necessary to overcome the obstacles in the path of making new boulevards, or resurrecting old ones, is the will to do it. The impetus could come from many levels, depending on the local situation. It could originate at the political level of the mayor or city council, at the professional level of a city administration, or from an entrepreneurial push by a developer or a business community operating along a stretch of a street.

The key to making boulevards happen, and overcoming the possible concerns of the different user groups, professionals, fire marshals, public works directors, and many others, lies in helping everyone understand the most special quality of multiway boulevards: the way they cater to many needs and purposes in a balanced way. Although they may not meet everyone's expectations all of the time, they represent a vast improvement over today's arterial roads, which acknowledge and meet only the needs of fast-moving automobiles. Our intention, here, has been to help add to the inventory of great streets. Multiway boulevards can do that.

NOTES

INTRODUCTION

1. We are advised by officials in Chico that a poll is regularly held to ascertain what residents regard as the best street in town and that The Esplanade comes out on top.

2. François Loyer, *Paris in the Nineteenth Century: Architecture and Urbanism,* trans. Charles L. Clark (New York: Abbeyville Press, 1988), 121.

3. See Mark H. Rose, *Interstate: Express Highway Politics, 1941–1956* (Lawrence: Regents Press of Kansas, 1978), 85–94. For a discussion of highway development financed by tolls and (in California) sales taxes before the 1956 Federal Highway Act and its emphasis on freeway construction, see also John B. Rae, *The Road and the Car in American Life* (Cambridge, Mass.: MIT Press, 1971), 170–94.

4. Allan B. Jacobs, *Great Streets* (Cambridge, Mass.: MIT Press, 1993).

5. See, for example, Allan B. Jacobs, E. Macdonald, D. Marsh, and C. Wilson, *The Uses and Reuses of Major Urban Arterials: A Study of Recycling, Revitalizing, and Restructuring "Gray Area" Transportation Corridors* (Berkeley: Institute of Urban and Regional Development, University of California, Berkeley, 1997).

PART ONE, CHAPTER 1

1. In 1995 a complete reconstruction of Avenue des Champs Elysées was concluded, one marked by the complete elimination of the side access roads. The new design is very elegant—a second row of trees on each side, new paving, new street furniture, underground parking—but the street is no longer a multiway boulevard.

2. Of the Paris multiway boulevards, only Avenue Foch is wider. It is not presented here because its wide medians, at approximately 100 feet, so completely separate side access roads from central traffic lanes that it feels like three separate streets rather than a single, unified avenue. Essentially, it is a different type of street altogether.

3. City of Paris map of traffic counts, 1986.

4. This is the street form illustrated in Adolphe Alphand's book, *Les Promenades de Paris* (reprint, Princeton, N.J.: Architectural Press, 1984).

5. Avenue Montaigne is also described in Allan Jacobs, *Great Streets* (Cambridge, Mass.: MIT Press, 1993).

6. Jacques Hillairet, *Dictionaire Historique des Rues de Paris,* vol. 2 (Paris: Editions de Minuit, 1985), 139.

7. Counts taken between 11:00 A.M. and 12:30 P.M., 28 March 1994.

8. Counts taken between 12:30 and 1:30 P.M., 28 March 1994.

9. Counts taken between 3 and 5 P.M., 29 March 1994; morning counts, taken between 10:30 and 11:45 A.M., were similar. In 1986 daily traffic on Avenue Marceau was 29,300, according the City of Paris map of traffic counts.

PART ONE, CHAPTER 2

1. Speeds measured at approximately 5:00 P.M., 31 March 1994.

2. Counts taken between 5:00 and 7:30 P.M., 4 April 1994.

3. Counts taken between 5:00 and 7:30 P.M., 4 April 1994.

4. Counts taken between 5:00 and 7:30 P.M., 4 April 1994.

5. Speeds measured at approximately 5:00 P.M., 31 March 1994, averaged 38 kilometers per hour on the access road and 55 kilometers per hour in the center lanes. Traffic counts were taken between 11:00 A.M. and 12:00 noon, 2 April 1994.

PART ONE, CHAPTER 3

1. See Robert Caro, *The Power Broker: Robert Moses and the Fall of New York* (New York: Alfred A. Knopf, 1974).

2. Surveys of residents were conducted as part of the research described in Peter Bosselmann and Elizabeth Macdonald, "Livable Streets Revisited," *Journal of the American Planning Association* 65 (1999):168–80.

3. Ibid.

4. These vehicle volumes are based on traffic counts taken on Ocean Parkway between 10:00 A.M. and 12:00 noon, 26 July 1994, and on Eastern Parkway between 2:30 and 4:30 P.M., 26 July 1994.

5. Donald Appleyard and Mark Lintell, "The Environmental Quality of City Streets: The Residents' Viewpoint," *Journal of the American Institute of Planners* 38 (1972): 89–101.

6. Bosselmann and Macdonald, "Livable Streets Revisited."

PART ONE, CHAPTER 4

1. For the history of the Grand Concourse by the engineer who designed it, see Louis A. Risse, "The True History of the Conception and Planning of the Grand Boulevard and Concourse in the Bronx" ([pamphlet] 1902).

2. Counts were taken between 3:00 and 4:00 P.M. on 25 July 1994.

3. New York City Department of Transportation, "Grand Concourse Traffic Safety Study," draft, December 1992.

4. The figure of 864 pedestrians per hour is derived from counts taken between 4:30 and 5:30 P.M. on 25 July 1994.

PART ONE, CHAPTER 5

1. The blocks of downtown Chico are typically 260 feet square—small in scale compared to those in most U.S. cities. The Portland, Oregon, grid, has blocks that are 200 feet square, as small as any found in major American cities. Downtown San Francisco blocks are often about 275 by 400 feet. Downtown Chico, then, may be characterized as both urban and pedestrian in scale. Block sizes of streets on both sides of The Esplanade are approximately 400 by 360 feet—also not large by U.S. standards.

2. These historical facts derive from conversations with local planners and traffic engineers and from historical photographs, newspapers, and journal articles in the Chico Public Library.

3. Speeds were measured at approximately 5:00 P.M., 19 August 1994.

4. For example at First Avenue, average northbound volumes of 896 vehicles per hour in the center and 20 in the access road were counted during the same period. An average southbound hourly volume of 844 was counted in the center, while only 24 vehicles moved on the access road. Counts were taken between 3:00 and 5:30 P.M., 19 August 1994.

5. Openings occur with some regularity as cars in the center travel in "platoons," having been stopped at the preceding light-controlled intersection.

6. In 1991, The Esplanade had an average daily traffic count (ADT) of 24,800, compared with 22,233 for Mangrove Street (City of Chico, Central Services Department of Engineering).

7. Accident data from City of Chico, Central Services Department of Engineering.

PART TWO

1. See Spiro Kostof, *The City Assembled: The Elements of Urban Form through History* (Boston: Bulfinch Press, 1982); and Mark Girouard, *Cities and People: A Social and Architectural History* (New Haven: Yale University Press, 1985).

2. See Henry W. Lawrence, "Origins of the Tree-Lined Boulevard," *Geographical Review* 78 (1988): 355–74, for a wonderfully detailed analysis of the landscape-form precedents of boulevards.

3. Girouard, *Cities and People,* 176.

4. Ibid., 177.

5. A marvelous little book called *Les Grands Boulevards,* published by the Musée Carnavalet in 1985, reprints both early engravings of the boulevards and texts of police ordinances.

6. See Spiro Kostof, *The City Shaped: Urban Patterns and Meanings through History* (Boston: Little Brown, 1991).

7. A book called *Les Promenades de Paris,* written by Haussmann's landscape architect Adolphe Alphand and published in 1867–1873, includes wonderfully illustrated detailed plans and sections of Paris's new boulevards. This book, which was available to designers elsewhere in Europe and America, was no doubt highly influential in disseminating the boulevard configuration (reprint ed., Princeton, N.J.: Princeton Architectural Press, 1984).

8. See David H. Pinkney, *Napoleon III and the Rebuilding of Paris* (Princeton: Princeton University Press, 1972) for a thorough description of the reconstruction of Paris.

9. See, for instance, Spiro Kostof, David Pinkney, Mark Girouard, and A. E. J. Morris, *History of Urban Form before the Industrial Revolution* (London: George Godwin Ltd., 1979).

10. Marshall Berman, *All That Is Solid Melts into Air: The Experience of Modernity* (New York: Viking Penguin, 1988), 150, 151.

11. See Pinkney, *Napoleon III.*

12. Splendid drawings of the Avenue de l'Impératrice can be found in Alphand, *Les Promenades de Paris.*

13. Norma Evenson, *Paris: A Century of Change, 1878–1978* (New Haven: Yale University Press, 1979).

14. See Robert Hughes, *Barcelona* (New York: Knopf, 1992).

15. For a series of essays that discusses and analyzes many aspects of Cerdà's plan and reproduces his drawings, see *Treballs sobre Cerdà i el seu Eixample a Barcelona* [Readings on Cerdà and the extension plan of Barcelona] (Barcelona: Ajuntament de Barcelona, Ministerio de Obras Publicas y Transportes, 1992).

16. Ibid., 190.

17. For a detailed description of Brooklyn's early development, see David Ment, *Building Blocks of Brooklyn: A Study of Urban Growth* (Brooklyn: Brooklyn Educational and Cultural Alliance, 1979), and Henry R. Stiles, *A History of the City of Brooklyn* (Brooklyn: by subscription, 1867–70.)

18. Ment, *Building Blocks of Brooklyn,* 44.

19. *Annual Report of the Brooklyn Park Commissioners,* 1867, 178–79.

20. Ibid., 192, 197.

21. Ibid., 198.

22. *New York State Laws,* 1868, chap. 631.

23. A plan describing this system is contained in *Annual Report of the Brooklyn Park Commissioners,* 1867.

24. These proceedings are chronicled in newspaper article of the times, especially in the *Brooklyn Eagle,* and also in a document found in the New York Public Library entitled "Petition from the Residents of Gravesend to the Legislature of the State of New York" (1879).

25. See *Brooklyn Eagle* articles and New York State laws of the time.

26. Berman, *All That Is Solid Melts into Air,* 165.

27. Charles Mulford Robinson, *City Planning, with Special Reference to the Planning of Streets and Lots* (New York: G. P. Putnam's Sons, 1916).

28. Institute of Traffic Engineers [hereafter ITE], *Traffic Engineering Handbook* (Washington, D.C.: ITE, 1992), 155.

29. Such publications include ITE, *The Traffic Engineers Handbook;* Transportation Research Board [hereafter TRB], *Highway Capacity Manual* (Washington, D.C.: TRB, 1985); and the American Association of State Highway and Transportation Officials [hereafter AASHTO], *A Policy on Geometric Design of Highways and Streets* (Washington, D.C.: AASHTO, 1990).

30. ITE, *Traffic Engineering Handbook,* 155–57.

31. ITE, Wolfgang F. Homburger et al., *Residential Street Design and Traffic Control* (Englewood Cliffs, N.J.: Prentice Hall, 1989), 22.

32. ITE, *Traffic Engineering Handbook,* 154.

33. Indeed, a recurring and troubling aspect of our inquiries has been the lack of actual data to accompany assertions or conclusions that one particular road or intersection configuration is unsafe or less safe than another—or, for that matter, more safe. Accident data is often blindly considered, without reference to particular conditions in which accidents occur.

Often when presenting designs to traffic officials, we were told that a particular arrangement would not be safe. If we asked officials how they knew that, they could not tell us. When we started our inquiries, we were advised on many occasions that both accident and traffic data was available for particular streets. The availability of such information was central to our choice of streets for research, but, sadly the safety information was rarely found. This raised the question: What was the basis of the conclusion that boulevards are unsafe relative to other streets? We have yet to find satisfactory answers to that question.

34. See, e.g., International Congress for Modern Architecture, *The Athens Charter in Practice* (Boulogne: Architecture d'Aujourd'Hui, 1948); Clarence Stein, *Towards New Towns for America* (Liverpool: University Press of Liverpool, 1951); Clarence A. Perry, *Neighborhood and Community Planning* (New York: Regional Plan of New York and Its Environs, 1929).

35. The concept of an imbalance of power on urban streets derives from ideas initially presented in Colin Buchanan's influential report, *Traffic in Towns* (London: British Ministry of Transport, 1963), which was taken up by planning professionals in Europe and United States, notably Donald Appleyard, Peter Bosselmann, and Terence O'Hare, in "Traffic in American Urban Neighborhoods: The Influence of Colin Buchanan," *Built Environment* 12 (1983): 127–39; Donald Appleyard, *Livable Streets* (Berkeley: University of California Press, 1980).

36. See Jane Jacobs, *The Death and Life of American Cities* (New York: Random House, 1961); Berman, *All That Is Solid Melts into Air;* Appleyard, *Livable Streets;* Ken Greenberg, "Making Choices," *Places* 11 (1997): 14–21; Carmen Hass-Klau, *The Pedestrian and City Traffic* (New York: Bechaven Press, 1990); Walter Kulash, "The Third Motor Age," *Places* 10 (1996): 42–49.

PART THREE, CHAPTER 1

1. For example, in the American Association of State Highway and Transportation Officials (AASHTO) 1957 policy document, *A Policy on Arterial Highways in Urban Areas* (Washington, DC: AASHTO), there are direct regulations concerning streets with access ways, while in AASHTO's 1990 policy document, *A Policy on Geometric Design of Highways and Streets* (Washington, DC: AASHTO, 1990), they have been dropped altogether.

2. In most cities we were able to obtain gross figures for traffic volumes measured by Average Daily Travel (ADT). Pedestrian traffic is usually not counted, and we had to estimate it from field counts. Cities or police departments also keep records of reported accidents, usually those including serious damage to property or bodily injury. Pedestrian accidents, though, are not always recorded as such.

3. For a detailed accounting of the research conducted, see Allan B. Jacobs, Yodan Rofé, and Elizabeth Macdonald, *Boulevards: A Study of Safety, Behavior, and Usefulness,* (Berkeley: Institute of Urban and Regional Development, University of California, 1994).

4. The pedestrian counts used are those taken as part of the research project. The assumption is made that pedestrian volumes were similar for the period for which the accident rate was collected.

5. One should note, however, that blocks on most of Linden Boulevard are much shorter than they are on either Eastern Parkway or Ocean Parkway. The accident rate on the part of Linden Boulevard with long blocks is 1.18, and the pedestrian accident rate is 0.09. Thus it can be seen that by controlling for the effect of the shorter blocks on the number of accidents per intersection and isolating the effect of the boulevard configuration, Eastern and Ocean Parkways are both safer than Linden Boulevard.

6. For Paris, a report from the municipality that lists all the locations (either intersections or street segments between intersections) that had more than 10 accidents between 1 January 1990 and 31 December 1992 was available (Maire de Paris, 1993). This report includes only accidents in which injury to persons was sustained. Locations with fewer than 10 accidents were not reported. A 1986 map showing ADT counts for central Paris within the Boulevard Périphérique, based on 1982–86 counts, was also available.

7. For more on Avenue Montaigne, see Allan B. Jacobs, *Great Streets* (Cambridge, Mass: MIT Press, 1993); accident data from Maire de Paris, 1993.

8. One must be aware, however, that we may be confounded here by different definitions of what is a reportable accident.

9. Data from the Municipality of Barcelona.

PART THREE, CHAPTER 2

1. No single body of norms and regulations governs the design of streets in the United States. Practice differs from state to state and from city to city. Perhaps the most representative source is Institute of Transportation Engineers (ITE), *Guidelines for Urban Major Street Design, A Recommended Practice* (Washington, D.C.: ITE, 1984). Because it relates to major roads, this publication is applicable to boulevards. Other sources for norms and standards include the policy publications of the American Association of State Highway and Transportation Officials (AASHTO), specifically *A Policy on Arterial Highways in Urban Areas,* (Washington, D.C.: AASHTO, 1990). Also useful are Wolfgang Homburger and James Kell, *Fundamentals of Traffic Engineering* (Berkeley: Institute of Transportation Studies, 1984), and Wolfgang Homburger, L. E. Keefer and W. R.

McGrath, eds., *Transportation and Traffic Engineering Handbook* (Englewood Cliffs, N.J.: Prentice-Hall, 1982).

2. Minimum and desirable roadway standards used are from ITE, *Guidelines for Urban Major Street Design,* Table 2.1.

3. A tree-diameter limitation is included in ibid.

4. Ibid., Table 7.1.

5. Ibid., 33.

6. AASHTO, *A Policy on Geometric Design of Highways and Streets* (Washington, D.C.: AASHTO, 1990), 838–39.

7. ITE, *Guidelines for Urban Major Street Design,* 36, Table 92.

8. Nicholas J. Garber and Lester A. Hoel, *Traffic and Highway Engineering,* 2d ed. (Boston, Mass.: PWS Publishing, 1997), 164–67.

9. ITE, *Guidelines for Urban Major Street Design,* 47.

PART FOUR

1. The street was designed by Bimal Patel in collaboration with Allan Jacobs and Elizabeth Macdonald. Patel, Jacobs, and Macdonald were coleaders of a 1996 workshop on street design held in Ahmedabad and sponsored by the Ahmedabad Environmental Design Collaborative and the Ahmedabad Municipal Corporation.

2. City of Melbourne, Urban Design and Architecture Division, *Grids and Greenery: The Character of Linear Melbourne* (Melbourne, 1987) 37–40.

3. Letter from Michael J. Wallwork, P.E., *Transportation Engineer,* March 1996.

4. City of Melbourne, Urban Design and Architecture Division, "Boulevard Street Section Case Studies."

5. Adriana Chirco and Marco di Liberto, *Via Libertá ieri e oggi: Ricostruzione storia e fotografica della piu bella passeggiata di Palermo* (Palermo: D. Flaccovio, 1998).

6. See Allan Jacobs and Cortus Koehler, "San Francisco Boulevard," *Journal of Urban Design* (2000): 3–18.

PART FIVE, CHAPTER 1

1. This issue is not unique to boulevards. It is a fundamental issue about streets and urban life that has enormous implications for the well-being of cities. It is connected to the issue of boulevards because the primary reasons why large stretches of urban roadways are not fronted by buildings and not enlivened by doorways or watched over by people from windows are a direct result of the functional categorization of streets, which was devised as a way to facilitate vehicular traffic.

2. Two examples in Paris exemplify this arrangement: the Boulevard de Courcelles, which runs in part along the Parc Monceau, and Avenue Franklin Roosevelt, which is completely one-sided and has two museums along one side.

3. The guideline of half is not meant to be an absolute; good judgment is needed to establish the dimensions of each realm. The figure does, however, reflect the importance of balance between the through-going functions and the local functions of the street. The more the balance is weighted toward the car and the center roadway, the less comfortable and safe the boulevard is likely to be for pedestrians. The more it is weighted toward the pedestrian realm, the less useful the street is likely to be as a way to move quickly from destination to destination.

4. The lane widths proposed in this discussion of the width of the boulevard and its constituent parts are narrower than the current norm in the United States. Earlier research conducted by the

authors has shown that larger lane widths on boulevards can reduce safety, particularly in the access ways. For a fuller discussion of the matter, see Allan B. Jacobs, Yodan Rofé, and Elizabeth Macdonald, *Boulevards: A Study of Safety, Behavior, and Usefulness* (Berkeley: Institute of Urban and Regional Development, University of California, 1994), 90–91, 111–14.

5. See, e.g., the prominent place of Commonwealth Avenue in mental maps of Boston shown in Kevin Lynch, *Image of the City* (Cambridge, Mass., MIT Press, 1960).

6. An example of a quick embarkation system is the bus-loading tubes used in Curitiba, Brazil.

7. See Robert Cervero, *Transit-Supportive Development in the United States: Experiences and Prospects* (Berkeley: Institute of Urban and Regional Development, University of California, 1994).

8. A good example is the Passeig de Gràcia in Barcelona. Besides having dedicated bus and taxi lanes in the center realm, with bus stations at every second intersection, it has a subway line running underneath it and includes a subterranean station for regional and national train networks. Passengers can board an international train there in the center of the city, or transfer easily from one mode to another.

9. See, for example, ITE, *Guidelines for Urban Major Street Design: A Recommended Practice* (Washington, D.C., 1984), 24.

10. See Jacobs et al., *Boulevards: A Study of Safety, Behavior and Usefulness,* 110–13.

11. For an alternative approach to emergency-vehicle access standards, see Terrence L. Bray and Victor F. Rhodes, "In Search of Cheap and Skinny Streets," *Places* 11 (1997): 32–39.

PART FIVE, CHAPTER 2

1. To be sure, the 1980s and 1990s witnessed the acceptance of many traffic calming practices—speed bumps, traffic diverters, wider sidewalks at intersections, to name only three—so there has been change in the direction of a more balanced approach to roadway redesign.

2. See Allan B. Jacobs, Yodan Rofé, and Elizabeth Macdonald, *Multiple Roadway Boulevards: Case Studies, Designs, Design Guidelines* (Berkeley: Institute of Urban and Regional Development, University of California, 1995).

3. See Terrence L. Bray and Victor F. Rhodes, "In Search of Cheap and Skinny Streets," *Places* 11 (1997): 32–39.

4. See Ken Greenberg, "Making Choices," *Places* 11 (1997): 14–21.

5. There was also a hybrid possibility, which had the entrances to the access lanes from intersecting streets, at the intersections, and exits returning traffic to the central lanes at median breaks before each intersection.

INDEX